Love and Politics

A New Commentary on the Song of Songs

LUIS STADELMANN

PAULIST PRESS
New York and Mahwah, N.J.

Nihil Obstat:
Marcelo F. de Aquino, S.J.

November 27, 1990

The Nihil Obstat is an official declaration that a book or pamphlet is free of doctrinal or moral error. No implication is contained therein that those who have granted the Nihil Obstat agree with the contents, opinions or statements expressed.

Library of Congress Cataloging-in-Publication Data

Stadelmann, Luis I. J.
Love and politics : a new commentary on the Song of songs / Luis Stadelmann.
p. cm.
Includes bibliographical references and index.
ISBN 0-8091-3290-7 (pbk.)
1. Bible. O.T. Song of Solomon—Commentaries. I. Title.
BS1485.3.S733 1992
223′.9077—dc20 92-17162
CIP

Published by Paulist Press
997 Macarthur Boulevard
Mahwah, New Jersey 07430

Printed and bound in the
United States of America

Contents

Abbreviations vii

Preface ix

Introduction 1
- 1. Hermeneutic Key 1
  - a. The Text in Code 1
  - b. The *Personae* 1
  - c. The Central Theme 2
- 2. Exegetical Method 3
- 3. Canonical Inspiration 3
- 4. Date and Author 4
- 5. Canonicity 5
- 6. The Masoretic Text and Versions 6
- 7. Hebrew Metrics 6
- 8. Literary Structure 7
- 9. Outline 10

Exposition of the Song of Songs 13
- Superscription (1:1) 13

Poem I: The Preludes of Love (1:2-17) 15
- 1. The Yearning of Love (1:2-4) 15
  - *Commentary: The Theme of the Monarchy* 26
- 2. The Self-esteem of Love (1:5-6) 29
  - *Commentary: The Theme of the Nation* 34
- 3. The Ambitions of Love (1:7-11) 37
  - *Commentary: The Theme of the Government* 45
- 4. Exultant Love (1:12-17) 47
  - *Commentary: The Theme of the Covenant* 53

Poem II: The Pledge of Love (2:1-17) 55
1. Under the Apple Tree (2:1-3) 55
Commentary: The Theme of Royalty 60
2. At Home (2:4-7) 61
Commentary: The Theme of the Capital 68
3. In the Countryside (2:8-15) 70
Commentary: The Theme of the Country 80
4. The Bond of Friendship (2:16-17) 82
Commentary: The Theme of the Covenant 85

Poem III: The Coming of the Bridegroom (3:1-11) 87
1. The Expected Coming (3:1-5) 87
Commentary: The Theme of the Restoration of the Monarchy 95
2. The Royal Procession (3:6-8) 96
Commentary: The Theme of the Repatriation of the King 100
3. The Royal Insignia (3:9-11) 102
Commentary: The Theme of the Coronation 106

Poem IV: The Beauty of the Bride (4:1–5:1) 109
1. The Comely Bride (4:1-7) 109
Commentary: The Theme of the Integrated Nation 115
2. The Privileged Bride (4:8) 116
Commentary: The Theme of Foreign Trade 118
3. The Wealthy Bride (4:9-11) 120
Commentary: The Theme of the Nation's Prosperity 123
4. The Assets of the Bride (4:12-15) 124
Commentary: The Theme of the Nation's Economic Independence 128
5. The Delights of the Bride (4:16–5:1) 129
Commentary: The Theme of the Nation Firmly Established 133

Poem V: The Presence of the Bridegroom (5:2–6:3) 135
1. The Call of the Bridegroom (5:2-8) 135
Commentary: The Theme of the Restoration of the Monarchy 141
2. The Attributes of the King (5:9-16) 143
Commentary: The Theme of the Enthronement 148
3. The Favorite Resort (6:1-3) 149
Commentary: The Theme of the King's Taking Charge of the Country 153

Poem VI: The Bride's Attractiveness (6:4–7:10) 155
1. The Charming Bride (6:4-7) 155
Commentary: The Theme of the Unified Nation 158
2. The Distinguished Bride (6:8-12) 159
Commentary: The Theme of Diplomatic Relations 167
3. The Attractive Bride (7:1-6) 169
Commentary: The Theme of the Judean Leadership 180
4. The Stately Bride (7:7-10) 181
Commentary: The Theme of the Union between King and Nation 186

Poem VII: The Bliss of Love (7:11–8:5) 189
1. The Bond of Friendship (7:11) 189
Commentary: The Theme of the Covenant 190
2. The Return to the Countryside (7:12-14) 191
Commentary: The Theme of the Country 194
3. The Return Home (8:1-4) 195
Commentary: The Theme of the Capital 200
4. The Return to the Apple Tree (8:5) 201
Commentary: The Theme of Royalty 204

Poem VIII: The Plenitude of Love (8:6-14) 207
1. The Power of Love (8:6-7) 207
Commentary: The Theme of the Covenant 211
2. The Legacy of Love (8:8-10) 213
Commentary: The Theme of the Government 218
3. The Treasure of Love (8:11-12) 220
Commentary: The Theme of the Nation 223
4. The Intimacy of Love (8:13-14) 225
Commentary: The Theme of the Monarchy 228

Bibliography of Works Cited 229

Index of Passages 233

General Index 239

Abbreviations

AE	*Archaeological Encyclopedia of the Holy Land*, see Bibl. NEGEV, A.
AEL	*Ancient Egyptian Literature*, see Bibl. LICHTHEIM, M.
AI	*Ancient Israel*, see Bibl. DE VAUX, R.
AJ	FLAVIUS JOSEPHUS, *Antiquitates Judaicae*
AnBib	*Analecta Biblica*, Rome
ANET	*Ancient Near Eastern Texts relating to the Old Testament*, ed. J. B. PRITCHARD (3rd ed. and including the *Supplement*), Princeton University Press, Princeton 1969
AOAT	*Alter Orient und Altes Testament*, Kevelaer/Neukirchen-Vluyn
AuS	*Arbeit und Sitte in Palästina*, see Bibl. DALMAN, G. H.
BAC	*Biblioteca de Autores Cristianos*, Madrid
BDB	BROWN, F.–DRIVER, S. R.–BRIGGS, C. A., *A Hebrew and English Lexicon of the Old Testament*, Clarendon, Oxford 1962
BHK	*Biblia Hebraica*, ed. R. KITTEL
BHS	*Biblia Hebraica Stuttgartensia*
Bib	*Biblica*, Roma
BJ	FLAVIUS JOSEPHUS, *Bellum Judaicum*
BKAT	*Biblischer Kommentar. Altes Testament*, Neukirchen-Vluyn
BL	BAUER, H.–LEANDER, P., *Historische Grammatik der hebräischen Sprache*, Olms, Hildesheim 1965
BR	*Biblisches Reallexikon*, see Bibl. GALLING, K.
CBQ	*Catholic Biblical Quarterly*, Washington
Ct	*Le Cantique des Cantiques*, see Bibl. JOÜON, P.
DB	*Dictionnaire de la Bible*, Paris
DBS	*Dictionnaire de la Bible. Supplément*, Paris
FWG	*Fischer Weltgeschichte*, Frankfurt–Hamburg
GK	GESENIUS, W.–KAUTZSCH, E., *Gesenius' Hebrew Grammar*, see Bibl.

Gr	*Grammaire de l'hébreu biblique,* see Bibl. JOÜON, P.
HAL	*Hebräisches und Aramäisches Lexikon zum Alten Testament,* KÖHLER, L.–BAUMGARTNER, W. 3rd edition thoroughly revised and expanded by W. BAUMGARTNER et al., 4 Lieferungen, Brill, Leiden 1967, 1974, 1983, 1990
HAT	*Handbuch zum Alten Testament,* Tübingen
IDB	*The Interpreter's Dictionary of the Bible,* Nashville
IDB.S	*The Interpreter's Dictionary of the Bible. Supplement,* Nashville
JSOT	*Journal for the Study of the Old Testament,* Sheffield
KAT	*Kommentar zum Alten Testament,* Gütersloh
Kl.P.	*Der Kleine Pauly,* see Bibl. ZIEGLER, K.–SONTHEIMER, W.
Kl.S.	*Kleine Schriften zur Geschichte des Volkes Israel,* see Bibl. ALT, A.
LXX	The Septuagint
MT	Masoretic Text
NEB	*New English Bible*
NT	New Testament
OT	Old Testament
PT	*Perspectiva Teológica,* Belo Horizonte
RB	*Revue biblique,* Paris
RSV	*Revised Standard Version*
SA	*Summa Artis,* see Bibl. PIJOÁN, J.
THAT	*Theologisches Handwörterbuch zum Alten Testament,* München–Zürich
TWAT	*Theologisches Wörterbuch zum Alten Testament,* Stuttgart
UT	*Ugaritic Textbook,* see Bibl. GORDON, C. H.
VAB	*Vorderasiatische Bibliothek,* Leipzig
Vg	Vulgate
VT	*Vetus Testamentum,* Leiden
XPa	Xerxes, Persepolis a, see Bibl. KENT, R. G.
ZAW	*Zeitschrift für die alttestamentliche Wissenschaft,* Berlin

Preface

Each generation seeks to understand the books of the Bible from the study of the commentaries which contemporary exegetes had produced on the basis of their scholarly investigation and grasp of the meaning of biblical texts. Thus there would result a widespread consensus on a given topic, leading to its deeper penetration in the centuries-long process of successively accumulating insights. While this is the case in relation to almost all the biblical books which have been expounded in the course of centuries, with revisions of conflicting interpretations and new insights incorporated in subsequent works, there is, however, one notable exception: the history of interpretation of the Song of Songs. The ground of the motley pattern of different viewpoints lies in some social, cultural, historical context, in the personal position or counter-position of given interpreters, and in the manner in which the method and task of exegetical investigation have been conceived. Thus divergent interpretations have arisen as each interpreter invites the reader to an encounter with his own personal stance and horizon rather than with the biblical text.

Our interpretation of the Song of Songs intends to elucidate the meaning of the text, to listen to the past, and to perceive the implications of the text for its contemporaries. From a judicious use of appropriate exegetical methods and the grasp of the thematic content of the book there emerges a clear understanding of ideas which the author couched in poetic language so as to convey a plan of intended proceedings for the social integration of repatriate and autochthonous Jews into the Judean community and the restoration of the Davidic monarchy in Judah in the post-exilic period of the history of Israel. This text about the cohesion of social groups in the restored monarchy leads to a reflection on the way in which the formation of social identity demands that individuals and cultures learn to transcend their particularities so as to forge a new cohesion and reach a clearer and more precise perception of the divine plan laid down for the communion of all mankind in the kingdom of God.

This commentary has been long in the making. It is the result of the literary analysis of the text, the study of the usage of the words in common, literary, and technical language, the search for a dominant theme running through other interconnected sections that thereby become subordinate themes, and the attempt to eliminate previously entertained perspectives and opinions in order to replace them with the perspectives and views that emerge from the cumulative interplay of data, insight, and evidence. These procedures have permitted a breakthrough leading to a grasp of the meaning which the author intended to convey to the reader.

With great appreciation I want to acknowledge the interest and support which my colleagues of the Jesuit School of Theology in Belo Horizonte have constantly demonstrated during this undertaking. I am also especially indebted to Fr. James N. F. Alison, O.P. for his assistance in editing this book. Finally, I am most grateful to the Stichting Benevolentia of Amsterdam, Holland, and the Fondation Argidius of Fribourg, Switzerland, for financial assistance in the publication of this book.

Luís I. J. Stadelmann, S.J.

Introduction

1. Hermeneutic Key

a. The Text in Code

The Song of Songs is a text in code whose meaning can only be penetrated with the help of a hermeneutic key. This enables the author's message to be decoded. The reason which led to the author couching his meaning in the disguise of love songs, wedding songs, nocturnes, bucolic songs, eclogues, idylls, etc., was not some poetic rapture in the face of the ineffable or an attempt to delve into the realms of fancy, but rather political prudence so as to cover Jewish nationalism from the eyes of the Persian authorities since they might suspect a burgeoning insurrection against their domination over Judah. While putting down the ideas in order to communicate them to those initiated in the plan of intended proceedings, he dressed them with suggestive images which impress themselves at the same time on our fantasy, our reason, and our feelings. From the ingenious combination of the subject matter with poetic intuition and aesthetic style a work of outstanding literary value has resulted in which the poet, while describing what he thought and experienced, became the spokesman for the aspirations of his community and one of the most enthusiastic voices of all times ever to extol social cohesion.

b. The Personae

The various scenes serve as background for the dialogues of the principal characters whose words and attitudes are related to their functions as bearers of a message. The topographical data are characteristic of the different regions of Palestine. The literary figure of personification lends life and corporate meaning to social groups. Thus, the Shulamite is the leading figure representative of the native population of Judah; the "daughters of Jerusalem" are an image of the the elite of the Jewish priesthood; the "daughters of Zion" personify the leaders of the urban population; "Solomon" is the representative of the monarchical state and the Davidic dynasty. Apart from these there stand out the "queens" who represent the kingdoms in vassalage to Persia; the "wives" symbolize the Persian provinces, and the "maidens" symbolize the Jewish communities of the diaspora. The mother of Solomon represents the royal house of David, and the mother of the Shulamite represents the Israelite nation from the pre-exilic period. The masculine characters, individual or collective, are representatives of the various functions carried out by those holding public office in the Judean community: the king, the retinue, the brothers, the sons, companions, shepherds, warriors, and keepers. We may also mention the chorus, even though it does not count as one of the characters quoted in the Song, but represents the mentors of the wisdom tradition.

c. The Central Theme

The content of the message is the restoration of the Davidic monarchy in Judah after the exile. It is not out of nostalgia for past glory that the poet deals with this matter but for the purpose of demonstrating that kingship is the most adequate institution to shape the future of the nation. Based on the allegiance of all the inhabitants to their sovereign, this institution could contribute most efficaciously toward the restoration and unification of the Judean community incorporating both repatriate and autochthonous Jews. The covenant between king and people, integrated into the fundamental relationship between Yahweh and the chosen people, is one of the constitutive principles of the Davidic monarchy as a political institution.

The author formulated this type of relationship not in the language of an intimate romanticism but in the juridical terminology of the political treaties of antiquity. One of those terms is "love" used as a synonym of the political pacts between states, kings, and social groups, when formalized by a written agreement. For this reason, the expressions of love of the Shulamite for Solomon point to a political covenant between king and people. The gestures of mutual appreciation—kisses, embraces, receptions at home, and meals shared in common—have the meaning of symbolic rites of the covenant as the non-verbal manifestation of mutual belonging.

The thematic content is meticulously worked out in all its aspects so as to instruct the initiates in the plan of intended proceedings. However, implementation of this plan must wait upon political events under Persian foreign policy and the economic and social circumstances of the post-exilic Judean community.

2. *Exegetical Method*

The exegesis of the Song of Songs demands the application of various methods of investigation so as to decode the language, the content, and the meaning of the written text. Since each exegetical method has its own focus, each must be applied in a differentiated way avoiding exclusivity and making use of the interrelation and complementarity of the techniques of methodological investigation. The *historical-critical method* analyzes the text as the expression of an author in the concrete circumstances of his time and with a directly intended meaning. Then, studying the literary aspect of the text, it points to the units, structured in poems and songs, and the themes which are developed in them. It relates the literary units amongst themselves on the basis of corresponding themes and it identifies the figures of speech which occur in each passage. The *sociological method* analyzes the faith-community under the aspect of a society that is being rebuilt, conditioned by social, cultural, economic, and political factors. The method of *semantic analysis* studies the concept of the word "love" in relationship to terms of correlative meaning situating it in the semantic field of the diplomatic texts of the ancient Near East where it expresses the relationship of a social and political covenant. We do not employ here other methods which have been used in recent or ancient commentaries, but limit ourselves to refer to the interpretations which are the result of their application to the analysis of the text, interpretations such as the cult-mythical, naturalistic, spiritual, allegorical, typological, etc.

3. *Canonical Inspiration*

Since the Song of Songs is to be found in the Bible, its message is not destined merely for a particular group of Jews contemporary to the author, but has a universal range because it is related to the history of salvation, and thus it is recognized as an "inspired" book. Although it mentions no interventions of Yahweh in history, has no theophany, and includes none of the biblical traditions of monotheism, the book deals with facts which translate and find their meaning in the word of God with respect to the divine designs toward the chosen people in the promised land. However, in place of religious categories the author uses terminology which is both appropriate to his aim to produce a coded text and has at the same time a personal resonance among repatriate and autochthonous Jews. Because of this he applies to the political sphere the thematic content found in the religious sphere, reformulating it in poetic language. Thus the country of Judah, as the territory of the Jewish community, represents the promised land, the religious expression of the geographical area which belonging to

Yahweh is a gift to the chosen people. The Jewish nation as the political community of citizens who profess their adherence to the religious traditions of Israel is the historical mediation of the chosen people. In addition to this, the four signs of the divine election of the people of Israel—Jerusalem and kingship, in the political sphere, and the temple and priesthood, in the religious sphere—represent the institutions of Israel.

This text is about the cohesion of social groups in the restored monarchy. It leads to a reflection on the way in which the formation of social identity demands that individuals and cultures learn to transcend their particularities so as to forge a new cohesion. This is the only way to reach a clearer and more precise perception of the divine plan laid down for the communion of all mankind in the kingdom of God.

4. Date and Author

Although there are no references for the date of the composition of the Song of Songs, we consider, with a basis in linguistic and historical criteria, that the book was probably composed around 500 B.C. To judge by the peculiarities of its grammar and syntax, the Hebrew language in which the book is written underwent the influence of Aramaic which had been adopted by the Persians as the *lingua franca* of their whole empire. Apart from Aramaic words there also occur some of Persian origin and there appear as well terms translated into Hebrew which are drawn from the administrative system of the Achaemenid kings. These linguistic elements are characteristic of the Hebrew language of the post-exilic period. So as to fix with more precision the date of composition of the book we situate its themes in the historical context relating them with those treated in other biblical books. Now, in two prophetic books (Haggai and Zechariah), which date from the year 520 B.C., there are prophecies concerning the important function which Zerubbabel, a descendant of the house of David, will carry out as representative of God in the organization of the Judean community. He was to exercise the royal functions even though not raised to kingship, since the crown, the symbol of royal power, would remain in store in the temple of Jerusalem (Hag 2:20–23; Zech 6:12–14). The prophecies about the reconstruction of Jerusalem foresee a glorious destiny for the city as the religious center of Judah (Zech 1:17; 2:14–16; 8:7–8) and as the sign of the divine election of Israel (Zech 1:16–17; 2:16; 3:2).

Just as these prophetic books preceded the beginning of the work of the rebuilding of the temple and gave impetus for the inhabitants of Judah to conclude it, culminating in its solemn inauguration in 515 B.C., in the same way the Song of Songs must have been written before the reconstruction of Jerusalem and the constitution of Judah as an independent province under the initiative of Nehemiah (445–433 B.C.).

To judge by the detailed data of the flora and the fauna, by the typical aspects of the various regions of Palestine, and by the apology for the local population, the author is a Jew native to Judah who wrote the book with the aim of winning over the repatriate Jews and conquering their sympathy for the aspirations of the autochthonous Jews so that mutual collaboration in carrying them out might lead to social cohesion and the irradiation of Israelite traditions in the homeland and the diaspora.

5. *Canonicity*

The objective criterion of the canonicity of the Song of Songs is the official seal which the religious authorities of the Jewish community attached to it, thus accepting it in the roll of the books of the Bible, and granting permission for it to be read in the community's worship. This seal is expressed in the title by the reference to Solomon which is used in the Hagiographa (*Ketubim*) in order to indicate the divine origin of the books of this third part of the holy scriptures of the Old Testament. This title although added later was already to be found in the heading of the book in Hebrew since it is included in the text of the Greek version of the Septuagint (LXX) which dates from the second century B.C. When the question of the canonicity of the Song was raised at the rabbinic Synod of Jamnia, around the year 90 A.D., there was no controversy as to whether it was to be reckoned amongst the inspired books, but there was discussion as to the validity of the reasons for its acceptance into the canon. In addition to this, the allegorical interpretation of the Song bears witness to the canonicity of the book, for, starting from the second century B.C., this exegetical method was applied to the canonical books so as to explain the meaning of parts that were unintelligible to the readers of that time. This was because the first generation of post-exilic Judaism, which possessed the hermeneutic key to decipher the meaning of this coded text, did not transmit it to the following generations at the same time as they handed down the book to them for reading in the community's worship. The interpreters who were later to expend great effort in deciphering it used the allegorical method not only to explain the book's meaning and relevance but also for polemical purposes between rival groups, e.g. Pharisees, Sadducees, Essenes, and Christians. They thus accommodated their interpretative method to the end of giving a basis for the biblical authenticity of their faith and their religious lifestyle. The Christian tradition, when it adopted the scriptures of the Old Testament, accepted also the canonicity of the Song; for this reason, the Second Council of Constantinople (553) rejected the interpretative method used by Theodore of Mopsuestia which minimized the divine inspiration of this book.

6. *The Masoretic Text and Versions*

The Masoretic text of the Song of Songs is well preserved and critically secure. Conjectures about the interpolation, duplication, omission, or transposition of words or phrases are based not on objective data but on the erroneous interpretation of the respective texts or on subjective criteria as to the division, into strophes and verses, of the literary units. The Greek version of the Septuagint (LXX) is faithful and literal, distancing itself from the original in the use of some Hebrew terms which it transcribes and does not translate and in the etymological interpretation of some geographical names out of context. To judge by these incoherences in the Greek version the thematic content of the book was enigmatic for the translator as also for his contemporaries. The Syriac version (Peshitta) is literal and faithful, closer to the MT than the LXX and Vg, although in passages that are difficult to translate, the Greek version was consulted. The Latin version (Vulgate), produced by Saint Jerome, is less literal than the version of the Septuagint. Faithful to the MT, the Vg supposes at times a different reading of the now vocalized Hebrew terms and underwent the influence of the LXX in some interpretations and translations. The Aramaic Targum which is of more recent origin, dating from the sixth or seventh century A.D., is not so much a version but rather an exposition of the Song treated as an historical allegory with reference to the principal events of the history of Israel from the exodus to the exile.

7. *Hebrew Metrics*

The lyric poetry of the Song of Songs is expressed in verses whose rhythm is determined by the recurrence of stressed and unstressed syllables repeated at regular intervals. Within the rhythmic regularity there are variations in the articulation of the verses, constituted by distichs or tristichs, in a rhythm which is sometimes symmetric sometimes asymmetric, and in the combination of similar sounding syllables or words. These intermittent variations do not offset the rhythmic strain of the songs; rather they enhance it by the application of various poetic devices, thus avoiding the monotony which results from the regularity of rhythmic patterns, especially in a long poem.

Three rhythmic systems have been proposed for the prosodic reading of the Song. The first is the accentual system, in which the verse foot is composed of a stressed syllable together with one or more unstressed syllables. Since only the stressed syllables are counted in the verse, their accentuation generally corresponds with the word stress. The second is the alternating system, based on the alternation of stressed and unstressed syllables. However, it is possible for the unstressed syllable to be absorbed into the stressed syllable preceding it, so that the verse foot can consist of one syllable. The third system takes word-units in every verse-line as the basis for the distribution of the stresses, since, as in Ugaritic, so also in the most ancient Hebrew poetry, it was assumed that the metric feet of the verse coincided with the words, because every Hebrew word was a poetic unit.

Here we adopt the accentual system as applied by L. KRINETZKI to the text in transliteration, though in certain respects differing from it. The regularity of the meter appears in the predominant occurrence of the meter called *qînâ* (3 + 2), and its reverse (2 + 3); there can also be found at times the binary meter (2 + 2), ternary (3 + 3), or quaternary (4 + 4) with variations. By the combination of different meters in the same strophe small units are highlighted which the poet wanted to emphasize for purposes of resonance; these present a different rhythmic pattern in the Masoretic system of accentuation, owing to its use for cantillation which takes into account grammatical rules, syntactic analysis, and the interpretation of the text.

8. *Literary Structure*

The Song of Songs is a homogeneous work of poetry structured in eight poems; the first four of these are related to the last four on the basis of corresponding themes. Poem I and poem II are in parallel with poem VII and poem VIII, according to the chiastic pattern A:B::B′:A′. The songs of poem I and poem VIII, as also those of poem II and poem VII, are related to each other according to the chiastic pattern A:B:C:D::D′:C′:B′:A′. Poem III and poem IV are in parallel with poem V and poem VI; the parallelism of these poems is analogic according to the pattern A:B::A′:B′, allowing it to be understood that these poems belong together.

Poem I. *The preludes of love* (1:2-17). This poem is composed of four songs which qualify the nature of love by means of four elements which are described in the respective songs. The first song about "the yearning of love" (1:2-4) has as its theme the monarchy; the second, about "the self-esteem of love" (1:5-6), deals with the theme of the Jewish nation; the third, about "the ambitions of love" (1:7-11), dwells on the theme of the government; the fourth, about "exultant love" (1:12-17), develops the theme of the covenant. In the final poem (8:6-14), the four elements corresponding to those in the initial poem are developed and their themes are taken up, in the inverse order, for the purpose of complementation. The themes of these poems are arranged according to the chiastic pattern A:B:C:D::D:C:B:A.

Poem II. *The pledge of love* (2:1-17). This poem is composed of four songs which present the different occasions of the meeting between bride and bridegroom. The first song deals with the meeting "under the apple tree" (2:1-3) and its theme is royalty; the second describes the meeting "at home" (2:4-7) with the theme of the capital; the third evokes a meeting "in the countryside" (2:8-15) and develops the theme of the country; the fourth refers to the meeting in which "the bond of friendship" (2:16-17) is confirmed in the context of the covenant. In the penultimate poem (7:11–8:5) there are taken up, in the inverse order, the same themes, related to each other according to the chiastic pattern A:B:C:D::D:C:B:A.

Poem III. *The coming of the bridegroom* (3:1-11). This poem includes three songs which describe the circumstances related to the return of the bridegroom and the reception which the inhabitants of Judah prepare for him. In the first song on "the expected coming" (3:1-5) his approach is visualized and its meaning is explained in the theme of the restoration of the monarchy; in the second, about "the royal procession" (3:6-8), the theme of the repatriation of the king is dealt with; in the third, on "the royal insignia" (3:9-11), the theme of the coronation is presented. The corresponding poem (5:2–6:3) takes up the same scene and adds two more referring to the accession of the heir apparent to the throne. The type of parallelism of these poems can be represented by the pattern A:B:C::A:C′:B′.

Poem IV. *The beauty of the bride* (4:1–5:1). This poem consists of five songs of which the fifth serves as a transition between the first and the second part of the book. The description of the bride aims to represent the Jewish nation. The first song about "the comely bride" (4:1-7) develops the theme of the integrated nation; the second, about "the privileged bride" (4:8), deals with the theme of foreign trade; the third, about "the wealthy bride" (4:9-11), takes up the theme of the prosperity of the nation; the fourth, on "the assets of the bride" (4:12-15), refers to the theme of the economic independence of the nation; the fifth, dealing with "the delights of the bride" (4:16–5:1), has as its theme the nation firmly established. The corresponding poem (6:4–7:10) dwells on related themes which are in parallel with those above according to the pattern A:B:C:D:E::A′:B′:C′:D′.

Poem V. *The presence of the bridegroom* (5:2–6:3). This poem is divided into three songs which relate the stages of his manifestation to the inhabitants of Judah. In the first song about "the call of the bridegroom" (5:2-8) there is developed the theme of the restoration of the monarchy; in the second, about "the attributes of the king" (5:9-16), the theme of his enthronement is set forth; the third, about "the favorite resort" (6:1-3), dwells on the theme of the king's taking charge of the country. This poem complements and amplifies the themes dealt with previously in poem III.

Poem VI. *The bride's attractiveness* (6:4–7:10). This poem consists of four songs which describe the qualities of the bride in terms of a person representing the Jewish nation. The first song about "the charming bride" (6:4-7) has as its theme the unified nation; the second, about "the distinguished bride" (6:8-12), takes up the theme of diplomatic relations; the third, about "the attractive bride" (7:1-6), develops the theme of the Judean leadership; the fourth, dealing with "the stately bride" (7:7-10), has as its theme the union between king and nation. The themes of this poem and those of poem IV represent the aims which the Jewish community must reach in order to become a nation.

Poem VII. *The bliss of love* (7:11–8:5). This poem is composed of four poetic units which highlight the function of the bridegroom in the organization of national life. The first, entitled "the bond of friendship" (7:11), serves as a point of reference to poem II and its respective songs, taking up once again the theme of the covenant; the second, about "the return to the countryside" (7:12-14), deals with the theme of the country; the third, about "the return home" (8:1-4), takes up the theme of the capital; the fourth, about "the return to the apple tree" (8:5), has as its theme royalty. With the repetition, in the inverse order, of these themes the same thematic content developed in poem II is complemented and amplified.

Poem VIII. *The plenitude of love* (8:6-14). This poem is divided into four songs which extol the lasting bond between the community of Judah and the Davidic dynasty. The first song about "the power of love" (8:6-7) develops the theme of the covenant; the second, about "the legacy of love" (8:8-10), deals with the theme of the government; the third, about "the treasure of love" (8:11-12), dwells on the theme of the Jewish nation; the fourth, on "the intimacy of love" (8:13-14), takes up the theme of the monarchy. The taking up, in the inverse order, of the same themes that were dealt with in poem I has as its aim to amplify and complete the respective themes.

9. *Outline*

Poem I. *The Preludes of Love* (1:2-17)
1. The yearning of love (1:2-4)
   The theme of the monarchy
2. The self-esteem of love (1:5-6)
   The theme of the nation
3. The ambitions of love (1:7-11) — A
   The theme of the government
4. Exultant love (1:12-17)
   The theme of the covenant

Poem II. *The Pledge of Love* (2:1-17)
1. Under the apple tree (2:1-3)
   The theme of royalty
2. At home (2:4-7)
   The theme of the capital — B
3. In the countryside (2:8-15)
   The theme of the country
4. The bond of friendship (2:16-17)
   The theme of the covenant

Poem III. *The Coming of the Bridegroom* (3:1-11)
1. The expected coming (3:1-5)
   The theme of the restoration of the monarchy
2. The royal procession (3:6-8) — C
   The theme of the repatriation of the king
3. The royal insignia (3:9-11)
   The theme of the coronation

Poem IV. *The Beauty of the Bride* (4:1–5:1)
1. The comely bride (4:1-7)
   The theme of the integrated nation
2. The privileged bride (4:8)
   The theme of foreign trade — D
3. The wealthy bride (4:9-11)
   The theme of the nation's prosperity
4. The assets of the bride (4:12-15)
   The theme of the nation's economic independence
5. The delights of the bride (4:16–5:1)
   The theme of the nation firmly established

A′

Poem VIII. *The Plenitude of Love* (8:6-14)
1. The power of love (8:6-7)
   The theme of the covenant
2. The legacy of love (8:8-10)
   The theme of the government
3. The treasure of love (8:11-12)
   The theme of the nation
4. The intimacy of love (8:13-14)
   The theme of the monarchy

B′

Poem VII. *The Bliss of Love* (7:11–8:5)
1. The bond of friendship (7:11)
   The theme of the covenant
2. The return to the countryside (7:12-14)
   The theme of the country
3. The return home (8:1-4)
   The theme of the capital
4. The return to the apple tree (8:5)
   The theme of royalty

D′

Poem VI. *The Bride's Attractiveness* (6:4–7:10)
1. The charming bride (6:4-7)
   The theme of the unified nation
2. The distinguished bride (6:8-12)
   The theme of diplomatic relations
3. The attractive bride (7:1-6)
   The theme of the Judean leadership
4. The stately bride (7:7-10)
   The theme of the union between king and nation

C′

Poem V. *The Presence of the Bridegroom* (5:2–6:3)
1. The call of the bridegroom (5:2-8)
   The theme of the restoration of the monarchy
2. The attributes of the king (5:9-16)
   The theme of the enthronement
3. The favorite resort (6:1-3)
   The theme of the king's taking charge of the country

Exposition of the Song of Songs

Superscription (1:1)

"The Song of Songs, which is Solomon's"

(*šîr haššîrîm ʾašer lišlōmōh*).

Vocabulary Analysis (1:1)

"Song" (*šîr*) is a lyric poem, which could be either for recital or chanting with or without musical accompaniment. According to its content, a song becomes suitable for religious or profane usage.

"Song of Songs" (*šîr haššîrîm*) is a Hebraism expressing the idea of the superlative, "the song par excellence." In an abstract sense it signifies the perfection attained by this poem in terms of its exquisite beauty, its deep emotional impact on the reader, or its merit as a masterpiece of Israelite literature; in an historical sense it means the most perfect of a series of poetic compositions. The superlative denotes the outstanding quality of this work of poetry. This quality is to be found in the harmony between form and content, in the suggestive force capable of stirring up and expressing the deepest emotions of the reader, and in the appeal to evaluate society in the light of the social structure as aspired to in the poems.

"Which is Solomon's" (*ʾašer lišlōmōh*). The periphrastic expression of the genitive indicates the author of the Song of Songs by means of the *lamed auctoris.* This excludes the possibility of Solomon being the object of the Song, in the sense of "songs about Solomon." The relative pronoun "which" (*ʾašer*) in its regular form, used in biblical Hebrew, occurs solely in the editorial heading, whereas in the poems the proclitic particle (*še*), regarded as a later form, used in the biblical books written in the second period of Hebrew literature, is employed. This difference of vocabulary in the expression of the same grammatical function seems to be a deliberate usage on the part of the author or redactor of the Song in order to distinguish between two meanings of Solomon's name: in the poems, Solomon stands for the representative of the monarchical state of Judah and the Davidic dynasty; in the superscription, Solomon indicates authority—not authorship—in terms of permission granted by the custodians of the Israelite religious tradition for the inclusion of the Song of Songs in the corpus of sacred writings which are read publicly at certain festivals of Jewish worship. This is because Solomon was held in biblical tradition to be the embodiment of the sage (1 Kgs 5:9-14). Even before that, the Song enjoyed wide acceptance among the sages who by consensus recognized its value and published it in order to preserve it for posterity and prevent it from falling into oblivion. The role of Solomon in the development of the wisdom literature was so emphasized in Israelite tradition that most of these books were attributed to him. Thus the association of the Song of Songs with Solomon indicates both the aesthetic affinity of this book to the type of poetry that is distinctive of wisdom usage, and the range of motifs reminiscent of Solomon's reign, such as the independent kingdom of united Israel, the royal court in Jerusalem, the king's statecraft, and diplomatic alliances. Wisdom tradition formulated and gave expression to the ideas which the autochthonous Jews elaborated in the post-exilic period in their endeavor to organize the Jewish nation along the lines of the Davidic monarchy.

Poem I The Preludes of Love (1:2-17)

1 ✦ *The Yearning of Love (1:2-4)*

2 Oh that he would kiss me with the kisses *Bride*
of his mouth!
Your friendship is better than wine.
3 Your perfumes are of a pleasant fragrance;
like perfume your name is diffused;
therefore the maidens love you.
4 Draw me after you, let us make haste!
May the king lead me into his chambers!
Let us exult and rejoice in you, *Chorus*
extol your friendship more than wine;
rightly do they love you.

Accented Transliteration (1:2-4)

2 *yiššāqḗnî minn^{e}šîqốt pî́hû*
kî́-ṭôbî́m dōdèkā miyyā́yin
3 *l^{e}rế^{a}ḥ š^{e}mānèkā ṭôbî́m*
šémen tûráq š^{e}mékā
ʻal-kḗn ʻ^{a}lāmốt ʼ^{a}hēbû́kā
4 *moškḗnî ʼaḥ^{a}rèkā nārû́ṣāh*
h^{e}bîʼánî hammélek ḥ^{a}dārấw
nāgî́lāh w^{e}niśm^{e}ḥā́h bā́k
nazkî́rāh dōdèkā miyyā́yin
mêšārî́m ʼ^{a}hēbû́kā

Literary Analysis (1:2-4)

Poem I on "the preludes of love" (1:2-17) is divided into four songs dealing with specific objects which qualify the nature of love by means of four elements described in these songs. Poem VIII on "the plenitude of love" (8:6-14) deals also with four elements which correspond to those of Poem I. Thus, both poems are correlated in view of their unfolding the same subject matter in its various aspects. One of these aspects dealt with in the first song (1:2-4) is "the yearning of love."

In order to ascertain the meaning of the word "love" we study it in its relationship with a set of correlated words that occur in the Song, e.g. "friendship," "my beloved," etc., and situate it in the semantic field of the treaty literature of the ancient Near East, where it is used to designate a socio-political alliance. The semantic field techniques applied to the textual analysis of the Song impose a conceptual framework on one's thinking and reconstructing—on the basis of historical information supplied by literary sources—the Judean community's *Sitz im Leben* in the post-exilic period. This hitherto unsuspected perspective stands in sharp contrast with the previous interpretation of the word "love" as an affection among lovers, an interpretation based on a reductionist view of love with a sentimental tinge inspired in the love songs extant in the literature of ancient and modern civilizations.

This song is composed of two strophes, structured in parallel form. Each strophe begins with an optative and/or imperative phrase and ends with a conclusion. In the first strophe (vss. 2-3), the bride enunciates, in three coordinate sentences, the attributes of the bridegroom; in the second strophe (vs. 4), the chorus takes up the content of the previous declarative sentences by rephrasing it in cohortative sentences.

As regards poetic and rhetorical devices that occur in the song we mention sound repetition: onomatopoeia *yiššāqēnî - minn*ᵉ*šîqôt;* alliteration, *š-m: šem - šemen - š*ᵉ*mekā;* assonance, *i-a: nāgîlāh - niśm*ᵉ*ḥāh - nazkîrah.* Rhetorical devices: synecdoche, e.g. "chambers" for palace; simile, "friendship is more than wine," "name like perfume"; etymological figure "kiss me with kisses"; enallage "he would kiss - your friendship."

Vocabulary Analysis (1:2-4)

Vs. 2: "Oh that he would kiss me with kisses!" (*yiššāqēnî minn*ᵉ*šîqôt*) The verb in the cohortative mood expresses the Shulamite's yearning for the arrival of Solomon from whom she expects a friendly reception. The subject of the verb is made explicit in vs. 4 which identifies the person as "king." Two objects in the accusative, "me" and "kisses," are governed by the same verb. The redundant expression "kiss me with kisses," grammatically, is an internal accusative; stylistically, it is an etymological figure of speech consisting of verb and noun of the same root. Poetic language relies on the manipulation of words for its effects on the reader's thoughts and emotions. The mention of the mouth instead of the lips is due to different meanings of two idiomatic expressions: "the kiss on the mouth" signifies greeting, while "the kiss on the lips" denotes response (Prv 24:26).

The particle *kî*, introducing vs. 2b, has an emphatic function, e.g. "in fact," to be omitted in the translation (JOÜON, *Gr.* § 164b). Thus, it is not an explicative or causal conjunction inserted for the purpose of explaining or justifying the invocation pronounced by the Shulamite. The clause whose subject is expressed by the 3rd person of the personal pronoun is followed by a series of clauses whose subject is the possessive pronoun of the 2nd person. The shift in person is due to enallage, a figure of speech common in poetry which contributes to variety in the sentence structure. These clauses specify in ascending order three attributes of Solomon and are linked to each other without conjunction by means of catchwords.

The adjective *tôb* (good, pleasant) qualifies all three nouns: "friendship," "wine," and "perfume," because of the same pleasant sensation produced in the person.

"Your friendship" (*dōdèkā*) designates a socio-political alliance between Solomon and the Shulamite. In the MT there are two spellings of this word in the plural in order to distinguish between two meanings: in *scriptio plena* occurs *dôdîm*, designating "lovers, uncles, cousins"; in *scriptio defectiva, dōdîm*, whose meaning in the abstract sense is "love" (Ez 16:8; 23:17; Prv 7:18) and "friendship" (Ct 1:2, 4; 4:10; 7:13), is used. In this text the stress is on the pleasant sensation caused to the persons, both by the ties of friendship and the tasting of wine. In order to establish a relationship between both terms of the comparison, the author considers friendship as being superior to the other.

"Wine" (*yayin*) is prefixed by the preposition *min* for the sake of comparison with "friendship." In Palestine, viticulture has been practiced from of old by a large part of its inhabitants, and its products, both raisins and wine, were widely commercialized among the population and constituted one of the principal sources of income; wine was the customary drink served at the main meal. On the basis of this dinner practice, wine represents the pleasures at table and the joy of commensal companionship and, by extension, it became a symbol of the bounty of nature's produce and of the prosperity of the country. In Israel it was customary to abstain from drinking wine during mourning, fasting, penance, and public calamity. After the destruction of Jerusalem in 587 B.C. there were days instituted as days of national mourning to be observed by the Jewish community four times per year: on the fourth month, for the fall of Jerusalem; on the fifth month, for the destruction of the temple; on the seventh month, for the death of Gedaliah; on the tenth month, for the extinction of the Jewish state (Zech 8:19). After exile, these commemorative dates of national catastrophe were no longer enforced by the Jewish community because they had already attained their objective, according to the teaching of the prophet Zechariah (Zech 7:1-7). With the return of the exiles to their native land, in 538 B.C., and the recuperation of national life, there was inaugurated the period of restoration. The days of mourning came to an end, commemorated up till then by fasting, and the time of joy arrived, celebrated with feasts and toasts of wine. Looking back to the period of exile which had ceased and forward to the period of restoration, now inaugurated, the inhabitants of Judah considered wine a symbol of a new prosperity opening up before the Jewish community. It is with this connotation that the term "wine" is used in the Song of Songs (Ct 1:2, 4; 2:4; 4:10; 5:1; 7:10; 8:2).

Vs. 3: "Your perfumes" (*šemānèkā*), lit. "your oils, ointments." The many uses of oil (*šemen*), extracted from olives, are determined by the degree of its quality and ingredients. "Pure" oil occurs in the Bible as an appreciated condiment for food seasoning. "Fresh" oil, obtained by pressing olives *in natura,* besides its nutritious value, was a lightly scented medicament serving as lineament applied on rough skin or dried up hair. Oil of inferior quality was obtained from a second pressing of olives. Residues deposited on the bottom of jars turned the oil rancid, leading to its being used as fuel oil. Manufacturers of perfumes and cosmetics added to "fresh" oil rare spices and resins from odoriferous plants producing various scented "oils" (*šemānîm*) of different types of fragrance for special use in cultic ceremonies and in exclusive circles among the wealthy.

The word "fragrance" (*rêaḥ*) refers to the aromatic substance, and not to the sense of smell. The *lamed* prefixed to *rêaḥ* is the *lamed* of reference, "as regards fragrance," without emphatic function (ROBERT-TOURNAY, 63), because in this sentence no specification of any particular type of fragrance is given, though varieties are mentioned elsewhere, i.e. "fragrance of nard" (1:12), "more fragrant perfumes than any spice" (4:10), "fragrance of Lebanon" (4:11), "fragrance of apples" (7:9), "fragrance of mandrakes" (7:14).

In the translation the adjective "pleasant" in the singular qualifies "fragrance," but in the Hebrew "pleasant" is in the plural qualifying "perfumes," i.e. "pleasant by their fragrance are your perfumes." Since the bodies may be identified by their odor, the more so the clothes sprinkled with perfume. The frequent allusions to perfume do not intend to differentiate the social rank of the bridegroom, the bride, and the maidens, but are meant to indicate Solomon's presence or proximity, perceptible as well to the sense of smell, which is attracted by the "pleasant" perfume of his clothes. The allusion to Solomon's presence is intended not to emphasize his charms but the function he exercises in the community.

"Your name" (*šᵉmekā*), more than just an identification of a person, is both a synonym of renown and a reference to his coronation name. The bridegroom's relevant services rendered to the community are publicly recognized, thus deserving the affection of countless maidens (6:8). In the Hebrew clause "you are diffused as to your name" (*tûraq šᵉmekā*), the expression "your name" is the complement of the subject of the verb whose function is to specify the verbal action: to be diffused as to the name, i.e. to be famous. The verb *ryq,* in the *Hophal,* means "to be emptied, shed, diffused." In the translation, "your name" becomes the subject of the phrase as the principal word of the clause. In the Hebrew, the word "perfume" (*šemen*) functions as an adverbial adjunct, viz. you are diffused in the manner of perfume.

"Therefore" (*ʿal-kēn*) expresses the conclusion of three clauses, which enunciate the epithets of the bridegroom, and indicates the reason for the maidens' affection for him. The anonymous "maidens" (*ʿᵃlāmôt*), without a definite article in Hebrew (1:3; 6:8), are a specific group of persons in the cast list of women mentioned in the Song of Songs: "daughters" (2:2; 6:9), "daughters of Jerusalem" (1:5; 2:7; 3:5, 10; 5:8, 16; 8:4), "daughters of Zion" (3:11), "queens and wives" (6:8-9). The word *ʿalmâ,* whose general meaning is "young woman," designates girls of different socio-juridical conditions: unmarried woman (Rebekah, Gn 24:43; sister of Moses, Ex 2:8), married woman (Is 7:14; Prv 30:19), virgin (Gn 24:43; Ex 2:8), non-virgin (Is 7:14; Prv 30:19), amateur dancers and singers (Ex 15:20; Jgs 21:21).

In order to determine the status of the "young women" they will be related to the categories of other women mentioned in the Song. The Israelite "daughters," although juridically *sub patria potestate,* had legally recognized prerogatives and were protected by the "right of the daughters," which secured them the right to life, freedom, honor, and inheritance. These legal measures constituted a safeguard of the daughters for their future marriage and a delimitation of paternal authority in order to prevent their being treated as slaves or prostitutes. The role of the "queens" and "wives" can be adequately understood in connection with diplomatic marriage. Treaties were given visible expression through royal marriages between the families of allied kings. Native and foreign wives retained a higher standing as "queens" (*mᵉlākôt*), "noble women" (*nāśîm śarôt,* 1 Kgs 11:3), if they were free-born and belonged to the nobility, or had a lower standing as "secondary wives" (*pîlagšîm*), if they were servants or slaves. To designate these secondary wives as "concubines" would be anachronistically to impose the image of a contemporary phenomenon upon a quite different situation from the past.

One distinctive feature which all these women have in common is their relationship with marriage, either already, or yet to be, accomplished. The "maidens" are longing to enter marriage with Solomon (1:3-4). The various categories of "daughters" are mentioned in the context of marriage alliance, but assume divergent attitudes as regards their relationship with Solomon.

Another characteristic feature differentiating these women is their attitude toward Solomon and the Shulamite: the "maidens" are on the side of Solomon; the "queens" and "wives" are on the side of the Shulamite; the "daughters," the "daughters of Jerusalem," and the "daughters of Zion" assume an intermediate posture. The "daughters" manifest initially some antipathy against the Shulamite, but gradually become sympathetic toward her (2:2; 6:9); the "daughters of Zion" are reserved in revealing their relationship with Solomon (3:11); finally, the "daughters of Jerusalem" are the Shulamite's rivals in securing leadership in Judah (1:5; 2:7; 3:5, 10; 5:8, 16; 8:4).

In order to discover the significance of these women, it is necessary to analyze the literary devices which the author employs so as to identify them. He does not limit himself to describing the characteristic features of each of them, but dramatizes their behavior in order to disclose their identity by means of attitudes which they assume in the social context. The personification of a city, community or nation by a woman is intended to represent a collective entity by means of attractive features which express her self-esteem and the sympathy of her admirers. Through the eyes of that woman the reader perceives the aspirations of a community, the tensions among these who share the same living conditions, the social structures, etc., and by looking at her reactions he is able to evaluate the events which have an impact on that society. The tendency to personify social groups, communities, and nations is partly due to the importance of life in common shared by certain social strata. This literary device, very much to the taste of the biblical authors, was used to emphasize the existential situation of certain persons, events, institutions, and themes, whose special significance can hardly become the object of abstract thought. The poetic personification of a collective entity brings it to life and endows it with a corporate dimension. According to the Semitic conception of society, it is the clan and the people which is the acting subject, as the corporate self of all its members. However, this corporative aspect does not erase the individuality of a particular person when described with the attributes of a collectivity. Thus, the *dramatis personae* of the Song of Songs refer to the corporate entity whose representatives they are. Their function is to dramatize and reinterpret the events and aspirations of the Jewish community in the period of restoration. Furthermore, it is typical of lyric poetry that the poet, while describing what he feels or experienced in the past, writes as spokesman of his community in order to generalize what he wants to express, so that others in similar situations may experience the same emotions. Therefore, the Song of Song contains individual experiences as well as the convictions and outlooks of the community, polarized around the specific interests of its social groups.

The "maidens," according to the analysis of their attitudes, the role they exercise in the context of the Song, and the relationship with other groups of women, represent the Jewish communities of the diaspora, situated in and outside Palestine. They existed in Gilead, Galilee, Babylonia, and Egypt. Those which maintained strong cultural and religious ties with the community of Judah later became flourishing centers of Jewish culture (AHARONI, 419).

The inhabitants of the territory of Judah, after the exile and the promulgation of Cyrus' edict in 538 B.C., were autochthonous Jews—a stable population which had remained after three deportations had assailed the country—and repatriate Jews who had returned from exile. Among the autochthonous population there stand out the leaders whose social status as landowners and chiefs of clans secured for them both ascendancy over the people dwelling in the territory of Judah and political influence in the provincial government. Among the repatriate Jews there were the leaders of Jerusalem who had administrative jurisdiction over the urban area of the former capital and the domains of the crown.

The incorporation of repatriate and autochthonous Jews in the Judean community did not happen by a process of fusion between two homogeneous components, but by integration of divergent groups into one social body which secured for all of them juridical, political, economic, and social equality. The divergency and even antagonism among these groups did not originate solely from their different provenance but was due above all to the different models of the socio-political structure proposed by each for the restored community. These two groups, while revindicating their rights, which had been in force during the previous monarchic period of Israel, demanded to participate in the organization of the community now under Persian rule. This was because, during the four centuries of political independence which the kingdom of Judah enjoyed up till the destruction of Jerusalem in 587 B.C., the power of the state was based, by constitutional law, upon two socio-political structures, separated geographically but equitative on the juridical level: i.e. the urban district of Jerusalem—where the house of David had its seat—whose leaders were the "inhabitants of Jerusalem," and the rural districts of Judah, represented by the "men of Judah" (Is 5:3). In view of the course which the Judean community was taking under the leadership of the repatriate Jews, the autochthonous Jews were claiming social equality and demanded the right to participate in the administration of the body politic, making heard their demand through the voice of their leadership. By designating itself "noble daughter" (7:2), this group of leaders evoked its former influential position in the government of the territory of Judah in order to assert its coresponsibility in the organization of the post-exilic

Jewish community. The model of political organization which it proposed was the restoration of the Davidic monarchy.

The repatriated Jews comprised three distinct groups according to the respective political objective which they aimed at consolidating in Judah in a situation of relative autonomy under Persian rule. The "daughters of Jerusalem" represent the elite of the Jewish priesthood, whose privileged position in the priestly hierarchy gave them ascendance over the servants of the Jerusalem temple, rebuilt in 515 B.C. In order to secure their political leadership in the community, these priests entered an alliance with prominent families which had control over the government in Samaria and the other neighboring provinces around Judah (Mal 2:11; Ezr 9–10; Neh 6:18; 10:31; 13:23-28). The model of political organization which they had in mind for the Jewish community was that of a theocracy, which later on developed into a theocratic hierocracy.

The "daughters of Zion" represent the leaders of the urban population. Some of its members exercised administrative functions under the jurisdiction of the provincial governor of Samaria. Previously, in the pre-exilic period, both the urban aristocracy and the leaders of both the urban and rural population had been attached to the monarchy of Judah by a formal pact. This gave them the right to ratify the nomination of the successor of the house of David and to grant him the executive power and authority to conduct the affairs of state (ALT, *Kl.S.* II, 126-134). By associating the leaders of the urban population with "Zion," a name which designates the older sector of the city of Jerusalem (2 Sm 5:7-9), the author probably meant to allude to the constitutional privilege which this group of repatriates inherited from their predecessors who had been deported from Jerusalem to Babylon in 587 B.C. The model of political organization which they sought to bring about for the Jewish community was the system of public administration they had known under the Persians.

Finally, the "daughters" do not seem to constitute a socially and politically well-delineated category. Although they do not fit into any of the other groups mentioned above, they sympathize with the political model proposed by the leaders of the autochthonous Jews.

While the women, described in terms of corporate personalities, represent the various segments of the Jewish community in the period of restoration, the men, either individually or collectively, personify the different functions carried out in the community of Judah. Since they will be analyzed in their respective contexts it will suffice just to list them: king, sons, companions, shepherds, retinue (*degel*), keepers, guards, warriors, and friends.

The second part of the sentence to be analyzed is the predicate expressed by the verb and the direct object "they love you" (*ʾahēbûkā*). The verb expresses the "maidens' " former and continuing high regard for the royalty. The frequent occurrence of the word "love" (seven times as a verb:

1:3, 4, 7; 3:1, 2, 3, 4; and eleven times as a noun: 2:4, 5, 7; 3: 5, 10; 5:8; 7:7; 8:4, 6, 7) is an indication of the importance of this concept as well as of its function as a keyword in the entire book. In all commentaries, past and present, the word "love" has invariably been taken in the sense of emotional affection between lovers. In addition to this, the history of interpretation of the Song of Songs displays the multiple variations of the theme of love, according to the subjective preference of the interpreter or the cultural tendencies of his time.

The divergent interpretations of the Song of Songs are owed to different opinions about the connection between this literary work and its historical context, to diverse explanations offered of the theme of love, and to extraneous views read into the conceptual content of love. This has given rise to extrapolations of different kinds: allegorical, spiritualizing, naturalistic, romantic, etc. In order to ascertain the specific meaning it is required to situate the Song of Songs in its historical context and in the tradition of the wisdom literature, to eliminate extrinsic presuppositions which determine the approach of the basic theme of the whole book, and to point out the exact meaning of the single word "love" as it is used by the biblical author. It is important to note that there is a univocal application of the term to the same conceptual content dealt with in various passages of the book and that its juridical connotation expresses a bond of fellowship. Now, the special kind of relationship intended here is not that of a subjective feeling but of a covenant (MORAN, *CBQ* 25, 77-87). Examining the word "love" in the respective passages in the Song we arrive at the conclusion that this word is used as a technical term expressing the covenant relationship between the house of David and the Jewish community. Thus, "love" may be taken as a synonym for covenant, since a covenant intends or brings about a bond of friendship.

A distinction must be made, however, between real and virtual covenants: in the first case, it refers to the one in force during the pre-exilic period; in the second, there is implied the possibility and desirability of establishing a covenant during the period of restoration. During the monarchic period of Israel's history, the covenant between king and people was a characteristic feature assumed by the state. Even after the extinction of the Jewish state, the destruction of Jerusalem, the deportation of the royal family and the inhabitants of the capital in 587 B.C., the relationship between the Davidic monarchy and the Jewish people was kept alive in the collective memory of the Jews and became a source of hope for the restoration of monarchy in Judah. Since the destiny of the people had always been associated with the destiny of their king, so too the future of the Jewish community would be linked to the future of the house of David. Thus complete restoration of the Jewish nation implied restoration of the monarchy. This is the task to be carried out by autochthonous and repatriate Jews with the caveat that no suspicion must be aroused in the Persian authorities of a burgeoning Jewish nationalism in defiance of their domination over Judah. For the communities located in the diaspora, facing the problem of survival as religious minorities surrounded by a population professing different creeds, it was a question of vital importance how to keep alive the traditions of the forebears. Therefore the Jews kept the king in their memory not on account of nostalgia but because of his function as a representative of the people of God and as a sign of divine election. In addition to this, the dispersed communities hoped that the prestige of the Davidic monarchy, restored in Judah, might benefit them in their social milieu as a source of influence which would pave the way for them to rise from a marginal position in the foreign cities in which they found themselves and would guarantee the enforcement of the religious laws of Israelite tradition. The reference to the "maidens," representing the Jewish communities of the diaspora, opens up to the Jews of Palestine a universalist perspective. This is because of the far-reaching impact which the restoration of national life and the organization of the community under the monarchic regime was to have, satisfying the expectations of the Jews at home and in the diaspora.

Vs. 4: The second strophe is introduced by the request of the bride that she be received in the company of the absent bridegroom. The verb in the imperative, "draw me!" (*moškēnî*), is followed by the adjunct "after you" (*'aḥarèkā*). The MT separates the adjunct from the verb, linking it to the verb "make haste" and taking the "maidens" as subject of the clause, in contradiction with logic which implies that the bridegroom, accompanied by the bride, is the subject at the verb "make haste."

The place of meeting is indicated by the terminative complement "into his chambers" (*ḥadārâw*), expressed in Hebrew by the accusative of direction without a preposition (JOÜON, *Gr* § 125n). The "chambers" signify, by synecdoche, the royal palace, seat of the head of the government.

The verb *hebî'anî* is to be parsed as a precative perfect and translated in the optative "may he lead me" (JOÜON, *Gr* § 112k); this balances with the imperative in the preceding colon "draw me after you!" The reference to "the king" (*hammelek*) designates the person (he, you) mentioned in the previous clauses (vss. 2; 3ab); the definite article identifies "the king" as the Davidic descendant raised to kingship.

Emendations of the MT try to eliminate the discordance between the subjects (you, the king) of the verbs "draw" and "lead" in this and in the previous sentence (vs. 2). The shift in person, known as enallage, is frequent in poetic language for variety in the sentence structure of a dialogue.

After the appeal of the bride, the chorus enters the stage; they manifest their presence at intervals by delivering a soliloquy. The chorus, as in Greek drama where they enuntiate the sapiential experience applied to concrete situations, has the function in the Song of Songs as counselors of the bride, using the categories of the wisdom tradition in order to divulge their project of social and political restoration under the monarchy. However, the presence of the chorus is so discreet that it is not even indicated in the Hebrew text, and the commentators diverge in identifying it in several passages, ascribed by some to other speakers. Taking into account both the sequence of ideas formulated in the texts and the nexus between the various dialogues and soliloquies, one perceives an interruption in the course of thought or an abrupt transition between passages containing exuberant feelings and those which express ideas in a sober and reflective mood. According to the form of composition, the texts recited by the chorus can be classified as introduction (5:9; 6:1, 10; 7:1; 8:5), transition (1:8; 8:10), conclusion (1:4), description (3:6-10), and apostrophe (3:11; 5:1). In addition to the literary function, the chorus exercises the role of representing the bride in social surroundings which are inaccessible to her, such as the crowded gatherings of spectators among whom she would not be able to gain sight of the approaching retinue (3:6-8), and the secluded circles of the elite (3:9-11).

The conclusion of the two strophes allude briefly to the persons mentioned before. The chorus does not restrict itself to being merely a narrator but adds a declaration of enthusiastic support to the bride's initiative (vs. 4c), and expresses a value judgment concerning the king's presence in the midst of the restored nation (vs. 4d) and the relationship between Judah's monarchy and the communities of the diaspora (vs. 4e).

The verbs expressing joy, "exult" (*gyl*) and "rejoice" (*śmḥ*) are constructed with *b*ᵉ to introduce the object (JOÜON, *Gr* § 133c). The object of the exulting and rejoicing which the chorus proclaims is the person of the bride, and not the solidarity between chorus and bride; for a distinction has to be made between "rejoicing in" and "rejoicing with." The sentence "let us exult and rejoice" (*nāgîlāh, niśmeḥāh*) expresses the will of the mentors of the wisdom tradition to support enthusiastically the movement in favor of the restoration of national life, undertaken by the leadership of the autochthonous Jews.

"Extol" (*nazkîrāh*), lit. "let us extol." The verb *zkr* (remember) in *Hiphil*, means "to awaken the memory," usually by means of manifestations of praise, and in this sense it is equivalent to "celebrate." In the expression "your friendship" (*dōdèkā*), the pronoun refers to the king. The reason for the chorus' extolling the king is the expectation of his return to his native land. The joy about the covenant between king and people is superior to the satisfaction resulting from economic prosperity—in poetic language, "your friendship is superior to wine" (*dōdèkā miyyayin*).

"Rightly" (*mêšārîm*) in Hebrew is an abstract plural, used as adverbial accusative to express a value judgment. The verb in the 3rd person plural of the phrase "they love you" (*ʾahēbûkā*) is governed either by an indefinite subject "one" or definite "they," i.e. the maidens. On the basis of the previously mentioned persons and the parallelism with vs. 3c, we conclude that the maidens are the implicit subject of the phrase. The mentors of the wisdom tradition give praise to the preservation of the monarchy in the memory of the Jews scattered in the diaspora, considering it a positive factor for the restoration of the monarchic regime in Judah.

Commentary: The Theme of the Monarchy (1:2-4)

The theme of the whole book is introduced by the song dealing with the bride's invocation, which presents the principal characters of most of the scenes, specifies the relationship between them, manifests the state of spirit which characterizes the entire book, and announces the theme to be developed in the dialogues. In applying the genre of lyric poetry to the topics mentioned above, the poet uses a medium capable of stirring up empathy between himself and the readers, beyond time and space. However, the aim of this poetic composition is not aesthetic pleasure but engagement in those movements which determine the course of history at a specific time. The author of the Song is a poet "engaged" in the restoration of socio-political structures which would bring about and uphold the cohesion of the chosen people in the post-exilic period. Such a contingent and temporal theme served as background for the artistic configuration of a perennial and universal theme, i.e. social cohesion. Historically, the author of the Song advocates the unity of a people, which is identified, from a synchronic view of Israelite history, as the Jewish people in the post-exilic period; artistically, from a symphronistic view of literature, he is one of the most enthusiastic voices of all times ever to extol social cohesion.

Among the socio-political institutions which would contribute most to the integration of autochthonous and repatriate Jews and to the organization of the post-exilic community of Judah, the author rates the monarchic regime as the most effective. This is because the representative of the Davidic monarchy embodies the national consciousness of the Jewish people. By virtue of the principle of corporate personality and the interrelation between individuals and social groups, one particular person could be the representative of collectivity. Thus the governor of Judah, being a descendant of the Davidic dynasty and a nominee of the Persians appointed to govern the Judean territory, is designated "king" whose function is to elevate the various social groups of Judah to the rank of an autonomous nation, although subordinate to Persian rule. He is not a mere poetic personage in a "royal travesty" (GERLEMAN, 96) who would be representing on stage the role of an enamored youth paying court to a damsel. There is never used in the Bible either the literary genre of drama or that of poetry of evasion. The recourse to love poetry happens to be an expedient dictated by reason of political caution to conceal from the eyes of the Persian authorities—who would suspect the rise of an insurrection against their domination over Judah—the intention to promote Jewish nationalism. Another reason for the use of this type of poetry is its particular resonance among Jewish readers who undoubtedly recognized in the characters of the Song corporate personalities representing specific social groups and perceived the meaning of the declarations of love as expressions of consent to a covenant. The cohesion among different groups of the community of Judah, a goal to be attained, imposed the initial task of solving the problem of discrimination and disunity among different groups; secondly, it was required of them to engage all the inhabitants of Judah in the common objective of restoring national life. According to the traditions of their forebears, the promises of future restoration are linked to the house of David and express the aspirations for a new kingdom like that of David (Ez 37:15-28).

The bride is the leading figure representative of the autochthonous Jews. Her invocation of the bridegroom expresses the yearning for the king's return to the seat of the Davidic dynasty in Jerusalem; the subjects will receive from him the confirmation of their social status (vs. 2a) and the recognition of their rights as citizens (vs. 4ab). The maidens represent the Jewish communities in the diaspora, located in and outside of Palestine, being associated to that of Judah by the heritage of the religious traditions of the chosen people. The dispersion of the Jews, in Old Testament times, was partly due to spontaneous emigration and partly the result of the deportation of the inhabitants of Jerusalem and neighboring towns at the time of the conquest of Judah by the Babylonians. Different factors contributed to the organization and flourishing of these communities dispersed in foreign countries; among these were: the policy of religious tolerance adopted by the Babylonian and Persian empires, permitting subjugated peoples and ethnic minorities to practice their national religions; the segregation of exiled Jews confined to restricted colonies, initially as a provisional measure and later on as a definitive one with the approval of the government; the internal organization carried out by the local leadership which acted as an integrating factor, and brought about the social cohesion which enabled them to face the challenge of acculturation and prevented a fragmentation of the community; the exchange of letters among scattered Jews (Jer 29; 51:39-64; Neh 1:1-3), made easier by the adoption of Aramaic as the official language of the Persian empire. This meant that the Jews kept alive the sense of belonging to the promised land and incentive was given to literary creativity among the mentors of these communities by means of the transcription of religious texts which were read in cultic meetings. As a result of exchanging letters, the events that took place in Judah had an impact on other Jewish communities located even in the farthest regions of the Persian empire. With the promulgation of Cyrus' edict in 538 B.C., concerning the reconstruction of the Jerusalem temple and the repatriation of exiled Jews, the exilic age had officially come to an end. At that time a new period of Israelite history began, marked by the restoration of the community of Judah. The symbols of the Jewish nation were the temple and the city of Jerusalem, which became factors of irradiation and convergence of all Jews in and outside of the homeland. Thus, for the Jews who remained in foreign countries it became a matter of personal responsibility to renew contacts with the leaders in Jerusalem and keep Israelite identity alive in the diaspora. Those who returned to the native land did not go in pursuit of adventures but embarked on an enterprise with a guarantee of success because they relied on official support from the Persian government. The token of such a guarantee was the nomination of Sheshbazzar and Zerubbabel, both prominent Jewish leaders, to hold office as provincial governors of Judah, provided with imperial authorization and safe conduct for the journey of the caravans of repatriates. These auspicious signs fueled aspirations for an immediate restoration of the monarchy (Hag 2:20-23; Zech 4:6-10) and kept it alive while the descendants of the Davidic dynasty lived in Judah.

From that time onward, the Jewish communities scattered in the diaspora possessed a center of convergence. The homeland of their ancestors, governed by the heirs of the house of David, would be enrolled among other nations as it regained its national independence. When the Jewish communities of the diaspora gave their support to the restoration of the monarchy in Judah they hoped that the prestige of this monarchy might benefit them in their own social milieu as a source of influence which would pave the way for them to get away from their marginal position in foreign cities and would guarantee the enforcement of the religious laws of Israelite tradition. In order to express the relationship between the Davidic monarchy and the communities of the diaspora, the Song uses the term "love" (vs. 3c), according to the terminology used in the ancient Near Eastern treaty literature. The nature of a particular treaty becomes clear from the context. In the Song, however, the communities of the diaspora ("maidens") do not speak for themselves, since they do not have active voice in the community of Judah, but are mentioned by the leadership of the native population of Judah.

The Davidic monarchy and its significance for the Jewish nation are described in terms which allude to the repatriation of the heir to the royal throne, after the exile. The condition necessary for establishing the monarchic regime in Judah is the arrival of the Davidic descendant in the country of his predecessors, provided with the authorization of the Persians to hold office. His return to the homeland is extolled by the inhabitants with festive greetings (vs. 2). His presence in the midst of the population is compared to air scented with perfume (vs. 3a), in allusion to a text which refers to "the Lord's anointed, the breath of our nostrils" (Lam 4:20). His coronation name, made known all over (vs. 3b), refers to the house of David and its special relationship to Yahweh. During the period of restoration it was hoped that the prestige of the Davidic monarchy would extend beyond the borders of the territory of Judah (vs. 3c), not in the form of political hegemony, impossible under Persian rule, but in the sense of an influence exercised by the monarch's delegates in the organization of the Jewish communities of the diaspora.

The leading figure representative of the autochthonous Jews engaged in the organization of the religious community was not, however, the only voice raised in Judah in favor of the monarchy. There appear on the scene the followers of the wisdom tradition who, through the words pronounced by the chorus, express their enthusiastic support for such an initiative (vs. 4c). They stress the regulatory function of the monarchy in the organization of socio-political structures which are not to be subordinated to economic structures (vs. 4d), and acclaim the efforts at linking the communities of the diaspora with the inhabitants of Judah by means of their allegiance to the monarchy (vs. 4e). According to such an universalist perspective, the institution of the monarchy exercises a decisive influence on all Jewish communities as an integrating force capable of bringing about and maintaining the cohesion of the chosen people.

The theme of the monarchy will be taken up again in the final song (8:13-14), in the context of a covenant being brought into existence.

2. ✦ *The Self-esteem of Love (1:5-6)*

5 I am black, but comely, *Bride*
O daughters of Jerusalem,
like the tents of Kedar,
like the pavilions of Solomon
6 Do not gaze at me because I am swarthy,
because the sun has scorched me.
My mother's sons were angry with me,
they made me keeper of the vineyards;
but, my own vineyard I could not keep.

Accented Transliteration (1:5-6)

5 *šeḥôrâ ʾanî wenāʾwâ*
benôt yerûšālāim
keʾoholê kēdār
kîrîʿôt šelōmōh

6. *'al-tir'únî še'ᵃní šeḥarḥóret*
šeššezā́fatnî haššā́meš
bené 'immî niḥᵃrû-bî́
śāmúnî nōṭērấ 'et-hakkerāmî́m
karmî́ šellî́ lō' nāṭā́rtî

Literary Analysis (1:5-6)

This song deals with the second aspect of love which consists in the self-esteem arising from the experience of the surety of one's innate value as the source of love. Thus, the bride's self-esteem is not diminished; rather it is enhanced in the face of the contempt which a dominant group dispenses on her as belonging to a subordinate group.

The bride's profile stands out in the midst of the landscape through the contrast between light and darkness, civilized life and desert, center and periphery. In the first strophe (vs. 5), the stress is on the features of her physiognomy and those of the landscape, as a literary device used for expressing the emotions arising from the innermost recesses of the heart. In the second strophe (vs. 6), the exposure to sunrays while on duty in the vineyards during the heat of the day is given as the cause of the woman's dark complexion.

As regards the meaning of "vineyard" it is to be noted that this word is used in the singular to designate a plantation of grapevines and, figuratively, the Jewish community, while in the plural it designates a plurality of such plantations and, in a figurative sense, the settlements of the local population of Judah.

Poetic and rhetorical devices which occur in this song are sound repetition: identical consonants: *k-k* (vs. 5cd), *š-š* (vs. 6ab); onomatopoeia *šeššezāfatnî haššāmeš* (vs. 6b); repetition of structural patterns: chiasmus (vs. 6a-b, d-e); isocolon (vs. 5b-d); epanodos "I am black . . . like the tents of Kedar, comely . . . like the pavilions of Solomon." Rhetorical devices: antithesis "black but comely"; simile "I am like the tents of Kedar, like the pavilions of Solomon."

Vocabulary Analysis (1:5-6)

Vs. 5: The bride's appearance is compared to the color of the Bedouin tents (*'oholê*) of Kedar, located in the region of Wadi as-Sirhan, in western Saudi Arabia. The name Kedar was also used in a figurative sense to designate desolate areas occupied by inhabitants opposed to any adjustment to civilized life. The canvas woven from wool of black goats provides the image for the black color of the skin or of the veil covering the woman's face. However, the silhouettes of jet black tents, nestling between sand dunes ablaze with the glare of the sun's rays, is not a likely comparison for a woman's complexion, but is rather a caricature of a person exposed to ridicule (LANDY, *JSOT* 1980, 63). Yet the reference to the "black" (*šeḥôrâ*) color of the skin is intended as an indication not of racial identity, but of social rank, and is linked with the opposition between Bedouins and townspeople. By enunciating the words "I am black . . . like the tents of Kedar," which is a disparaging remark made by the "daughters of Jerusalem," the bride raises her voice in protest against discrimination in a soliloquy of complaint against the persistent hostility present in society. In the following verse, she mentions that sunburn and rustic toil rather than any genetic factor are the causes of her dark-hued complexion.

In contrast with the hostile attitude of the "daughters of Jerusalem," who represent the townspeople's aversion for the Bedouins, the bride instead approaches them without a hint of confrontation but, on the contrary, with an expression of empathy. The term "comely" (*nāʾwâ*), employed to qualify herself, expresses her gentle reply to the pejorative comment on her rustic aspect. It would be utterly mistaken and completely out of context to interpret this verse in the sense of the slogan "Black Is Beautiful" as it is used in today's black liberation movements. Thus, the Hebrew particle *we* is not a copulative conjunction "and," but adversative, "but," "though," whose function is to connect words that are in opposition. Since beauty is something to be looked at, the bride's comeliness is compared with the splendor of Solomon's "pavilions" (*yerîʿôt*), which are a metonymy for his palace. By analogy with the aesthetic function of the pavilions annexed to the stately mansion of the king, the bride revindicates for herself an influential position in the political heart of the country. Therefore she does not tolerate being treated as a rural outsider like the Bedouins whom the townspeople kept at a distance from civilized society.

The emendation of a word in the MT which replaces Solomon by Salmah is unwarranted for two reasons: first, the poetic sentence structure consists in an antithetic parallelism: black–Kedar, comely–Solomon; second, the idea expressed in these clauses is formulated by opposite terms: "black" with a pejorative connotation, and "comely" denoting appreciation. Furthermore, Salmah is an Assyrian term designating a Bedouin tribe dwelling in the desert region of Jordan, between the Dead Sea and the Gulf of Akaba.

The "daughters of Jerusalem," as a corporate personality, represent the elite of the Jewish priesthood brought to Judah by caravans of exiles coming from Babylon. Their provenance from a cohesive Jewish community and their improved cultural milieu were determining factors in their self-esteem and one of the reasons for their attitude of superiority with relation to the native Jews in Judah.

Vs. 6: The second strophe mentions the cause of the "swarthy" complexion of the bride. By addressing the "daughters of Jerusalem," she demands that they should not stare at her with a look of contempt. The verb *rā'āh* (to stare) is conjugated in Hebrew in the masculine, *tir'ûnî* (you stare at me), although the subject is feminine. According to the rules of verbal agreement in Hebrew, the feminine forms of the 2nd person plural of verbs with suffixes are replaced by masculine forms (JOÜON, *Gr* § 150a). The prohibitive particle *'al* (not) is used in this sentence to express a request that they should not stare at her with contempt. Another alternative interpretation of this sentence is based on the asseverative meaning of *'al*, e.g. "indeed do look at me!" This rendering is based on the supposition that the two strophes express the bride's attempt to put the beauty of both blackness and whiteness on level pegging (EXUM, *Bib* 62, 416–419). This interpretation however is to be dismissed because the song does not deal with a racial conflict but with socio-political discrimination.

The sentence introduced by the Hebrew conjunction *še* states the cause of her dark-hued complexion, "because the sun has scorched me." The *hapax legomenon šeḥarḥōret* (swarthy) is an attenuating adjective of *šeḥôrâ* (black). The effect of the sunrays on the skin is expressed by the verb *šzp* (to see, look at) or *šdp* (to scorch). By a permutation of the consonants *z* and *d*, frequent in Aramaic, the verb *šzp* would have been used instead of *šdp* (ROBERT-TOURNAY, 72). The feminine verbal form *šezāpatnî* (she has scorched me) occurs as the predicate of a feminine subject; the "sun" (*šemeš*) can be either masculine or feminine; here, the "sun" is a feminine noun on account of parallelism with the "daughters of Jerusalem," in order to stress the analogy between the "glare" of the sun which has a physical effect on the body, and the "glaring look" of the "daughters of Jerusalem" which causes a moral effect on the soul. In both cases, the result is temporary, since the swarthy skin becomes white again, and likewise the grief of the soul ceases as soon as the cause of grief is eliminated.

The task to be carried out by the bride was not of her choosing, but was imposed by other members of the community, i.e., "my mother's sons" (*bené 'immî*), who are mentioned indirectly by a circumlocution in another text (8:8). The term "brother" is employed in the Semitic languages to designate, first, a blood relative belonging to a family circle; second, a partner of a social covenant fellowship between different groups or tribes; third, an ally of a political treaty relationship between king and people, vassal and overlord. In the Song, the term "brother" (8:1), applied to Solomon by the Shulamite, occurs once. However, the correlate term "sister" is mentioned more frequently to designate the reciprocal relationship between the two principal characters of the poems: in the dialogue between Solomon and the Shulamite— "my sister, my bride" (4:9, 10, 12; 5:1); "my sister, my friend" (5:2)—and in the text dealing with the brothers and the Shulamite— "little sister" (8:8). By applying the term "brother/sister" to designate exclusively

Solomon/Shulamite, the author gives a hint of his intention to use these terms in a strict sense, i.e. as official titles. Thus, the covenant relationship is restricted to the king and the people of Judah, represented respectively by Solomon and the Shulamite. There was no bond of fellowship to be established between Jews and Ashdodites, Ammonites, Moabites, and Samaritans (Neh 13:23-28).

The text referring to the mother of the bride is to be analyzed in order to explain her role and relationship with the other persons of the poems. Like the other women mentioned in the Song, so too the mother of the bride is a poetic personification. As a corporate personality she represents the pre-exilic Israelite nation into which the social groups of Judah were integrated. The descendants of these groups are called "daughters"; they stand for the segments of the restored nation, unified in the post-exilic period.

"My mother's sons" (*bᵉnê 'immî*) symbolize a specific social group in authority over the community of Judah. The complaint made against the domineering attitude of these "sons," who try to hold sway over other groups, indicates them as repatriate Jews who were trying to deprive the autochthonous Jews of their legitimate right to participate in the government of the community. The refusal to grant their request is expressed by an upsurge of anger: "they were angry with me" (*niḥᵃrû-bî*). Morphologically, the verbal form is regarded either as an irregular perfect, in *Niphal,* of the root *ḥrh,* or as a perfect, in *Piel,* of the root *nḥr.* In both cases the meaning is that of anger which flared up in the hearts of these sons.

In order to stifle any further attempt to challenge their leadership, "the sons" put the leaders of the native population of Judah in charge of their local domains—"they made me keeper of the vineyards" (*śāmmunî nōṭērâ 'et-hakkᵉrāmîm*). The verb *nṭr* (to keep) is not to be taken in the sense of guarding the vineyards from being robbed of their produce by thieves or damaged by animals, but rather that of administering them.

The expression "my own vineyard" (*karmî šellî*) has double determination to indicate possession and emphasis. Most commentators identify the vineyard with the bride. This interpretation contradicts, however, the meaning of the text and the sense of the term "vineyard" which signifies a plantation of grapevines and, figuratively, the community. Thus, this noun in the singular represents either the Jewish community of Judah (1:6; 8:12), or that of Babylon (8:11); in the plural, "vineyards" denote plantations of grapevines (1:14; 2:15; 7:13) or, in a figurative sense, settlements of autochthonous Jews located in various districts of the Judean territory. "Vineyard," as a collective noun, designates the sum total of the integrating parts; in a figurative sense, it acquires different connotations according to the different ways in which people are integrated into the social body. Thus, on the religious level, "vineyard" designates the chosen people (Is 5:1-7, etc.); on the social level, it denotes the community (Ct 1:6; 8:11-12); on the political level, it signifies the nation (Ct 1:6; 8:12).

The distinction between "vineyard" and "vineyards" not only sets in contrast the nation and the settlements, but underscores too the antagonism between the elite occupying the center of the stage and the peasantry edged off to the side.

The statement of the bride saying "I could not keep" (*lō' nāṭārtî*) is neither an admission of negligence in fulfilling her duties nor a complaint against excessive work-load; on the contrary, it denounces the stratagem devised by some repatriate Jews to deprive their autochthonous brethren of the right to participate in the administration of the community. But what is the purpose of their voicing the demands in the presence of the elite of the Jewish priesthood ("daughters of Jerusalem")? The answer to this question lies in a common quest for overcoming socio-cultural estrangement by working together in the promotion of the common good. This objective should inspire both repatriate and autochthonous Jews to abdicate from the selfish pursuit of private interests. The organization of national life, expressed in poetic language in terms of administration of the vineyard, represents an inspiring goal for all segments of society which are invited to take part in the restoration of the Jewish nation.

Commentary: The Theme of the Nation (1:5-6)

This song expresses an invitation to all members of the Judean community to get involved in the restoration of the Jewish nation. The immediate objective is the organization of a cohesive community and, concomitantly, the elimination of any social and cultural discrimination. If this goal, transcending private interests, were not inspiring to all the inhabitants of Judah, it would hardly be possible for them to overcome internal division arising from the assemblage of heterogeneous groups whose provenance and customs were different. The return of exiles brought about a displacement of native people in Judah as those who had occupied the exiles' homes in their absence were now dislodged from them. Other types of tension were caused by internal factors which had deeply marked the Jewish communities during the exilic period. As a matter of fact, both repatriate and autochthonous Jews maintained their socio-religious identity during a period of half a century by virtue of their resistance to any attempt at assimilation whereby a minority would be absorbed by a surrounding majority. But with the promulgation of Cyrus' edict of repatriation and the constitution of an integrated Judean community, whose territorial integrity was secured by imperial decree, the inhabitants of Judah did not need any longer to live in continuous confrontation with other nations or groups of people. The socio-political organization of the community made it necessary from then on that concrete measures be taken in order to harmonize the pursuit of private interests with those of the community as well as to overcome divergent tendencies.

Given the social and cultural differences, it was inevitable that tensions should arise. It is important to note, though, that the leaders of Judah's native population did not repay the insult which the elite of the Jewish priesthood leveled against the natives by demeaning their social status to the lifestyle of uncultured Bedouins; rather they tried to create an atmosphere of empathy which would bring them closer to one another under the auspices of the king. Indeed, no more suitable place of meeting for the two delegations would be available than the pavilions of the royal palace, where the "uncivilized" peasantry would have an opportunity to demonstrate their gracious manners in the presence of high society. The scene intends not only to focus on the problem of the tense relationship but also to offer a possible solution. Since decorative features have the function of revealing the thematic content and to make manifest the significance of the scenario, one perceives that kingship, mentioned in reference to Solomon, acts as a catalyst in that it brings about the integration of two equidistant social groups. The allusion to Solomon is also a link between the theme of the monarchy, dealt with in the preceding song, and that of the nation in the present one.

The transition from one scene to the other takes up, in dark colors, the external aspect of the bride and adds to the psychological reaction of the audience. The contemptuous staring of the leading figures of the Jewish priesthood is an eloquent sign of their censure of the outsiders' intrusion into the secluded circles of the elite. Its focus, aimed at the garment and the color of the skin, brings into the range of vision the bride's social condition. By her appearance she belongs to a group of Bedouins who live at a distance from civilized society. The lifestyle of the Bedouins is labeled by the townspeople as primitive. But all of this is mere conjecture on the part of the townspeople, which leads to an erroneous opinion about her. In fact, the bride does not argue in favor of nomadism as the only viable form of life on the frontier between the desert and cultivated land. On the contrary, she rejects being lumped in with Bedouins. Her toil as keeper of vineyards proves that long ago she had advanced toward settled life and managed to contribute to the growth of the country's economy by supplying the local markets with products of considerable commercial value. The reference to viticulture refutes the insinuation of her being a parasite of society and a menace to the security of the inhabitants as if she were an alien to settled life and uncooperative with any engagement in the organization of social structures.

The autochthonous population of the territory of Judah is not, then, a group of Bedouins, as the repatriate Jews insinuate, although in some regions of the Edomite province there were Jews dwelling in the countryside, given over to nomadic life or agriculture. However, these inhabitants did not belong to the territory of Judah (AHARONI, 416). The cultural imbalance among the different Jewish groups is not the result of a primitive socio-economic structure, but of the fiscal system imposed by the Babylonian government (586-539 B.C.), which gradually impoverished the rural population. In spite of adverse conditions under Babylonian occupation, the autochthonous Jews deserved special merit for having defended the territorial integrity of their native soil against fragmentation, annexation by neighboring countries, and massive infiltration of non-Jewish groups into the land of Judah. The reorganization of the community had been entrusted to persons in authority under the monarchy prior to the extinction of the kingdom of Judah: officials, clergy of the rural sanctuaries, sages, and scribes who had escaped from the siege of Jerusalem and from the deportation to Babylon. Their role as mentors of community life was decisive in the spiritual and religious restoration of a population left in a state of humiliation and hopelessness in the face of a devastated country with the temple in ruins, the royal family in exile, and the nation scattered abroad (STADELMANN, *PT* 1987, 181–202). By this retrospective view of all that had happened in the past, the people of Judah were reminded of the service they had rendered to the country and thus encouraged to refuse being ostracized from the "vineyard" by repatriate Jews and relegated to the administration of "vineyards," a term which designates, by synecdoche, the settlements of native Jews.

As a result of the repatriation of exiles, the social organization of Judah underwent some drastic changes. Its leadership was taken over by delegates of the exiles who tried to consolidate their position by ousting those who had been in command of the community of Judah. Since the people of Judah denounced this trend before the elite of the Jewish priesthood, it is because they recognized its share of responsibility for the common good. At first sight, this would seem to be a case of rivalry between political parties each trying to secure its own interest. However, what is at stake is the very future of the Jewish nation, designated by the term "vineyard." Therefore, by depriving the leaders of the native population of the right to take part in the government of Judah, the native Jewish groups dwelling in the districts of the "vineyards" are deprived of their political equality along with the recent arrivals. Now, if there were no socio-political structures upholding the community so as to prevent power from becoming overbearing and obstruct the road to tyrannical domination, all citizens would be deprived of their rights and reduced to mere puppet figures. Thus, the voice raised in protest against this kind of discrimination is a warning against the rise of a despotic regime and a demand that the community of Judah be formally constituted as a state with a legal foundation. The society composed of repatriate and autochthonous Jews, intended to secure political rights for each citizen, was now to be constituted as an ethical community, destined to become a nation. The theme of the nation is taken up and amplified in the corresponding song about Solomon's vineyard (8:11-12).

3. ✦ *The Ambitions of Love (1:7-11)*

7 Tell me, you whom my soul loves, *Bride*
where you go forth to pasture,
where you rest your flock at noon;
that I may not appear as one veiled
beside the flocks of your companions.
8 If you do not know, *Chorus*
O fairest among women,
follow the tracks of the sheep,
and pasture your kids
beside the shepherds' huts.
9 To my mare amongst Pharaoh's chariots *Bridegroom*
I compare you, my friend.
10 Your cheeks are comely with pendants,
your neck with beads.
11 We will make you pendants of gold,
with droplets of silver.

Accented Transliteration (1:7-11)

7 *haggî́dāh lî́ šeʾāh^{a}bā́ nafšî́*
ʾêkā́ tirʿéh
ʾêkā́ tarbî́ṣ baṣṣoh^{o}rā́yim
šallāmā́ ʾehyéh k^{e}ʿōṭ^{e}yā́
ʿal ʿedrḗ ḥ^{a}bērékā
8 *ʾim-lṓʾ tēd^{e}ʿî lā́k*
hayyāfā́h bannāšî́m
ṣ^{e}ʾî-lā́k b^{e}ʿiqbê haṣṣṓʾn
ûr^{e}ʿî́ ʾet-g^{e}diyyōtáyik
ʿal mišk^{e}nôt hārōʿî́m
9 *l^{e}susātî́ b^{e}rikbê farʿṓh*
dimmîtî́k raʿyātî́

10 *nā'wû leḥāyáyik battōrîm*
ṣawwā'rék baḥarûzîm
11 *tôrê zāhāb na'aśeh-lāk*
'im nequddôt hakkāsef

Literary Analysis (1:7-11)

This song deals with the third aspect of love viewed as the source of ambitions, illustrated by the aspirations of the bride to share with the bridegroom in the tasks related to public administration. The song, composed of three strophes, presents two scenes: pasture and parade. The quiet atmosphere of rural simplicity, typical of the countryside given over to shepherds and their flocks, pervades the environment of the first scene in which the dialogue is carried on in two strophes (vss. 8 and 9). The third strophe (vss. 9-11) is couched in a scene which has as its setting the mews where horses are harnessed, hitched on chariots, and made ready for an official parade. The principal character in the song is the bride who moves from one scene to another and starts the chorus and the bridegroom engaging in a lively dialogue about administrative affairs which are described in analogy with pasture and parade. Each strophe ends with a circumstantial complement of place (vss. 7f, 8e) or quality (vs. 11) related both to the function which the bride exercises in the community and the relationship between her and the other characters of the song.

Poetic and rhetorical devices that are used in the song are sound repetition: assonance *e-i: tēde'î–ṣe'î–be'iqbê–ûre'î;* word repetition: anaphora "where–where." Rhetorical devices: parallelism "your cheeks with pendants–your neck with beads"; "pendants of gold–droplets of silver"; simile "you are like one veiled, like my mare"; hyperbole "fairest among women."

Vocabulary Analysis (1:7-11)

Vs. 7: The first strophe opens up with a pastoral scene where bride, bridegroom, and companions are presented in the pursuit of their interests. The dialogue is introduced by a request from the bride to the absent bridegroom entreating him to tell her his whereabouts. "Tell me" (*haggîdāh-lî*) governs two adverbial clauses; the interrogative adverb of place *'êkâ* (where), as regards its form and meaning, is borrowed from Aramaic (Krinetzki, 44), whereas in Hebrew it signifies "how." The verb *ngd* (to tell) is used here as a literary device in order to introduce a dialogue and to point at the main subject to be dealt with in these strophes. The wording of "he whom my soul loves" (*še'āhabâ nafšî*) is a circumlocution of "my beloved" (*dôdî*): the former occurs less frequently in passages which express a feeling of nostalgia for the absent bridegroom (1:7; 3:1, 2, 3, 4), whereas the latter term *dôdî* is used twenty-six times in the Song when the woman addresses him in her presence, whether real or virtual. The identification of the bridegroom by this circumlocution is intended as an indication of the covenant relationship to be established between Solomon and the Shulamite. However, the idea of belonging-to-the-other is not conceived of in terms of a romantic attachment between two lovers enraptured with love for one another, but signifies a political covenant between the future king and the people of Judah, represented, respectively, by bridegroom and bride.

The pasturing of flocks is designated by the verbs *r'h* (to pasture) and *rbṣ* (to lie down), in *Hiphil,* "to let (the flock) lie down." By leaving out the reference to the direct object, the verbal action gains additional emphasis, intended specifically to qualify the function of the shepherd. Yet the purpose of this scene is not to romanticize pastoral life nor to draw a picture of pastoral economy, but to employ an image traditional to the ancient Near East which represents the king governing the people like a shepherd who tends his flock. This image illustrates both the cohesion among inhabitants in analogy to sheep gathered in a flock as well as the leadership of the king over the people in comparison with the shepherd tending his sheep. In the same way as the shepherd is solicitous in providing sustenance and rest for the flock, so should the king be caring for the subsistence and welfare of the nation. This is highlighted by the allusion to the time for repose "at noon" (*baṣṣohorāyim*), in order to gather the sheep scattered all around the countryside and to convene the shepherds from different regions.

The subordinate clause expresses the reason for the request for information. The conjunction "that not" (*šallāmâ*) is equivalent to the Aramaic *di lemâ* and to the Greek *mēpote* (JOÜON, *Gr* 161h). The emphatic construction of the negative proposition is an indication that it is not a mere case of a humiliating situation which the bride wishes to avoid, but a precautionary measure against the upsurge of antagonism which her presence might stir up among the companions of the bridegroom. In the preceding song mention is made of such antagonism between repatriate and autochthonous Jews on account of tensions arising from different lifestyles, and this antagonism is compared with the townspeople's discrimination against the Bedouins. Here the causes of antagonism are more serious, since the discrimination against the autochthonous Jews implies their being deprived of the right to participate in the administration of the affairs of state. This socio-political situation is described in figurative language which presents the shepherds in a privileged position, whereas the woman is compared to a Bedouin being edged out from the pastures. However, this antagonism will disappear as soon as both of them convene under the auspices of the bridegroom. The appropriate moment for a meeting is the siesta time at noon when the sheep lie down to rest and the shepherds assemble.

In order to achieve this goal, the generation of Jews living in the period of restoration has to put an end to the discrimination against that part of the population that is compared to a "woman whose face is veiled" (*'ōṭᵉyâ*), lit. "one veiled," like a Bedouin woman whose face is covered with a non-transparent veil. The attempt at emendation of the MT, on the basis of old versions, replaces the verb *'ṭh* (to cover, veil) with another verb *t'h* / *ṭ'h* (to stray), whose feminine participle *ṭō'iyyâ* means "one who strays." On the ground of any of these meanings, commentators proposed various interpretations of a woman with these externals (cf. POPE, 331). The explanation adopted by most is based on the emendation of MT, since allegedly the meaning would be the same (RUDOLPH, 125). Against this opinion we adduce the argument that the text does not deal with an errant shepherdess in search of pastures for her flock, but with a woman whom the shepherds identify as a Bedouin, and whose appearance is described by the typical non-transparent veil covering her face. As is manifest from the third strophe, the shepherds are mistaken in their opinion about her, since the woman is not a Bedouin at all because there her face is completely uncovered showing all kinds of ornaments. If one were to ask about the external appearance of a shepherdess who is not a Bedouin, the answer is given in other texts (4:1, 3; 6:7) where the bride either does not wear a veil or, when she does, wears a diaphanous veil as an elegant accessory of a woman's attire in refined circles, or proper to the time of betrothal and the wedding ceremony.

The circumstantial complement of place "beside the flocks of your companions" (*'al 'edrê ḥᵃbērèkā*) situates on the political level the range of interrelations among the leaders of Judah's population. In figurative language, the "flocks" represent the groups of the social body organized as a political community. The designation of the leaders of these groups as "companions" of the bridegroom is an indication of an administrative hierarchy in which the king occupies the first place in the nation's government and the ministers are his subordinates. The same administrative terminology was used among the Persians who designated those who were the king's immediate auxiliaries as his "friends" and "companions" (OLMSTEAD, 74). Alexander the Great conferred the title of "companions" to the members of his general staff, a practice which was adopted by the Hellenistic kings (GAUDEMET, 227). The title of "companions" conferred upon high-ranking government officials in Judah is an implicit allusion to the provenance of the leaders and of the respective social groups, by referring to Persian customs whose nomenclature entered the vocabulary of the repatriate Jews. It is owing neither to special deference for these government officials nor to subservience that the bride addresses them as "companions" of the bridegroom, but for political reasons since she is demanding both recognition of her rights and equal opportunity for all social groups.

Vs. 8: The second strophe develops with more details the pastoral scene, underlining the elements which qualify the shepherds and their flocks. The chorus enters the stage to give the answer to the bride's request in lieu of the absent bridegroom. The clause introduced by "if not" (*'im lō'*) is the protasis of a negative condition. The verb in the clause "you know" (*tēdeʿî lāk*) is construed with the *lamed* of the *dativus commodi,* "you know for yourself" (JOÜON, *Gr* § 133d); therefore the *lamed* is not introducing the object "you know yourself," as it is translated in the old versions. The expression "fairest among women" (*hayyāfāh bannāšîm*) denotes the superlative beauty ascribed to her by the chorus, in opposition to the negative opinion held by the "companions" based on her externals. The praise given her is intended to stir up her self-esteem as an incentive for her to continue looking for the bridegroom in spite of obstacles (1:8; 5:9; 6:1). Thus she should "go out" (*yṣ'*) of her restricted milieu and take the initiative to go in pursuit of an ambitious project. "Follow in the tracks" (*ṣe'î-lāk beʿiqbê*): the verb construed with the *lamed* of the *dativus commodi* has a reflexive nuance, with a shade of cordiality, "follow by yourself" without fear. The word *ṣô'n* is a collective noun signifying ovine or caprine animals. Unlike adult animals which the shepherds lead to pasture, the shepherdess leads forth kids and lambs (*gediyyôt*). But her occupation is identical to theirs as regards responsibility for providing security and sustenance for the flocks. In fact, the differences that exist are outweighed by the points they have in common, because the animals are of the same species, they pasture in the same area, and the shepherds belong to the same population dwelling in the same territory. The place "beside the shepherds' huts" (*ʿal miškenôt hārōʿîm*) represents the destination and the end of her journey. However, if it were of her choosing, she would rather go in a different direction in order to avoid coming into contact with the shepherds, for the sake of peace.

The historical background of the pastoral scene is the social, political, and economic situation of the Judean community during the period of restoration. As a result of the repatriation of exiled Jews and their integration into the native population, a new page of the history of Israel was opened up. The course which the chosen people will take from then on depends on the organization of a unified community and on the institution of sociopolitical structures which will guarantee equal status for all citizens in spite of differences. In order to achieve these objectives on a collective level, it was required of the different leaders to articulate the transition from particularism to a political society, taking into account the profound transformation of the social groups, as regards living conditions, economic opportunities, and ethical values. Although some of the measures to be taken would initially be provisional, the delay in providing definitive solutions would create other problems. Thus, the immigration of repatriate Jews brought about relocation of groups within the local population; cultural differences caused segregation between foreign-born and native Jews; in the social and political organization there originated a distinction between privileged repatriates and marginalized autochthonous Jews with the result that the latter were deprived of social equality and the political right to participate in the government. Under the prevailing circumstances it was an issue of fundamental importance to provide for all the social groups in the Judean territory the necessary space for human self-realization. On account of this, the intellectual mentors of the local population, represented by the chorus, made an effective effort to promote a rapprochement between autochthonous and repatriate Jews, solidarity among different social groups, and active participation in the organization of the government.

Vs. 9: The third strophe (vss. 9-11) presents the "companions" compared to horses hitched to chariots. The scene moves from the preceding rural environment to urban surroundings, where the royal stables and sheds for chariotry are located. Amid the bustle of high-spirited stallions being harnessed and lined up for an official parade, the bridegroom catches sight of the bride among the enthralled onlookers. As he addresses her from a distance he tells of his admiration for her by drawing a comparison with his highly esteemed mare which stands out among the stallions hitched to chariots.

The singular *rekeb*, "chariotry," is regularly employed as a collective noun, whereas for a single chariot a common term *merkābâ* is used (6:12). Since the plural *rikbê* occurs only here, it seems that the author intended to convey a special meaning by it. As will be seen, the nexus between mare and chariots is not based on the richly adorned mare and the high-priced chariots imported from Egypt, but on the single mare and the stallions hitched to the chariots. Yet the purpose of juxtaposing mare with stallions is not to indicate the procreative function of male and female animals, but to compare the mare (used for riding) with the stallions (used for drawing chariots). On the basis of texts and pictographic representations from Egypt, it becomes clear that combat chariots are not drawn by mares but by stallions (Keel, 62–66).

The reference to Pharaoh is not intended as an indication of the custom in vogue among Egyptian kings to use horses and chariots in parades, since this would be drawing on material from outside of Judah to make a comparison between the bridegroom and Pharaoh. Rather, the name Pharaoh is used as a qualifying term both for a specific type of war chariot, whose manufacture was monopolized by the Egyptian kings, and for a special strain of horses, bred in royal stud farms. Thus, Pharaoh's name, qualifying both chariots and horses, is a component element of the comparison between the Jewish leaders and the horses hitched to chariots. In view of the highly-priced imported chariots, as manufacturers of which the Egyptians were unequaled in antiquity until the Persian period, and of the Egyptian horses which excelled all other breeds in size (GALLING, 251), this imagery pays tribute to the leaders' self-esteem.

A question arises about the mention of a mare among chariots. It is certainly not an animal kept in reserve; the rich ornaments fastened on it and the designation with the possessive suffix *susātî* (my mare) indicate that it is an animal held in esteem by the bridegroom. However, many commentators assume that the suffix *-î* is merely an obsolete case-ending, called *ḥireq compaginis,* since they do not take into account the meaning of the possessive pronoun nor do they discern the relation between the mare and the chariots. In fact, the mare is reserved for riding by the bridegroom, while the chariots are employed to carry his entourage.

Since these commentators are not concerned with the particular function of the mare and the stallions, they mistakenly translate the preposition *b^e*, "amongst," prefixed to *rikbê* (chariots), by "of chariots." The incongruity between a single mare and a plurality of chariots is smoothed over by an emendation of the MT by replacing the plural *rikbê* for the singular *rekeb* with the explanation that the termination in *yod* of the plural *rikbê* is to be regarded as a *ḥireq compaginis.* By adjusting the numerical imbalance between mare and chariots there arose another unforeseen problem of a chariot that should be drawn by a team, being drawn instead by a single mare. The expedient they tried to apply was the unusual hitching of stallion and mare to the same chariot.

The use of the horse for riding is attested in texts of the late period of the history of Egypt, while in former times it was employed only as a draught-horse (GERLEMAN, 106). The inscription of the victory stela of Pharaoh Piye (715-664 B.C.) mentions that "he rode a horse, because he did not trust his chariot" in his flight for escape from the advancing armies (LICHTHEIM, *AEL* III, 75).

The designation of the bride, *raʿyātî* (my friend), is not used here as a term of endearment, but as a title applied to her by the bridegroom. Although the same word occurs both in love songs and in this book, its significance is different. In order to find out the exact meaning of this word we relate it to the masculine form *rē^aʿ* (friend) and determine the meaning from its use as a technical term applied both to high officials appointed by the king and to partners of a covenant relationship. Legal texts of the ancient Near East use the word "friend" to designate the partner of a parity treaty (KALLUVEETTIL, 101). By addressing his bride as "friend," the bridegroom ascribes to her the status of a covenant relationship in anticipation of its ratification in the future. In addition to this, the word "friend" is used as a title denoting high-ranking officials attached to the king.

Since certain leading members of the repatriate Jews are designated as "companions" of the bridegroom, owing to their appointment to administrative office, so too the autochthonous Jewish leaders are called "friends" as an equivalent title which implies an official rank in the administrative branch of the government. Thus the leaders of both groups of Judah's inhabitants are entitled to take part in public administration. The feminine form *raʿyâ* (friend), as a designation of the bride who represents Judah's native population, cannot be adduced as proof that women were appointed to administrative offices at that time, since it is merely a case of the gender agreement of two feminine nouns in Hebrew, i.e. woman and friend.

The comparison between mare and bride implies an analogy between the mare's special place in the parade and the bride's high position in government circles. The next two verses amplify the comparison with a description of ornaments offered to the bride.

Vs. 10: The puzzling impression produced by the comparison between mare and bride is in striking contrast with the fascination caused by the rich ornaments that add to the beauty of the woman's face. The harmonious combination of details underlines her features that are "comely" (*nāʾwû*), specified by two expressions in the bridegroom's apostrophe: "your cheeks with pendants" (*ḥāyayik battōrîm*) and "your neck with beads" (*ṣawwāʾrēk baḥ^{a}rûzîm*). The explicit reference to the woman's cheek and neck is intended to call the companions' attention to the woman whom they had previously treated as someone "without face," i.e. without social prestige, like a Bedouin woman who covers her face in public (*ʿōṭ^{e}yâ*).

The word *tôrîm* (pendants) is a *hapax legomenon*, signifying an artifact worn as an ornament. The diggings have brought to light such ornaments made of metal and ivory which had been fastened on the horse's headgear, viz. female figurines carved in ivory to be tied on the front strap and pendants of ivory with relief engravings of sphinxes (GALLING, 254). The word "pendant" renders the Hebrew noun *tôr*, which some commentators relate to *tôr* (row) or to its homonym "turtledove." In the first case it would indicate a necklace of beads; in the second, a lamella cut out in the shape of a dove with outstretched wings like the wing-shaped symbol of Ra. A reference to stamped dove-shaped jewelry occurs in Psalm 68:14, "the wings of a dove covered with silver, and its pinions with glittering gold." Among ornaments discovered in Gaza antiqua are earrings of gold wire modeled in the shape of a dove (GALLING, 283). The representation of doves appears frequently on coins as an heraldic symbol. Although from archeological evidence we know that jewelry existed in the shape of doves, there is still some doubt as to its use as a necklace, earring, or pendant; that is why we render the word *tôr* by "pendant," which adorns the woman's face.

The ornament worn on the neck is called *ḥ^{a}rûzîm*, a *hapax legomenon*, whose meaning is determined by etymological analogy with Arabic *ḵaraza* (to perforate) and *ḵaraz*, a noun which designates a necklace made up of more than a single strand of beads strung together (POPE, 344). Ornaments have been worn by women as a sign of social rank, as a talisman to avert evil and bring good luck, or as a decorative accessory; men have worn jewelry as a sign of social rank and insignia of office, forbidden by sumptuary laws to all but the ruling classes. In this text no reference is made to the bridegroom's insignia but instead to his mare's ornaments compared with those worn by the bride. As an illustration of a richly adorned horse, one can mention the sculpture of Ashurbanipal (669-627 B.C.) whose riding horse is represented with a necklace of several strands of beads, whereas the horse of his subordinate has no such ornament (*DB* I.2, 1145).

Vs. 11: The strophe which compares similar elements at the beginning concludes with a contrast. Cheap ornaments worn by the bride are replaced by expensive ones. Precious metals—"gold" (*zāhāb*) and "silver" (*kesep*)—are used for jewelry, and increased in value and quality by the technical processes applied by goldsmiths. Granulation as a decorative technique is referred to by the word *neqqudôt,* a *hapax legomenon,* derived from *nqd* I (to prick, punctuate). This very fine technique and virtuosity in miniature is reflected in the decoration of gold pendants covered with granulated silver dust, called *neqqudôt* (droplets). These are minute silver balls welded onto the surface of objects made of gold. Welding is a technique belonging to a more highly developed stage of ancient goldworking, since two different metals are combined by silver being heated up to its point of fusion at 960.5° C while the temperature of gold is kept below its point of fusion at 1063° C.

At the beginning of this strophe (vs. 9), the subject of the verb is in the singular, whereas in the final verse the subject is in the plural, "we will make" (*na'aśeh*). The plural form is not to be regarded as a *pluralis maiestatis,* which does not exist in Hebrew (JOÜON, *Gr* § 114e), but as referring to a composite subject, i.e. the king and his retinue. The mention of apparently insignificant details indicates the significance of the bridegoom's gift, viz. the replacement of the bride's cheap ornaments by expensive ones signifies her promotion to an exalted social rank. A person wearing jewelry as a sign of social rank and insignia of authority is entitled to be on equal terms with his peers and to participate in the government.

Commentary: The Theme of the Government (1:7-11)

This song deals with the government of the Judean community during the period of restoration after exile. It starts with a survey of the people's way of life in Judah and focuses on the conditions needed for the organization of community life. The basic assumption is that the fundamental structure of political life is not a test of strength between social groups but rather an effective participation of all citizens, under equal conditions before the law, carrying out the project of socio-political organization. Thus the objective of this song is to make the inhabitants aware of the need that their life in common be structured as a political community. Indeed, the awareness that they constitute an assembly of citizens who are co-responsible for the body politic presupposes that all inhabitants have the necessary space for human self-realization and the right to participate in the organization of community life.

Two scenes in rural and urban surroundings illustrate two social groups and their leaders as they attempt to organize their government. The first compares the groups with shepherds who lead their flocks to pasture in the countryside of Judah. The peaceful atmosphere is not disturbed by the barking of watchdogs or the voices of shepherds. In this idyllic environment a shepherdess appears, in search of pasture for her flock in the neighborhood of the shepherds' camps. These look on her as an intruder. She already perceives that a problem in providing pasture for the flocks will arise as the number of sheep increase, and that this will lead to tensions among the shepherds. The solution will have to be found in regulations concerning the access of all inhabitants to the sources of income for their livelihood, and a system of social organization to guarantee the right of each citizen to existence.

The chorus, as intellectual mentors of the native population, suggest that a meeting should be held of all shepherds in order to negotiate free access to pasture land. But the shepherdess does not ignore that she would be discriminated against since she received no friendly welcome at the shepherds' camp. Though a full citizen, who is entitled to dwell in the country, she is kept at a distance as if she were a wandering Bedouin. In her claim for recognition of her legitimate rights she turns to an authority higher in the ranks of government. The governor of Judah, appointed by the Persian king, is held responsible for the establishment of a social organization under Persian rule. His local officials, designated as "companions," have been selected from among repatriated Jews. On account of their privileged position in the government, they take advantage of their political influence to promote the interests of the social groups they represent at the expense of the autochthonous Jews. These are exposed to dire hardship by an economic imbalance caused by the immigration en masse of Jewish repatriates. This had led to the forced relocation of native inhabitants and the transference of their homesteads to the recent arrivals. Thus, new sources of income had to be assigned to them and protected by common rights. This would mean that the organization of the community could be conceived of in terms of a corporate pursuit of the common good and this as a free response to the challenge of building up a community without coercion from pressure groups.

The second scene takes place in an urban environment with the mews in the foreground, amidst the bustle of preparation for an official parade. The thematic content is presented in the form of a comparison between horse and man. The analogy had special resonance among the Judean inhabitants who recalled the related circumstances of the return of Jewish exiles from Babylon. From another source we know an account of their arrival in Judah that tells of 736 horses, used for riding by the leaders of the various groups, accompanied by their entourage (Ezr 2:66). The stately aspect and impetuous behavior of the horse illustrate the leaders' prominence. The official parade is an allusion to caravans of repatriate Jews arriving in Judah. Combat chariots, imported from Egypt, are an image of the people's expectation of a splendid future like the past glories which their forebears had enjoyed. However, the description of chariots drawn by stallions is not intended to represent a cavalry squadron ready for war, since no province of the Persian empire was allowed to recruit an army nor would there be a chance to engage the horses, brought from Babylon, in warfare. The reference to a single mare standing close to the chariots and the care taken for sprucing it up with all kinds of ornaments is an indication of its being used for riding by the person leading the parade. The meaning of the scene is easily understood by the Judean inhabitants who recognized in the portrayal of these stallions, hitched to chariots, the leaders of the repatriate Jews, and, in the mare, the leader of the autochthonous Jews.

The title qualifying her as "friend" of the bridegroom is a designation of her new status in the ranks of government on equal terms with the "companions" who also are high officials. The description of her ornaments and the reference to the former cheap ones being replaced by expensive ones, with an explicit mention of the authority invested in him who bestows them upon her, illustrate her high social rank and insignia of office.

The political circumstances of the post-exilic period determine the administrative structure of the community within the limitations imposed on provincial governments by Persian rule, which appointed a governor to administer each territory of the empire. The form of government proposed by the author of the Song for the Jewish community is the constitution of an assembly of free citizens entitled to make decisions about affairs concerning the common good. These decisions are to be executed by representatives elected by the assembly and appointed to administrative office in the government. Thus, equal status of all citizens and equal rights granted to all also implies equal status for the leaders of the different social groups and equal right of participation in decisions concerning community life. The theme of the government will be taken up and developed in another song (8:8-10).

4. ✦ *Exultant Love (1:12-17)*

12 While the king was among his retinue, *Bride*
my nard gave forth its fragrance.
13 My beloved is to me a sachet of myrrh,
that lies between my breasts.

14 My beloved is to me a cluster of henna blossoms
from the vineyards of En-gedi.
15 Behold, you are beautiful, my friend, *Bridegroom*
behold, you are beautiful;
your eyes are doves.
16 Behold, you are beautiful, my beloved, *Bride*
truly pleasant.
Foliage will be our couch;
17 cedars, the beams of our house,
cypresses, our rafters.

Accented Transliteration (1:12-17)

12 *'ad-šehammélek bimsibbố*
nirdî́ nātán rêḥố
13 *ṣerốr hammṓr dôdî lî́*
bên šādáy yālî́n
14 *'eškṓl hakkṓfer dôdî lî́*
bekarmế 'ên gedî́
15 *hinnā́k yāfā́h ra'yātî́*
hinnā́k yāfā́h 'ênáyik yônî́m
16 *hinnekā́ yāféh dôdî́*
'áf nā'î́m
'af-'aršḗnû ra'anānā́
17 *qōrốt bātếnû 'arāzî́m*
raḥîtḗnû berôtî́m

Literary Analysis (1:12-17)

This song, composed of two strophes, deals with the fourth aspect of love which consists in the mutual admiration between the Shulamite and Solomon. The first strophe (vss. 12-14) presents the Shulamite expectantly waiting for admission to the king's presence. As she ponders his significance to her she becomes aware of her deep appreciation for him which is compared with her fondness for fragrant perfumes. The second strophe (vss. 15-17) dwells on the covenant relationship between the king and his ally, addressed as "friend." The concluding stanza (vss. 16c-17) describes the country house where the king is invited to pay a call on his tour of inspection as ruler of the country.

Poetic and rhetorical devices that occur in this song are sound repetition: alliteration *m–n* (vs. 12); echo verse with end rhyme in *-î* (vss. 13-15a) and *-îm* (vs. 17); word repetition: anaphora "behold, you are beautiful—behold, you are beautiful" (vs. 15). Rhetorical devices: metaphor "my beloved is a sachet of myrrh, a cluster of henna blossoms"; "the friend's eyes are doves"; hyperbole (vs. 17).

Vocabulary Analysis (1:12-17)

Vs. 12: The scene is introduced by an account of the king's presence and the bride's perception of pleasant fragrances pervading the air. While she waits for the meeting to begin she entertains her mind by comparing the influence of the king on the people around him with the soothing effect which precious perfumes have on her. The identification of the bridegroom as "the king" (*hammelek*) is not meant to be an indication of a role ascribed to a theatric figure on stage in a "royal travesty" (GERLEMAN, 110), but is the specification of his Davidic descendance and royal authority as head of state.

The usage of the masculine form of the noun *mēsab* in other biblical texts has led some commentators to interpret its meaning as a dinner party, on the assumption that the scene here described takes place in the dining room (GERLEMAN, 111; KEEL, 67). Others suggest its being a round table (DELITZSCH, 36), or a couch on which participants in a banquet recline (POPE, 347), or else a divan in the bedroom of the palace (RAVASI, 57). However, there is no indication of any change of scenery from the previous scene to this one. This leads us to conclude that the meeting is being held at the mews after the royal parade. The same members of the royal entourage who were present on the occasion of the king's promising the bride expensive jewelry are those now gathered in front of him. Their function is to act as witnesses at the ceremony at which a covenant is ratified by the king and the bride, who is the leading figure representative of the Jewish population. Therefore, the meaning of *bimsibbô* is not applied to specify a place but rather the king's entourage and is rendered "among his retinue."

The king's presence is compared to the emanation of the nard's fragrance. This is to suggest the idea of simultaneous perception by the senses of sight and smell. Nard and myrrh were not commonly used in antiquity as perfumes to enhance female charm; since they were rare and precious their use was reserved for special occasions and official ceremonies. Nard (*nērd*) is an aromatic balsam extracted from the valerian *Nardostachys jatamansi* which grows in the Himalayan region. The fragrant substance was obtained from roots and spike-like woolly young stems which were dried and ground to powder, which was used for making perfume. Because of the long distance from which it had to be imported, it was obviously quite expensive (MOLDENKE, 148).

Vs. 13: Myrrh (*mōr*) is a resinous gum obtained from *Commiphora abessinica,* a thorny shrub or small tree native to southern Arabia, Ethiopia, and Somalia. To judge from the use of myrrh on special occasions in royal courts, temples, and social meetings, this aromatic substance was valued as perfume and also as medicine. The Persians held it in such high regard as a perfume that they had inserted some grains of this resin on the emperor's crown (MOLDENKE, 84). This verse presents the Shulamite carrying a sachet of myrrh (*ṣᵉrôr hammōr*) on the bosom. As if her fragrant attire were not sufficiently effective for calling attention to her person, she ostentatiously displays a sachet of myrrh lying between her breasts (*yālîn bên šāday*). The verb *lyn* signifies "to spend the night," or in a general sense, "to remain, stay, repose." In spite of the realism of the expression, it does not mean that she had worn this sachet while asleep at night. The description of a sachet of myrrh kept on her bosom is intended as an illustration of the high esteem for the covenant between the king and the leading figure representative of Judah's population.

The designation of the king as "my beloved" (*dôdî*) is not an expression of loving devotion for him implying a subjective experience, but is an official title applied to an ally in a pact of friendship. In the previous verse it is the same person referred to as "king" whom the bride is looking at from a distance. She does not publicly address him as king in order to avoid suspicions being aroused in Persian officials of a burgeoning Jewish nationalism. The identification of the bridegroom as king meant that authority exists and is recognized as such, and authority recognized implies a relationship between the person with authority and the person under it (MCCARTHY, 263). Such relationship extends beyond the kinship sphere by establishing a covenant of a political nature. The initiative for the effecting of a covenant is to be taken by the king, because he is expected to assume the reins of government of the nation and not just a single social group. Before the auspicious meeting to be held with the king, described in the following strophe, the leadership of the native Jews muses over the type of relationship to be established between the house of David and the Jewish population. With the designation of the monarch as "my beloved" there is indicated a relationship of amity, which is specified by reference to the indirect object "to me" (*lî*), intended as an indication of the king's rule for the benefit of the community.

Vs. 14: In continuation of the thought developed in the previous verse mention is made of the henna-plant for comparison with the king's presence. This well-known shrub, *Lawsonia inermis,* called in Arabic *al-ḥinna,* grows throughout the Orient. Clusters (*'eškōl*) of its white or yellow flowers, whose fragrance is much like that of roses, were gathered by eastern beauties in large bouquets which they carried in their hands and on their bosoms. A nosegay of henna flowers was one of the most elegant gifts that a girl could receive from a friend (MOLDENKE, 125).

"The vineyards of En-gedi" (*karmê ʿên gedî*) are located in an oasis on the western border of the Dead Sea. After the destruction of the settlement in 582 B.C. it had been reconstructed at the beginning of the Persian period. Diggings brought to light large storage jars and vessels of a non-domestic type which were probably connected with the perfume industry (NEGEV, 102). Its location below sea level and its hot summer and balmy winter climate are conducive to the growth of semi-tropical vegetation, of palm trees, grapevines, and balsam shrubs, watered by a fountain flowing from rocky slopes one hundred meters above the oasis.

The significance of aromatic substances in this song is derived from their supply by import or local production. Thus the mention of myrrh is an implicit reference to the economic resources at the disposal of the autochthonous Jews, permitting them to acquire expensive perfumes imported from the Orient; henna from the vineyards of En-gedi symbolizes cultivation of different varieties of plants. The comparison of the king's presence with henna flowers from the vineyards illustrates a prosperous future to be inaugurated through the government lending support to the enterprises of the autochthonous Jews.

Vs. 15: The second strophe deals with a rite preceding the pact of alliance between the king and the leading figure representative of Judah's population. The pact-enacting episode takes place on the occasion of a public event and thus has official connotation on account of the presence of the royal entourage acting as witnesses.

The interjection "behold" (*hinnê*) has formal significance in the pact-enacting rite (KALLUVEETTIL, 13n). Negotiations for a pact are opened with a formal calling forth of the ally, "behold, there you are" (***hinnāk–hinnᵉkā***). There follows a declaration of the new status which each attributes to the other and of setting forth the nature of the alliance. While ancient diplomatic documents contain specific tasks assigned by the lord to the underling and admonitions to acknowledge his overlordship and confide in his power, the Song confines itself to mentioning, further on, some symbolic rites related to the covenant-making procedure. Since a covenant enacted by government leaders affects public life, the ceremony was held in the presence of official witnesses, i.e. the king's retinue (*bimsibbô*). As negotiations for the pact draw to a close, those involved express their satisfaction with the relationship established by declaring their high regard for one another, i.e. "you, my friend, are beautiful" (***hinnāk yāfāh raʿyātî***) and "you, my beloved, are beautiful" (***hinnᵉkā yāfeh dôdî***). These statements are not meant to extol physical traits but the merits of the ally whose new status is a source of mutual delight.

The statement "your eyes are doves" (*'ênayik yônîm*), a comparison based on analogy, refers to specific qualities of the ally, i.e. candor and gentleness. Some commentators suggest that this sentence should be eliminated from the Hebrew text on the assumption that it is an unnecessary gloss (RUDOLPH, 127; WÜRTHWEIN, 42). However, such qualities inherent in an ally are fundamental to an association based on mutual trust.

Vs. 16: The acceptance of the new status conferred upon the leadership of the native population is expressed by the same words as in the declaration formula enunciated by the ally. Foregoing a comparison, the attitude of the king is defined as "truly pleasant" (*'af nā'îm*) which enhances his popularity among the country's inhabitants.

The pact-enacting episode takes place in the spring, at the time when outdoor activities are carried out in orchards and vineyards located on the terraced hillsides. While the farmers are away from home, they build shelters where they lodge temporarily (DALMAN, *AuS* I/2, 566). The description of such a shelter in terms of a country house is intended as an implicit invitation for the king to pay a visit to the population dwelling in the countryside given over to husbandry. The king's tour of inspection of the rural districts is meant to give incentive to productive activities whose growth will be fostered by government subsidizing agriculture and fruit-growing. During his stay in the countryside he will share the hospitality of the farmers living in rustic shelters and reclining on a "couch" (*'ereś*) made of green leaves.

The scenery described in this song has led most commentators to interpret the scene as a wedding feast. The "couch" would be a bedstead, adorned with garlands and festoons, set up in the inner chamber of the royal palace constructed with timber imported from Phoenicia, i.e. cedar and cypress. The dialogue between the king and his friend would be a love-duet of mutual devotion. Such an interpretation is based on parallel texts from extra-biblical literature on a falacious assumption that similar texts automatically express similar ideas.

Vs. 17: The structure of rustic shelters, used as a temporary dwelling place by farmers sleeping away from home, consists of four poles stuck into the ground with boughs fastened horizontally on top and covered with twigs. These temporary shelters were not intended for protection against inclement weather conditions nor to resist storms as they were hastily built with pieces of wood readily at hand. But the description of the king's lodge is all but a simple shelter, since it is solidly built with timber imported from Phoenicia; the "beams" (*qôrôt*) are "cedars" (*'ărāzîm*) from Lebanon. The term *'erez* designates two coniferous trees: the cedar, *Cedrus libani,* and the pine-tree, *Abies cilicica,* both native to Phoenicia.

By designating these shelters as "our houses" (*bāttênû*) it was thought that the landowners' town mansions are referred to. However, only one house is meant here because the plural of the first noun, *qôrôt,* influenced the second, *bāttênû*, which is a peculiar Hebrew construction explained as grammatical attraction (JOÜON, *Gr* § 136 o). The rafters are made of "cypress" (*b^e^rôtîm*); this word is a *hapax legomenon* borrowed from Aramaic, equivalent to *b^e^rôšîm* in Hebrew. The specific word for cypress, *Cupressus sempervirens*, is *t^e^'aššûr*, while *b^e^rôš* denotes a coniferous tree known as *Juniperus phoenicia*. Because they are similar in aspect and wood texture, both are named "cypress," used in building and furniture.

The word *rāḥît*, read with the Kethib, or *rāhîṭ*, with the Qere, is a *hapax legomenon* to be translated as "rafter," designating the roofing as *pars pro toto*. Obviously a house built with rafters of cypress is typical of a permanent residence in a cold climate, a far cry from temporary shelters used only in springtime.

The meaning of this stanza becomes clear by distinguishing between the underlying description of a shelter, and that of a palace, superimposed on it. The description of a shelter in terms of a stately residence is a literary device called hyperbole, and as such it is understood by the bride and the king. Moreover, the mentioning of cedar and cypress used as building material is not likely to go unnoticed by the king, since it is employed for the construction of the royal palace. The statement about a house built with wood of cedar and cypress, located in the countryside, implies the idea that any shelter at which the king stops over while on his tour through the country is his royal residence. Thus, the description of this house is intended as an invitation for the king to pay a visit to the farming districts of Judah. As regards the grammatical structure of this stanza, the sentence is made up of three noun clauses in which the syntactical relationship between the subject and predicate is expressed in Hebrew by simple juxtaposition. To what period or time the statements apply must be inferred from the context. Since the king's visit is thought of as a future event, the linking verb used in the translation is put in the future tense: "foliage will be our couch, cedars will be the beams of our house, cypresses will be our rafters."

Commentary: The Theme of the Covenant (1:12-17)

The theme of this song is that of the covenant between the king of Judah and the Jewish population, represented by its leadership. Among the requirements to be met before the covenant can be enacted, three are mentioned here: the first is the presence of the Davidic king in Judah as ruler of the country; the second is the willingness of the Jewish population to enter a covenant with the house of David; the third is the legally binding nature of the pact on account of its ratification and confirmation by the royal entourage acting as witnesses. The appropriate occasion for such an official ceremony to be performed is a civic festival when the population of Judah and their leaders are assembled for a public celebration of an event commemorated by all the members of the community. On such festivities the people are attired in their best and women carry a sachet of rare perfumes and a nosegay of fragrant flowers.

According to formal procedures, the pact-enacting ceremony begins with the calling forth of the ally. There follows a declaration of the new status which each attributes to the other and setting forth the nature of the covenant. By this very act the participants are tied to one another by a bond of friendship. After the ceremony the king is invited to pay a visit to the population dwelling in the countryside while making his tour of inspection of the rural districts. His visit to the farming communities is meant to give incentive to productive activities which will be fostered by government subsidies to agriculture and fruit-growing. Since the king is to begin his journey in the spring, when the farmers are engaged in outdoor activities in orchards and vineyards, he is invited to share their hospitality while staying with them. They will be honored to have him as their guest, and they mention the temporary shelter, where he would stop over, as if it were his royal palace built with cedar and cypress.

In contrast with the rustic shelters used temporarily by the farmers while in the fields away from their homes, the leadership of the Judean population is proud publicly to display their costly imported perfumes of nard and myrrh. They can afford to acquire luxury items because the annual yield of orchards and vineyards provides them with the means for subsistence and brings in a substantial surplus. The conditions of the country's economy will be dealt with in another song (4:9-11). As for the theme of the covenant, it will be taken up further on (8:6-7) and developed in two passages (2:16-17; 7:11).

POEM II *The Pledge of Love* (2:1-17)

1 ✦ *Under the Apple Tree (2:1-3)*

1 I am a narcissus of Sharon, *Bride*
a lily of the valleys.
2 As a lily among brambles, *Bridegroom*
so is my friend among the daughters.
3 As an apple tree among the trees of the wood, *Bride*
so is my beloved among the sons.
In his shade I want to sit
and delight in its fruit, sweet to my palate.

Accented Transliteration (2:1-3)

1 *ʾanî́ ḥabaṣṣélet haššārôn*
šôšannát hāʿamāqî́m
2 *kešôšannấ bên ḥôḥî́m*
kēn raʿyātî́ bên habbānnôt
3 *ketappû́aḥ baʿaṣế hayyáʿar*
kēn dôdî́ bên habbānî́m
beṣillố ḥimmádtî weyāšábtî
ûfiryố mātốq leḥikkî́

Literary Analysis (2:1-3)

Poem II on "the pledge of love" (2:1-17) is divided into four songs dealing with the different occasions of the meeting between bride and bridegroom, in which she assures him of her love for him by means of expressions with figurative meaning. The corresponding poem (7:11–8:5) takes up, in the inverse order, the same thematic content.

This song of two strophes, with two distichs each, expresses in a lively dialogue the mutual attachment of bride and bridegroom. Personal feelings are related to plants of the countryside resulting in a pleasant harmony between external sensations and internal emotions. The female figure is described with aesthetic qualities compared to flowers in the first strophe (vss. 1-2), while the male is qualified by his usefulness in the comparison with a fruit tree in the second strophe (vs. 3).

Poetic and rhetorical devices occurring in the song are sound repetition: assonance *a–i: ḥimmadtî–yāšabtî;* end rhyme *-îm* (vss. 1b, 2a) and *-î* (vs. 3cd); repetition of structural patterns: repetitive parallelism *k^e^–bên* (vs. 2a), *kēn–bên* (vs. 2b, 3b); syntactic chiasmus: statement (vs. 1ab)–comparison (vs. 2ab) // comparison (vs. 3ab)–statement (vs. 3cd). Figures of resemblance: metaphor "I am a narcissus of Sharon, a lily of the valleys"; simile "she is like a lily"; "he is like an apple tree."

Vocabulary Analysis (2:1-3)

Vs. 1: The bride is compared to a narcissus (*ḥ^a^baṣṣelet*), known as *Narcissus tazetta,* a favorite flower throughout the Orient on account of its white or cream color and sweet-smelling fragrance. During its flowering season bouquets of narcissus are to be found in almost every house (MOLDENKE, 147). The narcissus blossoms after winter until the end of March and thus is a welcome harbinger of spring. However, there is no consensus among commentators about the exact nature of the flower designated by the Hebrew word, also identified as *Asphodelus microcarpa, Urginea maritima, Cistus, Tulipa montana, Anemone coronaria, Colchium autumnale, Anemone fulgens,* or *Corchorus olitorius.*

The plain of Sharon (*šārôn*), a coastal area from Jaffa northward to Athlit, is noted for its fertile soil, suiting it for vineyards and cattle grazing. There was also another area designated by this name referring to a district located between Mount Tabor and the Lake of Tiberias. The plain intended here is not the one in Galilee, but the coastal area. This is because of its location on the western border of the Judean territory, as the corresponding song (8:5) mentions the desert on the eastern border.

The flower which occurs more often in the song is the "lily" (*šôšannâ*), *Lilium candidum.* This plant, indigenous to the mountains of upper Galilee and Lebanon, was found to be flowering among shrubs in humid recesses of the valleys even in mid-May. Some specimens with inflorescence on a 121 cm. tall stem were found to be growing on the slopes of Mount Carmel, blossoming among the limestone rocks and the shrubs (MOLDENKE, 279).

Before this information had been published, the Hebrew word was interpreted as a name of different flowers, e.g. *Anemone coronaria, Hyacinthus orientalis, Nymphaea lotus,* etc. The lily, valued for its pleasant fragrance and large white flowers which brighten their drab surroundings, is an appropriate image of the woman's beauty. Since this flower is indigenous to Palestine, it is used in the Song as an image of the native population of Judah. While the narcissus blooms after the winter, and the lily from the beginning of the spring until summer, all other plants have a shorter flowering season. The lily thrives among shrubs, sheltered from heat and dryness, enclosed in the recesses of the "valleys" (*ʿamāqîm*).

Vs. 2: The comparison between the woman and a lily is taken up so as to illustrate her attributes and relate the lily's habitat among "brambles" (*ḥôḥîm*) to the existential context of the "friend" (*raʿyâ*) among other social groups in Judah, designated as "daughters" (*bānôt*). To judge from the sympathy which these daughters express later on (6:9) toward the "friend," the relationship between the different groups of inhabitants undergoes various phases of polarization. During the first phase there predominates a common effort in the attempt to integrate groups of repatriate Jews into the autochthonous population of Judah, and to pacify the conflicts arising from cultural, social, and economic differences. During the second phase the endeavor to unite these groups by means of a political organization which recognizes as citizens all the inhabitants of the country and guarantees their right to participate in the government prevails. Initially the return of exiles from Babylon to Judah imposed the task of settling these various social groups among those dwelling in Judah. Thus geographical proximity was expected to turn into a mutual sharing of their different lifestyles. It is not surprising that frictions arose and the relationship between these groups showed some traces of antagonism which the native Jews liken to the harsh environment of a lily "among brambles." It is to be noted, however, that the tension between the "friend" and the repatriates is not only of a cultural, social, and economic nature, but also political. Thus, those designated as "daughters of Zion" are reserved toward her and also to the bridegroom (3:11). Strained relations exist too between the "daughters of Jerusalem" and the bride on account of the attempt by the former to extend their leadership to other groups (1:5; 2:7; 3:5, 10; 5:8, 16; 8:4) and to establish a political system suitable to their interests in the territory of Judah.

Vs. 3: The second strophe continues to praise the outstanding qualities of the bridegroom by extolling his useful attributes compared to those of the apple tree. The significance of the comparison and its application to the political situation of the Judean community are indicative of the thematic content of this Song. The beloved's preeminence excelling the "sons" (*bānîm*) is illustrated by a comparison of the "apple tree" (*tappûaḥ*) with the "trees of the wood" (*ʿaṣê hayyaʿar*). In contrast with these trees of sparse crowns which afford almost no shade and bear no edible fruits, the apple tree is highly valued for its delicious fruits and pleasant shade under its widespreading branches. The apple tree has been cultivated in antiquity in Palestine and especially in Assyria, as reported in written records referring to this tree (GALLING, 34). On a monumental sculpture of the Persian imperial palace in Persepolis, built during 512 to 494 B.C., is represented a nobleman holding a large apple in his hand which attracts the attention of those near him (OLMSTEAD, 180). As regards the region of Palestine, reference is made to two villages (Jos 15:34, 53; 16:8; 17:7-8) in the highlands of Judah and in the territory of Ephraim, whose name Tappuah is given after the apple tree or its fruit. Furthermore, the quotations in Jl 1:12 and Ct 2:3; 8:5 attest to the existence of the apple tree in Judah. In spite of this information from biblical sources, some commentators insist on asserting that the common apple, *Malus pumila,* was not found at all in the area of the Levant in antiquity and suppose that the Hebrew word would refer to *Prunus armeniaca, Cydonia oblonga,* or *Citrus sinensis.*

In the mountainous region of Judah with its annual rainfall varying from fifteen to twenty-five inches—which amounts to three times more than what is needed for the growth of trees—the extensions of forest were far greater in antiquity than today, owing to less erosion and a more favorable climatic regime. Terraced hillsides covered by a moderately deep layer of rich soil lend themselves to cultivation of vineyards, olive trees, nut trees, and apple trees. The owner of an orchard values its trees as a source of income. Thus, in a rural setting it is meaningful to use the expression "to sit in the shade of the apple tree" as an allusion to the people's enjoyment of the blessings of peace and prosperity shared by the entire nation reestablished in the land. Likewise, to eat delicious apples has a proverbial connotation in the sense of someone getting his sustenance from the product of his labor. However, the idyllic description of rural life hints at a future situation which will prevail after certain conditions have been fulfilled. Indeed there is no social, economic, and political structure other than the monarchy which is conducive to the economic development of the country.

Such an auspicious future seen to be close at hand gives rise to an ardent desire, expressed by the verb *ḥmd* (to desire, delight) and by the verbal form *weyāšabtî* "and I want to sit" (JOÜON, *Gr* § 119w). As a literary device used in poetry, the terms of the sentence are displaced. Thus the verb *ḥimmadtî* (I delight) does not have any syntactic function in the first stich but only in the second, where it modifies the complement *ûfiryô* (and its fruit). As regards Hebrew verbs denoting affections, although in the past, they are rendered by the present; thus *ḥimmadtî* signifies "I delight."

The apple tree is an image of the monarchy, visualized in its function as providing security and vitality for the inhabitants of Judah. In prophetic literature, the house of David is compared to a cedar whose shoot growing on the top of the tree represents the heir to the throne. In the shade of its branches all kinds of birds will nest, which symbolize vassal kingdoms.

Other dynasties are like trees of the field as compared to the Davidic dynasty pictured as a magnificent cedar (Ez 17:3-4, 22-24). The cedar of Lebanon is used too in a comparison with Pharaoh, the king of Egypt, whose royal power is represented by this tree of unusually large dimension, whereas smaller cedars, cypresses, planes, and trees of the field symbolize foreign kings (Ez 31:3-9). The image of the great world tree, as described by Ezekiel, has inspired Daniel to picture Nebuchadnezzar's extensive rule by a spreading tree. The beneficent function of kingship in providing food and shelter to all living beings is illustrated by the tree with its spreading branches bearing fruits (Dn 4:7-9, 11-19). Another image of kingship is that of the vine described by Ezekiel. The stem represents the Davidic dynasty, and its branches, laden with clusters of grapes, symbolize the king's fostering the nation's prosperity (Ez 19:10-14). There are two more images of kingship to be mentioned, i.e. the olive tree and fig tree, whose rural environment is related to a scene which takes place in an urban setting. In contrast with these fruit trees, brambles neither afford shade nor bear any fruit except thorns. This is mentioned in an apologue adduced to discredit Jotham's attempt to become king of Shechem (Jgs 9:7-15).

Of all fruit trees, the apple tree was most rare and thus it was highly valued. Its use as an image of the monarchy was quite appropriate to evoke in the Jews familiar resonances of the prestige of the royal institution in Israel's monarchic period, when the destiny of the people was linked to the destiny of the king. In the period of restoration, the leaders of the Judean community were faced with the task of reestablishing those institutions which are constitutive of the Jewish nation with a caveat that they should not conform their national life to the socio-political structures of other provinces of the Persian empire. Among the institutions of Israel, the Davidic monarchy ranked high in the hierarchy of the state, as the depository of supreme authority and dignity as God's representative, whose function was to canalize divine blessings to the entire realm. On account of the king's duty to foster the welfare of the nation, kingship was thought of as a means by which the salvific designs of God are accomplished in history.

As regards the identification of the "sons" (*banîm*), in a subordinate position in relation to the "beloved" (*dôd*), the text gives a hint of what they might be in the metaphor where they are compared to the trees of the wood. What is the meaning of this metaphor in the context of the Judean community? In other biblical texts quoted above, both types of trees, i.e. the trees of the field and the trees of the wood, represent vassal kings governing the domains outside of Judah. Since the Song is not a repertory of poetic expressions drawn from other biblical books, but is a literary work which contains the experience and intuition of a poet who described his community, it is evident that the terminology and imagery refer to the specific context of the population of Judah. The subjects treated here are strictly related to the life of this community, while other questions referring to neighboring countries are not dealt with. Therefore, the "sons" represent officials in charge of administrative affairs of the Judean community, recruited among repatriated Jews. As auxiliaries of the king, they have no authority of their own to act at will in carrying out their administrative office and thus they are not supposed to favor certain social groups or political parties. Indeed, the political integration of various social groups is not accomplished by favoring some and discriminating against others, but rather by the constitution of a state with a legal foundation. Now, kingship in Israelite history always held a decisive role in establishing and maintaining mutual cooperation among citizens. On account of this, the leader of the autochthonous Jews seeks to proceed toward the enactment of a covenant between the heir to the Davidic throne and the population of Judah.

Commentary: The Theme of Royalty (2:1-3)

The thematic content of this song is the Davidic royalty which played a major role during the history of Israel in the process of incorporating the tribes into a nation whose constitution as an independent state was decisive in maintaining its autonomy in relation to other nations.

During the period of restoration, it became evident that factors which would bring about the constitution of national life should be given priority over against ethnic values and territorial rights to areas now allocated to neighboring provinces. In fact, with the extinction of the southern kingdom, its territory had been reduced, and with the deportation of the upper classes the distinguishing signs of remnants and deportees belonging together were not connected any longer with the tribal system but with social and religious customs. As a result of the repatriation of exiles and their integration into the community of the autochthonous population, the idea of a restored Jewish nation, whose political organization would be modeled on the pre-exilic monarchy, came alive again. Among Israel's institutions none was better suited to carry this through than the Davidic monarchy, because it was maintained by the people's allegiance to the king and empowered with authority to take measures to implement the unity among different social groups and bring about the restoration of the Jewish nation. The fact is, however, that the monarchy was not restored in Judah, probably owing to the Persian policy of keeping control over territories near the military route to Egypt. Initially there were auspicious signs of a proximate restoration of the monarchy, since the first two Jewish governors commissioned by the Persian ruler to reorganize the community of Judah were members of the house of David. Of the four symbols of the Jewish nation there were two which were still missing for restoration to be complete, after the homeland and the Jerusalem temple had been restored by imperial decree, i.e. royalty and the city of Jerusalem. Yet a social group, even though its territorial integrity and religious identity are recognized by other nations, still needs to be organized as a political community in order to become a nation. In order to achieve this goal, the citizens had to be given the right to determine the form of government appropriate to the type of community they chose to adopt.

The preference for monarchic rule was voiced not only by a minority group, but by people from all social strata of society. By virtue of the authority invested in kingship based on divine right, the king was empowered to take measures to maintain peace and security in the country and foster the prosperity of its inhabitants. Moreover, the monarchy implies the bond of loyalty, which links the subjects to the king, and as a consequence brings about the association among different social groups and their integration into one nation. The symbols drawn from native flora are used here in a comparison both of tensions on the social level and rivalry on the political level. Both cases are to be solved by the reinstatement of the Davidic royalty in Judah as a means of mediation and balance between different groups integrated into the nation. The theme of royalty is taken up later on in the description of the Davidic dynasty (8:5).

2 ✦ *At Home (2:4-7)*

4 He brought me to the banqueting hall *Bride*
    and his escort before me for the sake of love.
5 Sustain me with raisin cakes
    and brace me with apples;
    for I am faint with love.
6 His left arm will be under my head,
    and his right arm will embrace me.
7 I adjure you, O daughters of Jerusalem,
    by the gazelles or the hinds of the field,
that you stir not up nor awaken love
    until it be propitious.

Accented Transliteration (2:4-7)

4 *h^{e}bîʾánî ʾel-bế̂t hayyā́yin*
    w^{e}diglố ʿāláy ʾah^{a}bấ
5 *samm^{e}kû́nî baʾ^{a}šîšố̂t*
    rapp^{e}dû́nî battappûḥî́m
    kî-ḥôlát ʾah^{a}bấ ʾānî́

6 *śemō'lô taḥat lerō'šî*
wîmînô teḥabbeqēnî
7 *hišba'tî 'etkem benôt yerûšālaim*
biṣbā'ôt 'ô be'ayelôt haśśādeh
'im-tā'îrû we'im-te'ôrerû
'et-hā'ahabâ 'ad šetteḥpāṣ

Literary Analysis (2:4-7)

The second meeting between bride and bridegroom takes place in the palace where high officials are gathered as qualified participants. The song is composed of two strophes (vss. 4-5 and vss. 6-7) phrased in parallel form: each strophe consists of a narrative (vs. 4 and vs. 6) and an apostrophe (vs. 5 and vs. 7). The bride is the one who relates the events and addresses the people close by. She is not mentioned by name, but is referred to with the feminine gender of the participle *ḥôlat 'anî* (I am faint). The rural surroundings of the previous scene are replaced by a setting within the palace. The reason for holding the meeting indoors is to confirm the covenant, expressed by the word "love" whose use as a synonym for covenant is attested in the treaty literature of the ancient Near East. The scene deals with the performance of symbolic rites related to the covenant which have special significance in the pact-enacting ceremony. Among these are: the reception at the home of the ally, the meal shared in common, and the embrace as a gesture of friendship.

Poetic and rhetorical devices used in the song are sound repetition: internal rhyme *sammekûnî–rappedûnî; śemō'lô–wîmînô; benôt–biṣbā'ôt–be'ayelôt;* alliteration *t–': tā'îrû–te'ôrerû;* end rhyme *-î* (vss. 5c-6b). Rhetorical devices: synonymous parallelism *sammekûnî–rappedûnî;* synecdoche "banqueting hall" for royal palace; the figure of "the gazelles and the hinds of the field" used for the rural population.

Vocabulary Analysis (2:4-7)

Vs. 4: The subject of "he brought me" (*hebî'anî*) is the bridegroom who assembled the bride and his entourage in the banqueting hall. The reference to the change of scenery—from an outdoor setting to the royal palace—provides additional information on the performance of a symbolic act, related to the pact-enacting ceremony, i.e. the covenant partner's admission to the house of his ally. In connection with formal proceedings, a reception is held for the honored guest in the banqueting hall of the palace. The

Hebrew name for a wing of a large building is *bayit* (house); *bêt hayyāyin* in a literal sense means "wine house," not to be confused with "wine-cellar" (*'ôṣâr*) nor "tavern" which does not occur anywhere in the OT (DALMAN, *AuS* IV, 390). In the residence of prominent families, guests were entertained in the reception room designed for supplying food and drink; hence its designation *bêt mišteh hayyāyin* (banqueting hall) [Est 7:8] or expressed in an abbreviated form *bêt hayyāyin* and *bêt mišteh*. In the banqueting hall joyful meetings were held, whereas in the room set for a funeral repast (*bêt marzēaḥ*) the visitors of the family met in mourning (Jer 16:5, 8). A single room may denote the house as *pars pro toto*, as e.g. in Eccl 7:2, "house of mourning" (*bêt 'ēbel*) and "house of feasting" (*bêt mišteh*).

The reference to the banqueting hall is intended to convey the meaning of the entire building and its location. Now, in rural settlements and villages there were no palaces found anywhere, for such large buildings were constructed only in the capital city, as mentioned above (1:4) where the "chambers" (*ḥadārîm*) denote the royal palace. Likewise, in the capital were located the officers' quarters of the king's "escort" (*degel*) and the residence of the "daughters of Jerusalem."

The word *degel* is a partitive noun of a collective whole. What is the category indicating a whole and its part? This word occurs in the Aramaic papyri from Elephantine designating a regiment of thousand soldiers whose centurions listed are mostly Persians (PORTEN, 32). In Hebrew, the word *degel* is used in military terminology to designate a "banner, signal," and in the context of Israelite clans where it signifies "tribal divisions." Some commentators render *degel* in this song as a flag fastened to a shaft or a signboard displayed by the wine house. However, the meaning of this word is to be determined by its context which reflects Persian influence in the use of terms applied to government officials. According to the Persian administrative system introduced in the provinces, high officials appointed by the emperor were given commissions to execute specific tasks. Although they were subordinate to the governor, they also had to report to the central government. Others were assigned to office by the governor himself who determined the extent of their jurisdiction. These officials always appear as a team entrusted with the administration of the province. The designation of this team as *degel* indicates the king's staff of high-ranking officials now acting as witnesses at the covenant ceremony. The rendering of *degel* by "escort" takes into account its connotation implied in its original military usage.

The king's escort is said to have been walking "in front of me" (*'ālay*), while the cortège made its entry into the banqueting hall. The members of the escort are not to be identified as waiters, since the fruits which are partaken at the ceremonial meal are already on the table.

The word "love" (*'ahabâ*) is used in the Hebrew sentence as *accusativus causae* (*GK* § 118 l), rendered "for the sake of love," which indicates the reason for the escort's presence in the banqueting hall. For the meaning of love as a synonym for covenant we refer to the explanation above (1:3). This precludes the interpretation of the officials' attitude in terms of affectionate devotion for the royal bride, since there is no emotional sentiment implied in the use of the word "love" nor do they have any part in the relationship of social and political alliance which is going to be established between king and people.

Vs. 5: Foregoing a transition from narrative style to direct address, the bride asks for fruits to be partaken at the ritual meal. No dinner is being served, except cakes and apples as refreshment. "Raisin cakes" (*'ašîšôt*) are mentioned in other biblical books as offerings to Canaanite deities (Hos 3:1 ; Is 16:7) and as dessert after a meal (2 Sm 6:19 // 1 Chr 16:3). The reason given here for her requesting these fruits is not the desire for an appetizer, but the need of energy, as expressed by the verbs "sustain me" (*sammekûnî*) and "brace me" (*rappedûnî*). The reference to "apples" (*tappûḥîm*) intends to allude to the preceding song in which the monarchy is compared to an apple tree whose shade and delicious fruits make visible the function of the royal institution to provide protection and vitality for the nation. Unlike the apple tree, the trees of the wood, bearing no edible fruits, represent the king's auxiliaries in charge of distributing the produce of the fruit tree. The reason for raisin cakes being mentioned in this context is due to the custom of people eating them on special occasions. Since the covenant meal partaken by the leading figure representative of Judah's inhabitants is such a memorable event, there ought to be served exquisite food. The prospect of the pact-enactment with the house of David is given as the cause for the bride's exalted state of mind, as she says: "I am faint" (*ḥôlat 'ānî*) "with love," i.e. "on account of love" (*'ahabâ*).

Vs. 6: The second strophe describes the embrace as a gesture of friendship between bridegroom and bride with special significance as a symbolic act related to the covenant. The meaning of the two antonymous words is specified by the context: *yāmîn* signifies "right hand, right arm, right side, southward"; *śemō'l* means "left hand, left arm, left side, northward." The specification of both words by "arm" is based on the meaning of the verb *ḥbq* (to embrace) in *Piel*, indicating a folding in the arms and not a handshake. In this context, the embrace is not a mere gesture of greeting, but a sign of friendship which is fundamental to the covenant (KALLUVEETTIL, 42).

Vs. 7: In the apostrophe addressed to the elite of the Jewish priesthood designated as "daughters of Jerusalem," the bride openly inveighs against their entering a covenant with the leaders of neighboring nations. In fact no treaty relationship with other countries should be established before Judah had become an independent state with its own government. Moreover, in accordance with the country's political system and the constitution of the state, it is the king's prerogative to carry through the foreign policy most beneficial to the nation.

The apostrophe is followed by the formula of adjuration which implies the imposition of an oath on the "daughters of Jerusalem" as a solemn corroboration of their promise to abstain from engaging in new alliances. The verb *šb'*, in *Hiphil,* signifies "to make swear"; the tense-form of *hišba'tî* is the perfect, which is used in the sense of a present (JOÜON, *Gr* § 112f). The pronoun *'etkem* (you) is in the masculine, although it denotes feminine persons, i.e. "daughters" (*bānôt*). This abnormal grammatical construction appears to be a peculiarity of a later period of biblical literature (ROBERT-TOURNAY, 106).

As regards the identity of the speaker who addresses the "daughters of Jerusalem" (*b*^e^*nôt y*^e^*rûšālaim*), there is no consensus among commentators. Most of them assume that the bridegroom is the one speaking here, since the bride languid with amorous passion would not be aware of other guests present in the room nor would she be able to say anything that sounds coherent. However, this hypothesis is unwarranted on two counts: first, the thematic content of the Song is not the courtship between damsel and suitor but the political alliance between the house of David and the Jewish community, as a prelude to the restoration of the monarchy in Judah; second, nowhere in the Song does the bridegroom address any person other than the bride, nor is he in a position to speak on his own authority before he is instituted as king and empowered to enact laws concerning the Judean community. Thus it is the bride who addresses the "daughters of Jerusalem."

The imposition of an oath implies a promise fidelity to which is a means of compelling the elite of the Jewish priesthood to abstain from entering further alliances with other nations. Since these alliances are intended to promote the interests of the partners with the exclusion of other social groups, strict measures are to be taken to prevent this course of action from becoming a customary practice. Indeed, a body of people engaged in restoring its national life can hardly tolerate a situation of a single group being absorbed in selfish pursuit of its own welfare in detriment of the sense of relationship with other less privileged groups of society. In order to prevent the social fabric from being torn apart, the leading figure representative of the Judean community peremptorily requests the elite of the Jewish priesthood to make common cause with the rural population, represented "by the gazelles or the hinds of the field" (*biṣbā'ôt 'ô b*^e^*'ay*^e^*lôt haśśādeh*). The conjunction "or" (*'ô*) introducing the second species distinguishes their respective habitats. The gazelles live in steppes and deserts, but usually in the plains, while some subspecies roam in mountainous regions; the hinds stay out of sight hidden in the forests during the day, coming out into the open at night to graze in the fields, pastures, orchards, and gardens. In literary analysis, a pair of related words such as "gazelles or hinds" is termed a merismus, a figure of speech used to give a conspectus of the variety of native fauna coexisting peacefully.

The significance of the animals mentioned in this text has been interpreted in different ways: according to one commentator, they represent the fascination of feminine beauty upon men (WINANDY, 112). Others consider these animals to be an allusion to the armies of angels and their commanders (JOÜON, *Ct* 161), or a sign of freedom (TOURNAY-NICOLAŸ, 55), or else an erotic symbol on the assumption that these animals are associated to the goddess of love (POPE, 386; WÜRTHWEIN, 44). However, none of these suggestions are pertinent to the matter at hand. The reference to animals as symbols of leaders or social classes is a literary device used in the ancient Near East: e.g. rams of Moab (Ex 15:15), he-goats (Is 14:9), cows of Bashan (Am 4:1), bulls and calves of the people (Ps 68:31), gazelles and bulls of Ugarit (GORDON, *UT,* Gl. 1045). In Ugarit, the nomadic population was designated as gazelles and the sedentary population as bulls (DUSSAUD, 363). In addition to these references contained in literary works there are a great many images representing such animals which were used in commerce to identify commodities delivered from feudal holdings as payment of taxes in kind, or to certify units of the measuring system adopted by the ruler of the country during his years in office. Numerous samples of clay vessels unearthed in Palestine bear the imprint of stamps in relief with representations of gazelles and hinds (GALLING, 105f).

The specific meaning of animal symbols, used for different purposes in commerce and literature, needs to be further specified. Thus the reference to "the field" (*haśśādeh*), an allusion to the habitat of "gazelles and hinds," indicates the rural area, as distinct from the urban area. Parallel to the "daughters of Jerusalem" who represent the leaders of the urban population, the "gazelles or the hinds of the field" symbolize the rural population.

What is the reason for mentioning these beasts in the formula of adjuration? Is it intended perhaps to invoke them as witnesses? From the context it becomes clear that such is not the case, since the formula expressing an oath calls on something held sacred to act as witness. The invocation of God as guarantor and witness gives the oath force and makes it irrevocable, incurring inevitable consequences in case of violation of the promise. It was suggested that gazelles and hinds were thought of as representing some goddess because no reference is made to God in this adjuration formula (KEEL, 94). However, this hypothesis is to be discarded. The motive for these animals being mentioned here is indicated by the preposition *bᵉ* with causal meaning, "on account of, in consideration of" (JOÜON, *Gr* § 170j). Indeed, the rural population, represented by gazelles and hinds, is the reason for the "daughters of Jerusalem" being compelled to make a solemn promise to side with them and abstain from selfish pursuit of their own welfare. This promise ought to be carried out, lest there be applied a severe sanction for violating the oath. Sanctions which are explicitly mentioned in imprecations are usually suppressed in adjuration formulae for fear of their malefic power in hunting down their victim. Although not expressed by word, the threat is implicit. The particle *'im* (certainly not) after the utterance of an oath (2:7; 3:5; 8:4) introduces the clauses expressing a prohibition, "that you stir not up" (*'im tā'îrû*) and "that you not awaken" (*'im tᵉ'ôrᵉrû*). Both verbs fundamentally have the same meaning of arousing or stirring someone to action. The repetition of the verb *'wr* II, in *Hiphil* and *Polel,* is intended to emphasize the prohibition. As for the inflexion of both verbs, it is to be noted that the masculine form is used instead of the feminine, although the subject is the "daughters" (JOÜON, *Gr* § 150a).

The object that receives the action of these verbs is the word "love," prefixed by the article, *hā'ahᵃbâ.* According to the hypothesis of a love scene being described here, the prohibition forbids the application of stimulants (POPE, 386). Contrary to this interpretation and taking into account the meaning of the word "love" as a synonym of "covenant," the adjuration compels the "daughters of Jerusalem" to give assurance that from now on they will not enter any alliance with the leaders of the neighboring countries. As a matter of fact, the elite of the Jewish priesthood (daughters of Jerusalem) tried to impose its leadership upon the group of repatriate Jews and to extend its hegemony to the population of autochthonous Jews, reinforcing its position by means of political alliances with influential families that were in control of the government in the provinces of Samaria, Ashdod, Ammon, and Moab (Neh 13:23-29). By mid-fifth century B.C., the prophet Malachi censured the priests for marrying women of foreign extraction in spite of strict regulations which prohibited such marriages, lest God's covenant with Levi be violated (Mal 2:10-16). For the social and religious integrity of the chosen people would become impaired if mixed marriages were to become a common practice among the population.

Diplomatic marriages served to reinforce the political relationship and to assure unwavering loyalty among allies, since they became members of one family. According to ancient custom, treaties were sealed by intermarriage unions. Although texts from antiquity do not always mention a formal treaty in connection with a diplomatic marriage, the marriage alliance with a woman of foreign extraction involved a political pact. Such an alliance with a political dimension was intended to build a legal friendship of a covenant-type (KALLUVEETTIL, 80).

The final clause "until it be propitious" (*'ad šetteḥpāṣ*) indicates the period at the end of which it will be permitted to enter political alliances. The conjunction "until" (*'ad še*), Lat. *priusquam,* designates the duration as well as the *terminus ad quem* after which something will be carried out (ZORELL, 572.2d). The verb *ḥpṣ* signifies "to want, desire, take pleasure, be agreeable, propitious." In connection with the noun *'ahᵃbâ,* in the sense of "covenant," the verb *ḥpṣ* qualifies this concept as "mutually expedient" (*TWAT* II, 104). The subject of the clause, rather than being, as is commonly assumed, the word *'ahᵃbâ* (a feminine noun in Hebrew), is in fact the general idea of the preceding clause, referred to by the verbal form in the third feminine used impersonally, "until this will be propitious" (JOÜON, *Gr* § 152c).

Some commentators suggest emending the text by replacing *'ahᵃbâ* (love) for *hā'ᵃhubâ* (the beloved) on the assumption that the concrete should be taken for the abstract, since the sense of volition implied in the verb "to want" postulates a subject capable of will. This interpretation is unacceptable because it is based on an arbitrary modification of a word which, in eleven passages of the Song, is invariably used in the sense of "love." Moreover, it is inadmissible to give different meanings to a recurrent word in the same text, i.e. taking it in the abstract sense (vss. 4b and 5c) and then subsequently in a concrete one (vs. 7e).

What is the decisive factor which is going to modify the status quo of the political situation in Judah? According to the opinion of the author of the Song this factor is the inauguration of the capital as the administrative center of the country, where the leaders of the different social groups have access to the executive branches of the government. There the affairs of state will be managed and the foreign policy to be adopted for the benefit of the country will be decided upon.

Commentary: The Theme of the Capital (2:4-7)

The theme dealt with in this song is the restoration of the capital city of the Judean territory. This city would have a role as the seat of government, as a symbol of political independence—although limited under the Persian domination—and as the center of convergence for the Jewish communities scattered in the diaspora. This would provide a concrete symbol with which to express the restoration of national prestige and would satisfy the nation's need for social and political organization. Since the beginning of the post-exilic period, the territory of Judah was subdivided into administrative districts which at the time of Nehemiah amounted to five with some subdistricts (Neh 3:1-32). However, the administrative division was conducive to a fragmentation of national cohesion and gave rise to an attempt by some local leaders to extend their leadership to groups in neighboring areas.

At that time the seat of government was located in Mizpah where the governor resided (Neh 3:7). But this town situated some way from the center of Judah, being on its northern border, should no longer be used as the governor's official residence, because the Babylonians had installed their administrative officials there after the conquest of Jerusalem and the extinction of the kingdom of Judah. Thus it was imperative to erase from the existing organization any vestige of the former national catastrophe and begin a new era by restoring the capital. Such a decision was reached by consensus of the country's leadership and ratified at an official meeting. It is to be noted that the initiative to restore the capital rests in the hands of the king and not of the elite of the Jewish priesthood so as to distinguish their respective competence in civil and religious matters and dissociate the political from the religious institution. Speaking in terms of political systems, a question arises concerning the viability of the diarchic government as proposed by the prophets Haggai and Zechariah in 520 B.C., according to which the state of Judah would be governed simultaneously by king and high priest, each presiding respectively over the political or the religious community.

The need for building a capital is the result of both internal factors arising from the political organization of the community by a ruler and external circumstance. Now, the body politic governed by a ruler implies a system of administrative organs which are not autarchies, in spite of their supervisory function over different districts. Those in charge of the administration of these districts are subordinate to the head of the government, no mere representative of this group of officials, but the heir of the house whose destiny is also that of the nation, the house of David. Thus these officials are subordinate to the king as his immediate auxiliaries, while the leaders of the different social groups are related to the monarch as his allies. This covenant relationship is described in the scene where the king meets the leading figure representative of the autochthonous Jews. The rites of hospitality assume special significance as symbolic acts related to the covenant, i.e. the welcome at the ally's home, the meal shared in common as a sign of the other party's acceptance of the pact, and the embrace as a gesture of friendship.

As a result of the political organization of the Judean community, the city of the sovereign's official residence becomes the administrative center of the country and the place of assembly for the people's delegates. There the question of the government's foreign policy is brought up for debate. The representative of the autochthonous Jews argues against the enactment of alliances with the leaders of neighboring countries. Since the elite of the Jewish priesthood has already joined partnership with them, a motion is being issued, formulated in terms of an adjuration with the imposition of an oath, to make them promise to abstain from engaging in new alliances. A time will come when it is suitable to enter alliances, though this will not be on the initiative of a single group in selfish pursuit of its own welfare, but at the discretion of the king, whose duty is to foster the prosperity of the nation. Because the court of representatives is assembled under the auspices of the king, and the administrative officials depend upon his royal authority for the exercise of their function, the initiative to restore the capital rests entirely upon the king. Indeed, no person other than the head of government, appointed by the Persian emperor to rule the country, will have a chance to succeed in an enterprise with political implications for the status of Judah as a dependent territory. Since the attempt to restore the capital is not intended as an insurrection against foreign domination, the king will have to reassert his unwavering loyalty and allegiance to the Persian overlord. The theme of the country's capital will be taken up in another song (8:1-4).

3 ✦ *In the Countryside (2:8-15)*

8 Hark, my beloved! *Bride*
Behold, there he comes,
leaping upon the mountains,
bounding over the hills.
9 My beloved is like a gazelle,
or a young stag.
Behold, there he stands
behind our wall,
gazing in at the windows,
looking through the lattice.
10 My beloved speaks and says to me:
"Arise, my friend, my fair one, *Bridegroom*
and come away;
11 for lo, the winter is past,
the rain is over and gone.
12 The flowers appear in the country,
the time of singing has come,
and the voice of the turtledove
is heard in our country.
13 The fig tree puts forth its figs,
and the vines are in blossom;
they give forth fragrance.
Arise, my friend, my fair one,
and come away.
14 O my dove, in the clefts of the rock,
in the covert of the escarpment,
let me see your face,
let me hear your voice,
for your voice is sweet,
and your face is comely."
15 Catch us the foxes, *Chorus*
the little foxes,
that spoil the vineyards,
for our vineyards are in blossom.

Accented Transliteration (2:8-15)

8 *qốl dôdî́*
hinnê-zéh bā́ʾ
m^{e}dallḗg ʿal-hehārím
m^{e}qappḗṣ ʿal hagg^{e}bāʿốt
9 *dôméh dôdî́ liṣbî́*
ʾô l^{e}ʿṓfer hāʾayyālî́m
hinnê-zéh ʿômḗd
ʾaḥár kotlḗnû
mašgî́^{a}ḥ min-haḥ^{a}llōnốt
mēṣî́ṣ min-haḥ^{a}rakî́m
10 *ʿānā́h dôdî́ w^{e}ʾāmar lî́*
qû́mî lā́k raʿyātî́
yāfātî́ ûl^{e}kî-lā́k
11 *kî-hinnḗ hass^{e}tā́w ʿābár*
haggéšem ḥāláf hālak lố
12 *hanniṣṣānî́m nirʾû́ bāʾā́reṣ*
ʿḗt hazzāmî́r higgî́^{a}ʿ
w^{e}qốl hattốr nišmáʿ b^{e}ʾarṣḗnû
13 *hatt^{e}ʾēnā́ ḥān^{e}ṭā́ faggèhā*
w^{e}hagg^{e}fānî́m s^{e}mādár nāt^{e}nû rḗ^{a}ḥ
qû́mî lā́k raʿyātî́
yāfātî́ ûl^{e}kî-lā́k
14 *yônātî́ b^{e}ḥagwḗ hasséla ʿ*
b^{e}sḗter hammadrēgā́
harʾî́nî ʾet-marʾáyik
hašmîʿî́nî ʾet-qôlḗk
kî-qôlḗk ʿārḗb
ûmarʾḗk nāʾwéh
15 *ʾeḥ^{e}zû-lā́nû šûʿālî́m*
šûʿālî́m q^{e}ṭannî́m
m^{e}ḥabb^{e}lî́m k^{e}rāmî́m
ûk^{e}rāmḗnû s^{e}mādár

Literary Analysis (2:8-15)

The countryside brightened by its flowering vegetation during the spring season is the setting of the third meeting between bride and bridegroom. The song describes, in six strophes, the landscape in springtime and compares the burgeoning vitality in nature at the approach of the first season of the year with the response of the inhabitants of Judah to the auspicious signs of the beginning of the period of restoration. Each strophe consists mostly of three couplets with two or three accented syllables in Hebrew, except for the last strophe, composed of two couplets.

The first strophe (vss. 8-9b) gives an account, in a lively monologue, of the sudden approach of the bridegroom, whose gladness at returning to the homeland makes him hasten along his way over the hills faster than the pace of his feet, because he is urged on by the longing of his heart. The second strophe (vss. 9c-10a) mentions his attempt to get in touch with the local population after his arrival in Judah. In the third strophe (vss. 10b-12b) the bridegroom's address begins: He bids the bride to give a cheerful welcome to the restoration that is close at hand. The fourth strophe (vss. 12c-13) depicts three signs of the beginning of spring as an illustration of favorable conditions on the social and political level especially to be valued in the light of the new era. The fifth strophe (vs. 14) makes an appeal to the population to relinquish its attitude of isolation within regional boundaries and adopt a policy of nationwide influence. The sixth strophe (vs. 15) is a hunting song with reference to fox-hunting practiced at this time of year, which consisted of trapping foxes in their lairs. The ideas expressed in the song are applied to a specific state of affairs in which the country finds itself. By calling on the leaders of Judah to hunt foxes seen as pests, the chorus appeals to these leaders to take active measures to rid the country of harmful factors which affect the life of the community.

Poetic and rhetorical devices which occur in the song are sound repetition: assonance *e-a-e: m^edallēg–m^eqappēṣ;* recurrence of homophonous word endings *-îm* (vs. 15a-c); alliteration *m^edallēg ʿal-hehārîm // m^eqappēṣ ʿal-hagg^ebāʿôt* (vs. 8cd); recurrence of stressed syllables with the same vowel *-e* (vs. 14d-f); repetition of words: *qôl* (four times), "my beloved" (three times); repetition of a sentence: refrain (vs. 10bc and 13cd); anadiplosis *qôlēk–qôlēk* (vs. 14de), *šûʿālîm–šûʿālîm* (vs. 15ab), *k^erāmîm–k^erāmênû* (vs. 15cd); repetition of structural patterns: syntactic parallelism, e.g. verb + object // verb + object (vs. 14cd), subject + complement // subject + complement (vs. 14ef); chiasmus *mar'ayik . . . qôlēk–qôlēk . . . mar'ēk* (vs. 14c-f). Rhetorical devices: merismus "mountains–hills" (vs. 8); hyperbole, e.g. speed of the lover (vs. 8); simile "my beloved is like a gazelle or a young stag."

Vocabulary Analysis (2:8-15)

Vs. 8: The strophe begins with an interjectional clause "hark, my beloved!" (*qôl dôdî*), which implies an auditory response, in parallel to the following clause, referring to a visual response to the approach of "my beloved." In relation to the preceding song, where the abstract noun "love" occurs three times, the concrete noun "my beloved" is used here instead, repeated thrice, in order to hint at related themes and link the scenes of both capital and country to the territory of Judah. In order to point at the beloved who is nearby, the demonstrative pronoun "this" (*zeh*) is given deictic force by its combination with the interjection "behold" (*hinnê*), used here and below (vs. 9c). This interjection used with the participle shows the action as present, "there he comes" (*hinnê-zeh bāʾ*) and below in vs. 9c, "there he stands" (*hinnê-zeh ʿômēd*). His approach is said to be swift despite the irregular terrain with "mountains" (*hārîm*) and "hills" (*gᵉbāʿôt*), typical of the Judean plateau. In literary analysis, the pair of related words "mountains and hills" is termed a merismus, a figure of speech used to include the diversified topographical features of the country. The route taken by the "beloved" toward the homeland does not follow the official road, but swerves off in a short-cut over hills and valleys, which he crosses over by leaps and bounds (*mᵉdallēg–mᵉqappēṣ*).

Vs. 9: The description of the swift motion is continued in this verse with the figure of gazelles and stags, whose proverbial swiftness is used in the comparison of a man with gazelle (*ṣᵉbî*) and "young stag" (*ʿofer hāʾayyālîm*). In the preceding song mention is made of these creatures in a comparison of the habitat of native fauna with the settlements of the rural population. In addition to the literary nexus between these songs indicated by a pair of related words designating those animals, there is also to be recognized a relationship between this and the final strophe. Both gazelles and stags are classified under the category of big game, whereas foxes are small game. According to the laws protecting wild animals, the hunting season of gazelles and stags was restricted to autumn and winter, while fox hunting was regarded as a necessary measure to prevent the proliferation of noxious animals.

The second strophe begins with the interjection "behold, there" (*hinnê-zeh*), as above in 8b, in order to indicate something that is close at hand. Mention is made again of the beloved's sudden arrival at a country-house, like a gazelle or a young stag descending upon a rural settlement. The word *kōtel* (wall) is borrowed from Aramaic with the suffixed possessive pronoun from Hebrew, *kotlēnû* (our wall). The use of the plural possessive pronoun instead of the singular is typical of the poetic language of the Song (JOÜON, *Ct*, n° 79). By referring to the wall, there is meant the house itself, to be understood as synecdoche *totius pro parte*, rather than an enclosure surrounding a building (Colombo, 64). Indeed, it is a country house of some importance to judge from its features, i.e. windows and lattices.

In the preceding strophe, the stress is laid on the verbs "leaping and bounding" to indicate the motion of swift legs; here the emphasis is on the keen eyes, expressed by the verbs "gazing" (*mašgîaḥ*) and "looking" (*mēṣîṣ*). The verb *hēṣîṣ*, in *Hiphil*, is a *hapax legomenon*, whose meaning is to be inferred from its relation to the preceding *hišgîaḥ*. The staring gaze of the gazelle scans over the "windows" (*ḥallōnôt*) and "lattices" (*ḥarakîm*), not out of mere curiosity, but with intense searching. The noun "lattices" (*ḥarakîm*) is a *hapax legomenon* whose signification is known from comparative philology.

The comparison of the recent arrival with a gazelle, representing the native fauna of Palestine, illustrates the presence of this person extending to all the regions of the country. Thus he is not thought of as a stranger to the inhabitants of Judah. An atmosphere of harmony and peace pervades the idyllic environment of the rural landscape without any sound of a hunting party chasing gazelles and stags in the countryside. The purpose of depicting this rural environment is to relate the capital, described in the preceding song, to the country. In the same way as the "beloved" is closely associated with the administrative organs, the assembly of delegates, and the urban population, so now he draws near to the rural population, whose settlements are scattered over different regions of the country. Under the present circumstances, his visits to the countryside are quite discreet, in analogy with the unobtrusive appearance of the gazelle, in order to avoid the Persian authorities suspecting a possible insurrection against their domination.

Vs. 10: The transition to the following strophe is mediated by two verbs, *ʿānāh* (to speak), lit. "to reply," and *ʾāmar* (to say), whose tense-form is the perfect used in the sense of a present. The scene of spring, in which events occurring every year are displayed, is presented under the form of an historical narrative transposed to the present. Distinguishable features of the Palestinian landscape are described in view of their symbolic value as an example of events occurring in the history of Israel. Thus the beginning of spring is an allusion to the dawn of a new historical period, in which the Jewish community will come to life as a nation.

In the third strophe, the protagonist calls upon the lady of the house to raise herself (*qûmî lāk*) from her stupor and to follow him (*lekî-lāk*). The significance of this occurrence for her is emphasized by the combination of both verbs with the pronoun and the *lamed* of the *dativus commodi* (*GK*, § 119s). Owing to poetic license, terms assume a particular connotation appropriate to the context: thus the verb *hālak* (to go) signifies "to come," here and below in vs. 13 (Joüon, *Ct*, n° 109). The word *raʿyātî* (my friend) is the feminine equivalent to the masculine *dôdî* (my beloved). Both are official titles attributed to allies of a pact of friendship. Likewise, the expression "my fair one" (*yāfātî*) is not meant for extolling her physical traits, but the status of an ally held in esteem, as explained above in 1:15.

Vs. 11: The reason why she should come out of the house is to see for herself that the winter is over and the new season has set in with spring flowers appearing in the countryside. The word *s*^e^*tāw* (winter), taken over from Aramaic, is a *hapax legomenon.* A feature of the winter in Judah is the occurrence of heavy rainfall (*gešem*) and cold temperature. The end of winter is expressed by three synonymous verbs: *'ābar* (is past), *ḥālaf* (is over), and *hālak* (is gone), while the beginning of spring is indicated by five verbs referring to the senses of vision, audition, and smell.

Vs. 12: Silent harbingers of spring are the "flowers" (*niṣṣānîm*), a *hapax legomenon;* "they appear" (*nir'û*) in "the land" (*hā'āreṣ*), i.e. the territory of Judah. This word is to be taken in the sense of "country," because this song does not intend to describe the topsoil, but the country of Judah, as indicated below in the reference to "our country" (*'arṣēnû*). Disregard for the thematic content of this song leads to different translations of the word *'ereṣ,* as e.g. "ground" (GERLEMAN, 124; RUDOLPH, 132), "fields" (PIATTI, 106), and "countryside" (*NEB*).

In contrast with the silence that reigns outdoors during the winter, the season of garden parties held throughout the country now begins. The verbal form of *higgîa'*, "arrived," is the masculine, used as predicate of *'ēt* (time), a noun which occurs in the masculine in later biblical books, whereas in earlier ones it is taken as a feminine noun. As regards the meaning of *zāmîr* either as "singing" or "pruning," there is no consensus among commentators about the one which suits the springtime setting. It is obvious, though, that country-folk do not need the townspeople to tell them about pruning time, as if they were averse to labor or inexperienced in viticulture. Thus, *zāmîr* refers to the time of singing as a sign of joy at the arrival of the era of restoration.

The fourth strophe describes three features typical of the arrival of spring in Palestine, symbolizing the beginning of a new era in Israelite history. These features serve as criteria for the local population to observe *in loco* the approach of this era as having already set in. The first is the "voice of the turtledove" (*qôl hattôr*), which is "heard in our country" (*nišma' b*^e^*'arṣēnû*). The turtledove is a migrating bird that moves to Africa before the winter and returns to the northern hemisphere in spring. Analogously, the successive groups of exiles returning home from Babylon, Egypt, and other countries are a sure indication of the restoration period having already begun.

Vs. 13: The second feature of the approach of spring is the ripening of early figs. The fig tree, *Ficus carica,* is one of the fruit trees most cultivated in all regions of Palestine. According to FLAVIUS JOSEPHUS, the territory of Galilee supplied the markets with figs during ten months in the year, owing to temperate climate, fertile soil, and irrigation (*BJ* III, 10,8). There are three kinds of figs produced in different seasons. The first produce of the trees are called "early figs" (*paggîm*), a *hapax legomenon;* they grow after autumn, though most of them are shaken off the tree by strong winds blowing in winter, but those which are left on the tree and withstand the frost ripen at the beginning of spring and are known for their delicious flavor and succulence. The second produce is actually the primary yield of figs (*bikkûrîm*) gathered in at the end of May. The third produce is the second yield of figs (*te'ēnîm*) harvested at the end of August (DALMAN, *AuS* I/2, 379). As regards the early figs, their ripening process is designated by *ḥāneṭâ*, a *hapax legomenon,* whose meaning is obtained by relating it to Arabic and Akkadian cognates signifying "to mature, put forth," with no relation of *ḥnṭ* (to embalm), a homonym in Hebrew.

In order to ascertain the significance of early figs used as an image of the beginning of the period of restoration, a distinction is to be made between the figurative and imaginative element. Now, the "fig tree" is never used in biblical literature as a figure of the chosen people as, e.g., the vine, but rather occurs in context with blissful conditions, in contrast with an unproductive fig tree taken as a picture of calamity (2 Kgs 18:31; Jer 8:13, etc.). Thus, the description of ripening figs suggests peaceful conditions prevailing in and around Judah. These conditions are indicative of the period of restoration already near at hand. Looking back to the exilic period, which is compared to inclement weather conditions during a harsh winter, and contemplating their ruined cities, which are constant reminders of times of war, the Jewish population might become a prey to discouragement if they did not take advantage of the time of peace to restore their homeland.

The third feature of the new season of the year is the fragrance of "the vines in blossom" (*haggefānîm semādar*) pervading the air of the countryside. The vine, *Vitis vinifera,* cultivated in Palestine, was renowned both for its exuberant growth and the large clusters of grapes which it produced (MOLDENKE, 243). In order to call attention to the vines in bloom, a special term is being used, *semādar,* whose grammatical function in Hebrew is explained as an attributive accusative. Elsewhere, the flowers of fruit trees are commonly designated by such terms as *nēṣ, niṣṣâ,* and *peraḥ*. From grapevines in blossom a pleasant "fragrance" (*rêaḥ*) drifts over the vineyards planted on the hillsides and pervades the air of the entire region. In the mild temperature of spring, the flowers on the tendrils open up almost simultaneously and are exuberantly plentiful owing to the quantity and productiveness of the vines cultivated everywhere in the country, where soil is ideal for their growth.

The image of blossoming vines in spring is applied to Judah at the beginning of the period of restoration. In order to grasp the meaning of this image, placed at the close of a series of typical features of spring, we must relate it to other flowers mentioned in the preceding verse. Both types of flowers are silent harbingers of spring, either by the profusion of colors or the diffusion of fragrance. Amidst this flowering landscape joyful songs resound to welcome the exiles on their arrival as they join in the singing, glad to be able to intone again the hymns which they would not sing in foreign countries (Ps 137:4). The idyllic rural setting suggests peaceful conditions prevailing in Judah conducive to the social and economic recovery of the Jewish community, this in analogy with early figs which, after a harsh winter, are ripening under the influence of the mild spring climate. As for the country, once ravaged by war, vineyards will again be planted on terraced hillsides and cultivated vines will abound everywhere.

At the close of the strophe the refrain mentioned in the opening of the preceding strophe is repeated, forming an inclusion like a frame around this exceedingly beautiful picture of the beginning of spring in Palestine. The form of the pronoun with *lamed* connected with the verb *qûmî lāk* (arise!) is read with the Qere for MT *lāky,* rather than with the Kethib *lᵉkî* (go!). The yod at the end of MT *lāky* after quiescent shewa is wholly rejected (*GK* § 24d).

Vs. 14: The fifth strophe expresses an appeal for the bride to appear before the bridegroom. Since she did not respond to two previous invitations, she is now called upon by an invocation of her status as an ally. In fact the transition from winter to spring, adduced as an image for the change from exilic to the post-exilic period, was not sufficiently convincing that she should alter the course of the community's lifestyle in Judah. Thus, she is addressed as "my dove" (*yônātî*) rather than "my fair one" (*yāfātî*), so as to motivate her to make herself seen and heard. The response to the appeal will be given in the following song (2:16-17).

What is the meaning of the designation "my dove" applied to her in this text and below in 5:2 and 6:9? The interpretation proposed as a term of endearment (GERLEMAN, 125) is to be discarded in view of the arguments adduced above (vs. 10) in the explanation of the usage of official titles. Most commentators interpret the image of the dove in relation to the place chosen by the bird to make its nest "in the clefts of the rock" and "in the covert of the escarpment." Thus, the nest inaccessible to the dove's natural enemies would be an allusion to the woman's home in the mountains (DELITZSCH, 52), a hermitage (RICCIOTTI, 65), isolation (WÜRTHWEIN, 46), or a reserved attitude (BUZY, 314; KRINETZKI, 131). However, the specific meaning of the image of the dove has to be derived from the relationship between bride and bridegroom. Now, the typical behavior of mated doves is their indissoluble bond and their jealous attachment to one another. The dove of Palestine, *Columba livia,* makes its nest in the clefts of the rock and in the covert of the retaining walls and does not migrate before the winter, as opposed to the turtledove, which is a migratory bird, returning home in spring, and which places its nest in branches of trees. The typical behavior of these birds is used in the comparison of the repatriate Jews with turtledoves and the autochthonous Jews with doves, with special emphasis on the native population's alliance with the royal house in analogy with the lasting bond between mated doves.

The dove native to Palestine has its nest "in the clefts of the rock" (*beḥagwê hassela'*) or "in the covert of the escarpment" (*besēter ham-madrēgâ*). By "escarpment" (*madrēgâ*) is meant the retaining wall made of rocks for protection of a terrace filled with fertile soil. Terraced hillsides prevent erosion and expand the area of cultivable land for cultivation of cereal crops and groves of fruit trees.

In the appeal made for the bride to appear before the bridegroom, the mode by which she has to get in touch with him is also indicated. First, he asks her "let me see your face" (*har'înî 'et-mar'ayik*). The noun *mar'ayik* in the plural is used in the sense of the singular, whereas the following *mar'ēyk* with *iod otians* is the singular and with the Qere it is to be read *mar'ēk* as a syncopated form. Second, he requests "let me hear your voice" (*hašmî'înî 'et-qôlēk*). Although her voice is said to be "sweet" (*'ārēb*) and her face, "comely" (*nā'weh*), the bridegroom is not interested in taking a look at her externals nor in listening to the timbre of her voice, but rather wants her to be close at hand and affirm her commitment to the royal house. "To show one's comely face" means to present oneself formally to the ally with a friendly attitude as a sign of covenant allegiance; "to hear someone's voice" expresses recognizing assent to the covenant relationship. The verbs *šm' 'et* "to hear" (2:14) and *šm' le* "to harken to" (8:13) appear in clauses of treaties as covenantal expressions (KALLUVEETTIL, 135n; *TWAT* I, 797).

Vs. 15: The sixth strophe is a hunting song with reference to fox-hunting as engaged in at this time of year. The strophe serves as a transition between the appeal of the bridegroom and the response of the bride stated in the following vss. 16-17. Who is the person coming forward to sing this short poem? According to most commentators it is the bride (BEA, 35; DELITZSCH, 53; GERLEMAN, 127; JOÜON, *Ct*, 168; PIATTI, 107; POUGET-GUITTON, 158; RICCIOTTI, 217; ROBERT-TOURNAY, 122; TOURNAY-NICOLAŸ, 66; WÜRTHWEIN, 46); others ascribe it to her companions (KRINETZKI, 133; RUDOLPH, 135; WINANDY, 114; ZAPLETAL, 86), to her mother (LYS, 127), or to the bridegroom (RAVASI, 75). Some suppose that a redactor had inserted this song in the text (BUZY, 314; COLOMBO, 66; KEEL, 102). But none of these suggestions are satisfactory, as will be seen below. It is the chorus who recites or intones this song (ASENSIO, 599) as a send-off ditty for the departing hunters. The chorus represents the wisdom tradition kept alive in Israel and acts as advisor to the bride on matters concerning the socio-political organization of the community. The texts of the Song ascribed to the chorus vary in form and function. They occur either as introduction, transition, conclusion, description, or apostrophe (cf. 1:4). As for the hunting song, its function is to serve as a transition to the following literary unit, linking the address of the bridegroom (vss. 10-14) to the response of the bride (vss. 16-17). By relating this passage to its context, attention is drawn to the bride's response which would otherwise be undervalued owing to the deep impression still lingering on in the reader's mind in consequence of the song's poetic description of a new spring.

In the scenes of the Song, the presence of the chorus is discreet, so much so that neither its entry on stage is announced, nor do its apostrophes, directed to the bride, bridegroom, or both, have any introduction. Thus, the verbal action expressed in the hunting song as an imperative "catch!" (*'eḥezû*) concerns the leading figures of the Song. If on the other hand the verb were in the cohortative, "let us catch," the chorus or whoever might join in the singing would be the ones engaged in fox-hunting. In this case, the passage in question would be a folk-song inserted in the present text without any specific relevance to its thematic content.

Fox-hunting practiced either for sport or as a necessary measure tending to prevent the proliferation of noxious animals consisted in catching them in the groves of fruit trees. Between the middle and the end of March, the cubs leave the lair and dig into the soft layers of topsoil in the vineyards in search of insects. The verb *ḥbl* (to damage, devastate) refers to the destructive effects on the vines, whose roots are laid bare. The word *šû'ālîm* designates either foxes or jackals, although in the OT, jackals are usually termed *'iyyîm* or *tannîm*. In early spring, the vineyards became prime fox-hunting ground as a measure necessary to prevent depredation of the vines in blossom. Fox-hunting was a sport engaged in by vinedressers, while the nobility hunted big game, i.e. gazelles and stags, but here the noble guest takes part in the hunt.

Several suggestions have been put forward to interpret this hunting song, but none of them suits the context. Thus, a new approach has to be made by examining the key word of the passage, i.e. "vineyards," a common word for plantations of grapevines (1:4; 2:15; 7:13), which in a figurative sense denotes the settlements of autochthonous Jews located in the various districts of the Judean territory, as explained above in 1:6. For the protection of these "vineyards," the chorus calls upon the leaders of Judah to take measures to prevent depredation of the settlements, whose population looks with expectation to the period of restoration, compared to vines blooming in spring. The depredation of vineyards caused by foxes is to be taken as a picture of the local population suffering from the effects of an oppressive fiscal system imposed on the country by the forces of foreign occupation at whose service the exactors exploited the people (Hag 1:6). Among other types of oppression to be mentioned are robbery committed by fellow citizens and perjury uttered by these when brought to trial for robbery or fraud (Zech 5:3-4). In order to prevent the social order from suffering further damage the Jewish leaders are called upon to ensure the security and welfare of these communities.

Commentary: The Theme of the Country (2:8-15)

The description of the countryside in spring exhibits an idyllic landscape with birds flying in the air and wild beasts ranging over fields and orchards amidst a sprouting vegetation covering the mountainous region of Judah. The upsurge of vitality in the animal and vegetable kingdom is an image of the country's rebirth owing not to spontaneous development but to creative response of the citizens to the signs of a new era in history opening up before them. During the exilic period it was up to the autochthonous Jews to ensure territorial integrity, but in post-exilic times it was expected of the repatriate Jews that they bring renewed vitality to the Judean communities. Thus the return of the exiles to Judah deserved to be acclaimed and not repudiated by the local population so that the country not be deprived of the determining factor of the renewal of national life, but enabled to be reborn like nature which after winter comes to life again with the approach of spring.

Nature's seasonal cycle is a picture of the course of Israelite history which entered a new stage with the promulgation of Cyrus' edict in 538 B.C. (Ezr 1:1) concerning the repatriation of Jewish exiles and the restoration of the community of Judah. The change of climate from winter to spring illustrates the reversal of the people's insecure situation to a life of peace, propitious for economic development. The three typical features of the beginning of spring in Palestine serve as criteria for the inhabitants to observe *in loco* the rebirth of their country as the result of favorable social, political, and economic conditions prevailing in Judah.

Among the leading figures of the song, the bridegroom stands out by his initiative in bringing the autochthonous population to assume an attitude both of acceptance of the changes, resulting from the arrival of exiles, and of willingness to participate in the political organization of the country. By comparing him to a gazelle or stag, the author indicates that his presence in the country is not that of an intruder, but as an immigrant already integrated into the community of Judah on equal terms with the citizens of the country. Like these animals native of the Judean countryside, so also the scion of the house of David is of fundamental importance to the political structure of the Jewish nation.

The bride, whose role as representative of the autochthonous Jews is that of one who occupies a leading position within the local population, is the second important figure in this scene. Her isolationist attitude in keeping herself confined to rural districts is censured by the bridegroom in view of a nationwide policy which from now on she has to adopt. Indeed, the country of Judah represents a rare case in ancient history in which territorial integrity was preserved in spite of foreign occupation, and restored to its inhabitants. Despite the extinction of the kingdom of Judah, the destruction of the national temple, and the deportation of the ruling class, the country was spared from the resettlement of depopulated cities by foreigners. The Jews rebuilt the Jerusalem temple with subsidies from the central government and obtained safe conduct for all exiles who wished to return to their homeland (Ezr 1:2-4; 6:3-12; 7:13; Neh 2:7). The inhabitants of Judah were aware of their privileged position in relation to neighboring countries and made the homeland into a center of convergence for the Jewish communities scattered in the diaspora.

Other figures appearing in this song are the members of the chorus who express the thoughts and intentions of bridegroom or bride, explain their leadership role, and introduce their discourses. The chorus' entry on stage is not described anywhere; only its voice is heard as it declaims a hunting song in order to remind the leaders to take measures tending to rid the country of harmful factors.

Owing to the importance attributed to the land of Israel in the history of the chosen people there arises a question whether the post-exilic Jewish community regarded the territory of Judah as the promised land, seen as a religious category. The answer is in the affirmative as attested in prophetic books and in the writings of wisdom literature (*TWAT* I, 235). In view of the experience of exile and the expectation of the restoration of the promised land, prophecies uttered by Jeremiah (30:3) and Ezekiel (36:28) open the prospect of the return of exiles to the country of their forebears. Some texts articulated in poetic style of the wisdom literature mention that the access to the promised land is granted to Jews of upright conduct (Ps 37:11, 22, 29, 34; Prv 2:21-22; 10:30).

It is to be noted, however, that the author of the Song does not turn to religious categories in order to express his ideas nor does he mention Yahweh as the Lord of history. This is because his purpose is to apply to the political sphere the corresponding subject matter which in other biblical books is set in the context of the religious sphere. Thus, the country of Judah, in which the Jewish community is established, corresponds to the promised land which in religious terminology designates the geographical area that rightfully belongs to Yahweh. Indeed, the promised land is his gift bestowed upon the chosen people. The Jewish nation, organized as a political community of citizens who profess fidelity to the religious traditions of Israel, is the historical mediation by which the chosen people exists. Moreover, the four signs of divine election, Jerusalem and the monarchy (in the political sphere), and the temple and priesthood (in the religious sphere), represent the institutions of ancient Israel.

In the post-exilic period, the temple and priesthood were restored and inaugurated in a solemn ceremony held in 515 B.C. (Ezr 6:16-18). At that time, the restoration of Jerusalem and the monarchy was not yet accomplished. These institutions belonging to the political sphere had a symbolic value for Judah and the Jewish people in the homeland and abroad: the

Davidic monarchy was the embodiment of supreme authority in the government of the people and was the instrument of mediation between God and people; Jerusalem was regarded as the capital of the country and seat of government. In fact the city of Jerusalem was rebuilt by Nehemiah and regained its status as a fortified city after the walls surrounding the urban center had been reconstructed and solemnly inaugurated c. 435 B.C. (Neh 12:27-43). In the historical context and under the circumstances which affected the course of events that took place in the period of restoration, the country of Judah, assigned to the Jewish population, is regarded as the land where its inhabitants are entitled to create a social organization in continuity with the traditions handed down by their forebears. This organization would have to be carried out in the face of the challenges arising from the effort to integrate repatriate and autochthonous Jewish groups into the Judean community, to constitute a treaty relationship with neighboring countries, and to establish the kingdom of Judah under the hegemony of the Persian empire. The theme of the country will be dealt with again in the corresponding song in 7:12-14.

4 ✦ *The Bond of Friendship (2:16-17)*

16 My beloved is mine and I am his, *Bride*
he is a shepherd among lilies.
17 Until the day expires
and the shadows flee,
turn, my beloved, like a gazelle
or a young stag,
toward the terraced mountains.

Accented Transliteration (2:16-17)

16 *dôdî lî́ wa’^{a}nî́ lố*
hārōʿéh baššôšannî́m
17 *ʿad šeyyāfû́^{a}ḥ hayyố́m*
w^{e}nā́sû haṣṣ^{e}lālî́m
sṓb d^{e}mēh-l^{e}kā́ dôdî liṣbî́
’ô l^{e}ʿṓfer hā’ayyālî́m
’al-hārế bā́ter

Literary Analysis (2:16-17)

The fourth meeting between bride and bridegroom aims at establishing a covenant relationship. This short song, composed of a monologue (vs. 16) and an apostrophe (vs. 17), expresses the bride's response to the bridegroom's previous invitation for a tour through the countryside to enjoy with him the sight of the spring season as described in the preceding song. Her acceptance of his companionship is expressed by the standard formula employed in ancient documents referring to a covenant relationship. The identification of the bridegroom as a shepherd indicates his role in society by means of an official title attributed to him. The bride's apostrophe gives an account of the circumstances related to the bridegroom's return to Judah.

The figure of speech used here is that of the simile: "my beloved is like a gazelle or a young stag."

Vocabulary Analysis (2:16-17)

Vs. 16: The relationship between bride and bridegroom is based on the pursuit of a common interest expressed by the formula of a covenant, "my beloved is mine and I am his" (*dôdî lî wa'ᵃnî lô*). This formula corresponds to similar declarations of relationship between allies used in documents of the treaty literature of the ancient Near East (KALLUVEETTIL, 102). Since the bride is the one who makes the declaration, in keeping with the practice then in vogue by which the inferior party pledged its fealty to the superior, the covenant to be concluded establishes a relationship between unequal partners. That is to say, the bridegroom represents the king, and the bride, the leaders of the autochthonous Jewish population. The former's function in society is specified by referring to him as a shepherd, an official title employed in antiquity to indicate the role of the king as ruler over the people; in liturgical usage this term is applied to Yahweh (*THAT* II, 793f). The translation of the participle *hārō'eh* as a noun, "the shepherd," diverges from the commonly accepted rendering of this participle as transitive with the flock as its unexpressed object, "he pastures his flock," or as intransitive, "he feeds himself" (JOÜON, *Ct*, 169; POPE, 406). The rendering of the participle by a verb phrase is based on the assumption that the bridegroom is now leading his sheep to pasture. On the other hand, translating the participle by a noun "shepherd," we take into account its relation with the formula of the covenant, in conformity with ancient covenant formulae. These contain a clause specifying the status of the covenant partner. The preposition *bᵉ*, "among," prefixed to *šôšannîm* (lilies), indicates the habitat of these flowers, growing in Judah where the shepherd is to be found. This plant, indigenous to the mountains of Palestine, is the figure used of the autochthonous Jewish population. A distinction must be made, however, between lilies in the plural, representing several communities of this population (2:16; 4:5; 6:2-3), and lily, in the singular, which designates the bride in regard to her role as leader of these communities (2:1-2). This phrase is repeated in reverse in a different context (6:3).

Vs. 17: The sentence introduced by the conjunction "until" (*'ad še*) gives an account of the circumstances related to the bridegroom's return to Judah. The time of the day is indicated by two idiomatic expressions referring to the breeze arising at sunrise and sunset, "the day breathes" (*yāfûaḥ hayyôm*), and to the shades that vanish at sunrise or stretch out, as if fleeing away, at sunset, "the shadows flee" (*nāsû haṣṣelālîm*). Since these expressions denote typical climatic features of that region, one has to infer from the context what part of the day is meant here. Now, the people's expectation that the king will return to Judah grows day by day. They hope that his arrival will not be too late, nor the opportunity for restoring the monarchy lost. This is condensed in the image of a moment for which they are waiting and which will come about before nightfall.

The verb *sbb* (to turn) is taken in the sense "to swerve" from the overland road and take a route that leads "across terraced mountains" (*'al-hārê bāter*). Along with the information about the road to be taken mention is made of the haste required of the king in his journey to the communities located in the mountainous region of Judah. It is the proverbial swiftness of the gazelle and the young stag which is the underlying idea of the comparison introduced by the verb *demēh-lekā* (be like) and rendered by "like."

Many divergent explanations have been proposed for the expression *hārê beter*. According to ancient versions, it is a proper name of a locale after which a range of mountains is named (Aquila, Symmachus, Vulgate), a descriptive term of cragged mountains (LXX), a reference word for a spice-producing wonderland like the land of Punt mentioned in Egyptian love lyrics (GERLEMAN, 128), or a hyperbolical expression for the body of the bride (HAUPT, quoted by POPE, 410). There may also be mentioned two emendations of the MT which replace *beter* either for *beśāmîm*, as a synonymous term (8:14), or for *malábathrōn*, as a contraction of two words from Greek and Latin, designating an unknown aromatic plant. It was suggested too that *beter* signifies "separation," in allusion to the procedure of cutting up a sacrificial victim. Since a covenant enactment entailed the offering of a sacrifice, the mountains in question would indicate the region where a covenant was to be established and thus would denote, by metonymy, the mountains of the covenant (ROBERT-TOURNAY, 129).

What is the meaning of *beter* used in this expression? It is to be noted that in other biblical books this word occurs in a sacrificial context, used both as a verb *btr*, "to cut up" (Gn 15:10) and as a noun *beter*, "a cut of meat" (Gn 15:10; Jer 34:18f). The use of this word in a topographical context denotes a flat terrace incised into the slopes of mountains and hills, enclosed by retaining walls to prevent the fertile soil from being washed downhill by heavy rains. It thus expanded the area of cultivable land for cereal crops and groves of fruit trees. The technique of terracing was also applied to the construction of cities, e.g. Jericho and Jerusalem, and of roads through rugged terrain (Is 40:3-4; 49:11). But it was agriculture that most benefited from the terracing of hillsides which increased the area of arable land (Is 42:16). Thus, the reference to topographical features of Judah is a means of indicating human settlements developed "upon terraced mountains" (*'al-hārê bāter*) which are of importance in the economic and social life of the country.

Commentary: The Theme of the Covenant (2:16-17)

The theme under consideration in this song is that of the covenant between the heir to the throne of David, identified as a "shepherd," and the Judean communities, designated as "lilies." While previous songs (1:12-17; 2:4-7) have dealt with symbolic rites performed at the pact-enacting ceremony, the subject now under consideration is the legally binding nature of the association between king and people as expressed in the covenant formula. The oral declaration effected the bond and defined its nature. From the juridical point of view, the covenant is a contract of cooperation between king and people. In other biblical texts mention is made of a formal act of covenant-ratification performed at the investiture ceremony of the king. Since the ceremony occurred in a religious context, the covenant had both religious connotation, and political dimension in the form of a pact (KALLUVEETTIL, 66). In fact, the covenant was regarded (by king and people) as one of the constitutive elements of the monarchies of both Israel and Judah during the period of political autonomy as independent states. With the annexation of the kingdom of Israel to the Assyrian empire in 722 B.C., and the incorporation of the kingdom of Judah into the domains of Babylon in 586 B.C., both monarchies were suppressed and the royal families deported into exile. But the heir to the throne of David was looking forward to his return to Judah with the same hope as that which the autochthonous Jews in the homeland nurtured, while awaiting his installation in the seat of government. This hope is expressed in terms of the people's entreating call that he hurry the pace of his homecoming like a gazelle bounding with startling speed through the countryside. He is expected to arrive as a "shepherd," i.e. a person clothed with royal authority to assume the reins of the government. The Judean population is engaged in agriculture and fruit-growing made possible by terracing the uplands of Judah and the gently sloping hills in order to expand the area of cultivable land. Thus the scenery typical of that region serves as an indication of the settlements of the autochthonous Jews who express their allegiance to the scion of the house of David. This implies that they are willing to lend their support to the project of restoring the monarchy. The theme of the covenent will be dealt with in another text (7:11).

Poem III

The Coming of the Bridegroom (3:1-11)

1 ✦ *The Expected Coming (3:1-5)*

1 Upon my bed by night *Bride*
I sought him whom my soul loves;
I sought him, but found him not;
2 "I will rise now and go about the city,
in the streets and in the squares;
I will seek him whom my soul loves."
I sought him, but found him not.
3 The watchmen found me,
as they went about in the city.
"Have you seen him whom my soul loves?"
4 Scarcely had I passed them,
when I found him whom my soul loves.
I held him, and would not let him go
until I had brought him into my mother's house,
and into the chamber of her that conceived me.
5 I adjure you, O daughters of Jerusalem,
by the gazelles or the hinds of the field,
that you stir not up nor awaken love
until it be propitious.

Accented Transliteration (3:1-5)

1 *ʿal-miškābî́ ballêlṓt biqqáštî*
ʾēt šeʾāhᵃbấ nafšî́

biqqaštîw welō' meṣā'tîw
2 *'aqûmāh nā' wa'asôbebāh bā'îr*
baššewāqîm ûbārehōbôt
'abaqšāh 'ēt še'āhabâ nafšî
biqqaštîw welō' meṣā'tîw
3 *meṣā'ûnî haššōmerîm*
hassōbebîm bā'îr
'ēt še'āhabâ nafšî re'îtem
4 *kim'aṭ še'ābartî mēhem*
'ad šemmāṣā'tî 'ēt še'āhabâ nafšî
'aḥaztîw welō' 'arpennû
'ad-šehabê'tîw 'el-bêt 'immî
we'el-ḥeder hôrātî
5 *hišba'tî 'etkem benôt yerûšālaim*
biṣbā'ôt 'ô be'ayelôt haśśādeh
'im-tā'îrû we'im-te'ôrerû
'et-hā'ahabâ 'ad šetteḥpāṣ

Literary Analysis (3:1-5)

Poem III on the coming of the bridegroom (3:1-11) is composed of three songs which describe his return to Judah and the reception which its inhabitants prepare for him. The corresponding poem (5:2–6:3) takes up the same scene and points to the role of the bridegroom in the Judean community.

This song relates a dream of the bride occasioned by her loneliness at the absence of the bridegroom and by her longing for his presence. Bride and bridegroom represent, respectively, the leading figure representative of the people of Judah and the Davidic king. The bride's desire for the bridegroom's return to Judah manifests itself in an oneiric experience in which his immediate arrival and its circumstances are disclosed. The object of her desire is represented in a dream about the arrival of the heir apparent in the city of Jerusalem, the capital of the country, and the investiture as king of the Jewish nation. These wishful thoughts are expressed in two subsequent songs whose thematic content is the repatriation of the king (3:6-8) and the coronation ceremony (3:9-11).

However, the absence of someone dearly loved may either give rise to a feeling of nostalgia or serve as an incentive to search. Now, the author of the Song does not nurture an inert longing but a solicitous concern, described in the scene of the bride's courageous seeking without retreat in the face of obstacles, e.g. the darkness of the night and the curfew enforced upon the city. After an unrelenting search a happy reunion is held.

The various scenes correspond to the five strophes of the song. Four strophes are composed of three verse lines with one (vs. 2d) or two additional lines (vs. 4de), while the fifth strophe consists of a couple of distichs (vs. 5). Some commentators suppress some verse lines of the MT in order to harmonize strophes of equal length with each other without taking into account the peculiarity of poetic style which employs the repetition of phrases and words as a figure of speech for the sake of emphasis. Thus, the idea of "love," repeated five times as either a noun or a verb, occurs in all strophes so as to link them to each other and to indicate the reason for the reference to seeking and finding, four times repeated. As regards the literary form, the song is an account of a past dream, related in the first person. For the sake of variety, sentences in narrative style interchange with a monologue (vs. 2), a question (vs. 3c), and an apostrophe (vs. 5).

Poetic and rhetorical devices that occur in the song are sound repetition: assonance *a-i* (vss. 1, 2cd, 4b); recurrence of homophonous word endings *-tîw* (vss. 1c, 2d); word repetition, e.g. "love" (five times), "to seek" (four times), "to find" (four times), "soul" (four times); repetition of the clause "whom my soul loves" (vss. 1b, 2c, 3c, 4b), refrain "I sought him, but found him not" (vss. 1c, 2d); repetition of structural patterns: parallelism, e.g. preposition + noun + noun // preposition + noun + participle (*'el-bêt 'immî* // *'el-ḥeder hôrātî*) (vs. 4de). Rhetorical devices: merismus "streets and squares" (vs. 2b), and the figure of "the gazelles and the hinds of the field" used for the rural population.

Vocabulary Analysis (3:1-5)

Vs. 1: The introductory verse gives an account of an inner experience which in the following verses is described with more details. The nature of an oneiric experience such as this is indicated by the circumstantial complement of place "upon my bed" (*'al miškābî*), the time of its occurrence, and the imaginative rehearsal of the episode. Exponents of the cult-mythical theory, applied to the interpretation of the Song, convince themselves of their viewpoint by relating this text with the myth of the goddess Ishtar's descent to the netherworld whence she rescues her consort Tammuz and brings him to the nuptial chamber. As regards this interpretation and refutation, see RUDOLPH (*KAT* XVII 1–3, 138).

Moreover, the circumstantial complement of time "by night" (*ballêlôt*) specifies the dream as having occurred by night to make clear that it is not a case of daydreaming. The form of the noun *lêlôt* (nights) is the plural of composition designating the duration of the night by the sum total of vigils (Joüon, *Gr* § 136b). Thus it is not to be thought of as a recurrent dream during several nights.

The absent king eagerly sought after is identified by the circumlocution "he whom my soul loves" (*šeʾāhᵃbâ nafšî*), i.e. "whom I love." In the corresponding song (5:2-8) he is referred to as "my beloved" (*dôdî*), six times repeated and followed by the abstract noun "love" (*ʾahᵃbâ*). In this song, the king is named by an equivalent expression in verbal form, four times repeated and also followed by the noun "love." The difference in terminology used in naming the same person is owed not to the need of variety in style but to the distinction between the circumstances affecting his relationship with the bride. Thus, the bridegroom is thought of as present when addressed as "my beloved," whereas in his absence he is referred to by the circumlocution "he whom my soul loves" (1:7): By identifying him with this verbal expression, the author indicates the covenant relationship to be established between bridegroom and bride. However, the idea of belonging-to-the-other is not conceived of in terms of a romantic attachment between man and woman enraptured with love for one another but signifies a political alliance between the future king and the people of Judah, represented, respectively, by bridegroom and bride.

The ardent desire for him to be present leads to an unrelenting search expressed by correlated verbs: to seek and to find. Although there is no reciprocal correlation between them, since there it is possible to seek without finding or find without seeking, the relation between these verbs results from their juxtaposition and from their connection by coordinating conjunctions, thus creating a proverbial expression. In this text, no relationship of convergence is stated but rather a polarity between these verbs by means of an adverb of negation which modifies the second verb: "I sought him, but found him not" (*biqqaštîw wᵉlōʾ mᵉṣāʾtîw*). This antithetical construction expresses the frustration at the lack of success in spite of all efforts that had been made.

Vs. 2: With this verse there begins the account of the dream related in three scenes: the search in the city, the approach of the watchmen, and the meeting with the bridegroom. The initiative to set out in search of the absent bridegroom is expressed as an act of the bride's intentionality: "I will rise now (*ʾāqûmāh nāʾ*). This is not a case of deliberation about an action to be taken in the future, but intentionality shown in the person engaged in action. Thus, it is out of the question to insert a verb proper to the cognitive faculty: "then I said" (*wāʾōmar*), as proposed by commentators (Zapletal, 94, et al.), because such a gloss presupposes that the woman in the scene would be in a state of vigilant consciousness. The purpose of mentioning the bride's intentionality may be to refute the objection that ideas presented in the form of a dream are nothing but fantasy.

The urban setting where the action takes place is immersed in the darkness of the night in contrast with the rural landscape bathed in sunlight, as described in the preceding songs. The city in question is not specified by name but instead by the definite article, i.e. the city. Moreover, the reference to watchmen and city walls (5:7) is an indication of its being an important city of the Judean territory. Other biblical books referring to the period of restoration (Zech 1–8; Ezr, Neh) mention various cities located in different regions of the country. Yet, from archeological remains that provide evidence from which a picture of the situation in Judah can be reconstructed, it is to be inferred that no urban culture developed during the post-exilic period. Thus the places that are designated as cities were towns with little in the way of substantial buildings, mostly obliterated by later building operations (KENYON, 296–302). There are, spread throughout the country, traces of a few official buildings which had been used as administrative edifices and as living quarters for the governor. Among the towns or fortresses which had been occupied by Persian officials, five administrative centers connected with their respective district (*pelek*) of the Judean territory are to be mentioned: Jerusalem, Mizpah, Beth-haccerem, Beth-zur, and Keilah (Neh 3:9-18).

The account of a search to be made in the city is related in a monologue. The verbal form *'ᵃsôbᵉbāh* (I will go about) is the cohortative of *sbb,* in *Polel,* expressing the resolution to go the rounds of the city by taking in the areas accessible to the public. This is borne out by the juxtaposition of two nouns: "streets" (*šᵉwāqîm*) and "squares" (*rᵉḥōbôt*), a figure of speech called merismus which includes different ways of transit within the city. With the itinerary there is also specified the purpose of setting out in search, expressed in Hebrew by the verb in the cohortative *'abaqšāh* (I will seek). For the sake of emphasizing the identity of the person sought after, the same circumlocution is used as above: "him whom my soul loves." Some commentators suppress the following stich of the MT: "I sought him, but found him not," with the explanation that strophic symmetry should prevail over the extant Hebrew text (RUDOLPH, 136; ZAPLETAL, 94).

Vs. 3: The second scene of the search begins with the same word as that which closed the preceding verse, but, because of its context, with a different meaning. This form of construction, called antimetabole, stresses the contrast between the leading figures. The verb *mṣ'* signifies "to find" and "to meet by chance," as is the case of the watchmen who happen by chance to meet with the single woman walking about the city. By proposing that MT *mᵉṣā'ûnî* (they found me) be emended to *māṣā'tî* (I found), RUDOLPH (*KAT* XVII 1–3, 137) forgets to take into account the fact that watchmen are trained soldiers who detect passers-by long before they are noticed by them. Watchmen (*šōmᵉrîm*) standing guard are quite common, but what is unusual here is to find them on patrol duty, as "they go about in the city" (*hassōbᵉbîm bā'îr*). As regards their attitude toward the local population, further details are given below in 5:7. On account of the watchmen walking in the streets no one else ventures to go outside. No wonder the search was unsuccessful, since none of the inhabitants was around to inform on the whereabouts of the illustrious visitor.

Before the watchmen have a chance to begin questioning, the woman asks them, "Have you seen him whom my soul loves?" (*'ēt še'āhᵃbâ nafšî reʾîtem*). In place of an interrogative particle to introduce the sentence, the direct object is put at the beginning for the sake of emphasis. No answer is given to the woman, because the watchmen do not know whom she is talking about nor are they allowed to commune with the inhabitants of the country.

The presence of a detachment of guards in the city adds a dramatic aspect to the nocturnal episode, rehearsed in the dream, and at the same time provides information about the political condition prevailing in the country. The circumstances described in the scene are quite abnormal, since the streets, where the people used to gather for conversation until late at night, are now totally deserted while watchmen are on patrol and keep everybody confined indoors. An exception to the rest of the people is this woman, whom the watchmen permit to go on her way as long as she does not raise her voice in the city square (5:7) and avoids wandering through the streets. To judge from these data, the city is under curfew, a repressive measure taken by the forces of occupation to keep the local population under control.

The reason for the Persian authorities taking such a drastic measure is their suspicion of a nationalist insurrection which the arrival of the Jewish governor might stir up among the inhabitants of the city. However, the local population did not even think of throwing off the yoke of Persian domination, but rather made plans for the organization of their national life and for the administration of their territory, which at that time was under the administrative jurisdiction of the Samaritan province. By laying claim to the right to administer their territory, the leaders of the Jewish population intended to get red of Samaritan interference in the internal affairs of Judah and raise their country to the rank of a self-governing province. In addition to these designs the leaders aspired to restore the monarchy in Judah. The hope of fulfillment of what they ardently desired is expressed in the general theme of the messages delivered by the prophets Haggai and Zechariah. Furthermore, the fact that Sheshbazzar (Ezr 5:14; 6:7) and Zerubbabel (Hag 1:1, 14; 2:1, 20)—the first two governors of Judah after the exilic period—were both princes of the Davidic line was interpreted by the autochthonous Jews as an auspicious sign of the restoration of the monarchy seen as close at hand. Although none of the succeeding governors were Davidids, the line of the Davidic dynasty was not interrupted since there were royal descendants living in Judah, so that the hope of restoring the monarchy was kept alive among the Jews in the land of their forebears.

The restoration of the Jewish nation, its political structure, and its administrative and social organization was seen by the Jews as fundamental for national life, but was regarded by the Persians as conflicting with their hegemony over Palestine. This explains why a detachment of soldiers was stationed in the city. It is not a case of some guard posts set up at strategic points, but of a detachment of watchmen patrolling the city as indicated by the rhythm of the verse, composed of a couplet of two stressed and unstressed syllables, imitating the uniform step of troops (vs. 3a + b). The function of these watchmen is to prevent both the governor from engaging in nationalistic endeavor and the local leadership from getting in touch with him. During the night they had to double their vigilance so as either to stop him from slipping secretly away from the official residence to meet with the leaders of the nationalist party, or to intercept the leaders on their way to the governor's residence.

Vs. 4: The third scene takes up the search which had been interrupted by the approach of the watchmen. As the woman goes on her way without being molested, she is left all to herself but only for a short while, because all of a sudden the person sought after falls in step with her: "scarcely had I passed them" (*kimeʿaṭ šeʿābartî mēhem*). The substantive with preposition *kimeʿaṭ* stands for a sentence: "it was a little that," connected to a subordinate clause by the conjunction "until" (*ʿad še*), rendered by "when."

The person sought after is now finally found and identified by the circumlocution "he whom my soul loves." Since this expression designates the absent bridegroom, it is used here to indicate that his presence is a transitory one, unless the bride succeeds in retaining him, which she tries to achieve, as expressed in the sentence: "I held him and would not let him go" (*'aḥaztîw welō' 'arpennû*). The verb *'arpennû* is rendered in the past tense, "I let him go" (JOÜON, *Gr* § 113h) and not in the future, because the event is related in the account of the dream. In the clause "until I had brought him" (*ʿad-šehabê'tîw*) the Hebrew verb is vocalized in defective spelling for the regular punctuation *habî'ōtîw*.

The bride's residence is designated by her as "my mother's house" (*bêt 'immî*). Her mother, as a corporate personality, is a poetic personification of the Israelite nation (1:6; 3:4; 6:9; 8:1-2), whose descendant, the community of Judah, is called her noble daughter (7:2). The mother's house is set in the territory of Judah, surrounded by the neighboring countries, while its political center is the capital, as the seat of government, and its religious center is the temple at Jerusalem, where God's presence becomes important for cultic worship and the social unity of the Jewish people (Zech 1:17; 2:6-9; 2:14-17; 8:2-7, 15; Ezr 1:3; 10:7-9; Neh 2:17; 12). Thus, her mother's house is the capital of the country, regarded as a center of convergence for all Jews living both in the homeland and in the diaspora. The expression *ḥered hôrātî* (the chamber of her that conceived me) is a synonym for *bêt 'immî* (my mother's house); both designate by synecdoche the capital taking the part for the whole. Both terms are correlated in a comparative relation: as the chamber stands for the house, so the house stands for the capital.

As to the identity of the city, it was argued that it need not be Jerusalem (Pope, 417). If this were true, what other city would then be referred to? According to the comments on this subject in vs. 2, there were five cities in Judah known as administrative centers during the period of restoration (Neh 3:9-18). To judge from their geographical location—on the roads linking the various regions of the country—each of these cities occupied a strategic position and had a specific function for its related district. Thus, Beth-zur, located near the Edomite border, had a defensive function to prevent infiltration of foreigners who constantly endangered the settlements of the southern district of the Judean territory. Keilah, ten kilometers to the west of Beth-zur, derived its importance from the surrounding groves of fruit trees cultivated in the region of the Sephalah and had the function of controlling the flow of mercantile caravans crossing the country from Jericho to Gaza. Mizpah was the seat of the governor (Neh 3:7) and the administrative center not only of the northern district, but of the entire territory of Judah. Beth-haccerem was located on an imposing elevation in the Judean mountains where a sedentary population and nomads contended in occupying the slopes of the hillsides for both agriculture and pasture. Jerusalem was situated on the principal junction of roads connecting all the regions of the country and the neighboring provinces. In addition to its strategic location, this city was the religious center and, as the former capital of the southern kingdom, was best suited to become once more the capital of Judah, since the temple was reconstructed on the same spot where it had previously stood in all its splendor.

Which of the five cities is the one designated as "my mother's house"? It certainly is not Mizpah, because no one would have to search for the governor's residence, obvious to all the people. As for the cities of Beth-zur, Keilah, and Beth-haccerem their importance was strictly of local concern and they could hardly be the stage for an event of social and political impact for all citizens. Thus it is Jerusalem referred to in this scene as the city which in due time will become again the capital of the country.

Vs. 5: This verse is identical to the passage above in 2:7; thus cf. the vocabulary analysis *ad loc.* With the apostrophe to the "daughters of Jerusalem," the account of the dream draws to a close. At first sight there does not seem to be a connection between the scene and the apostrophe. Yet there is a common element underlying the bride's search and the endeavor of the daughters of Jerusalem: both are in pursuit of their interests. While the bride, the leading figure representative of the autochthonous Jews, is engaged in restoring the monarchy for the benefit of the Judean community, the "daughters of Jerusalem," representing the elite of the Jewish priesthood, seek to promote their own welfare at the expense of other social groups. Moreover, the priestly hierarchy is not favorably inclined toward the local leading party because of its growing influence in the community and its decisive role in the organization of national life (2:7; 3:5; 5:8; 8:4).

Commentary: The Theme of the Restoration of the Monarchy (3:1-5)

The theme of this song is that of the restoration of the monarchy in Judah after the exilic period. Such an initiative arose from the need to give continuity to an institution which was in force during four centuries and was not abolished by popular uprising against it, but suppressed by force at the time of the conquest of Jerusalem and the extinction of the southern kingdom by the Babylonian armies in 587 B.C. When the Babylonian empire fell under Persian supremacy a new phase in the history of Judah began, as Cyrus promulgated an imperial decree in 538 B.C. granting the exiled Jews the right to return to Judah and to reconstruct the Jerusalem temple. By means of such innovative measures the emperor intended to gather repatriate and autochthonous Jews into a homogenous population whose religious traditions would receive their authorized interpretation from the priesthood and have their cultic expression in the temple.

Furthermore, the administrative organization of the territory of Judah was adjusted to the needs of its inhabitants and to the interests of the central government. In order to secure the allegiance of its subject people, the Persian rulers would appoint courtiers or members of local royal houses, of proven loyalty to the overlord, to administer provinces, territories, or city-states. Thus, Sheshbazzar, a Davidid, was commissioned as governor of Judah, although of limited executive power and for one term of office. That Zerubbabel succeeded him as governor gave further incentive to Jewish expectations of such a procedure being continued, and the government of Judah continuing to be in the hands of members of the house of David. Since the royal family had survived in Babylonia and was repatriated after exile, it was expected that the succeeding governors would be chosen from among the Davidic descendants living in the homeland. As a result of these administrative measures the unification of all social groups living in Judah was gradually being achieved. It was their need for consolidation which brought about the attempts to restore the monarchy. This is because monarchy was regarded as an effective means of achieving national unity and as the form of government best suited to the different social groups anxious to be organized into a political community.

The monarchy had as its most strenuous supporters the leader of the autochthonous Jews and the prophets Haggai and Zechariah, with whom the mentors of the wisdom tradition and the rural population sided. As a precautionary measure they did not divulge their plan of intended proceedings in order to avoid the Persian authorities suspecting a possible insurrection against their domination. The scenes of the dream give a descriptive notice of a series of events connected with the program of the restoration movement: first, a meeting is to be held between the Jewish governor and the leading figure representative of the autochthonous population (vs. 1); second, the meeting is to take place in the city (vs. 2); third, precaution should be taken to avoid the watchmen becoming suspicious (vs. 3); fourth, the seat of government should be transferred to the restored capital of the country (vs. 4); fifth, the leaders of the repatriate Jews are to be compelled to abstain from entering into alliance with foreign rulers (vs. 5).

Whatever steps were to be taken to achieve the restoration of the monarchy, the most important one was to obtain, in due time, approval from the Persian overlord. As soon as this nationalistic movement began to gather momentum all possible precaution was needed so that nothing of this transpired to non-initiates. Therefore, the plan of proceedings was outlined in a descriptive account of a dream which evokes the longing of the bride for her absent bridegroom. Of the initiates it was required to decipher the meaning of words and images used in this poetic narrative. The scene has special significance, since the city represents the capital of the country and seat of government. The female characters stand for the leaders of repatriate and autochthonous Jews. As long as the country was deprived of its own ruler, instituted as supreme authority, the nation lacked the sign of unity, the state was bereft of personality, and its institutions were destitute of power. No wonder that the elite of the Jewish priesthood entered into alliances with foreign countries, since there was no policy enforced to prevent the pursuit of private interests in detriment of the common good. In order to avoid the social unity among the different groups of the Judean community being dissolved by the hegemonic ambitions of their leaders, the representative of the autochthonous Jews advocated the project of restoring the monarchy as an effective means of mediation and balance between these groups which were to be integrated into the future Jewish nation. The theme of restoring the monarchy will be dealt with in another song (5:2-8).

2. ✦ *The Royal Procession (3:6-8)*

6 What is that coming up from the desert, *Chorus*
like a column of smoke,
perfumed with myrrh and frankincense,
with all the fragrant powders of the merchant?
7 Behold, it is the litter of Solomon!
About it are sixty warriors
of the warriors of Israel,
8 all are girt with swords
and expert in war,
each with his sword at his thigh,
against dangers by night.

Accented Transliteration (3:6-8)

6 *mî zṓ't 'ōlā́h min-hammidbā́r*
keṭîmarṓt 'āšā́n
mequṭṭéret môr ûlebônấ
mikkṓl 'abqát rôkḗl
7 *hinnḗ miṭṭātṓ šellišlōmṓh*
šiššî́m gibbōrî́m sābîb lā́h
miggibbōrḗ yiśrā'ḗl
8 *kullā́m 'aḥuzḗ ḥéreb*
melummedḗ milḥāmā́
'î́š ḥarbṓ 'al-yerēkṓ
mippáḥad ballêlṓt

Literary Analysis (3:6-8)

This song deals with the approach of the royal procession whose central figure is the future king accompanied by his escort. The three strophes, recited by the chorus, are linked to each other by means of their reference to the royal procession, by the emphasis on the presence of the king, as insinuated by the mention of Solomon in the middle strophe (vs. 7), and by two descriptions of related circumstances: one in the first strophe (vs. 6) and the other in the third (vs. 8).

Poetic and rhetorical devices occurring here are sound repetition: internal rhyme *miṭṭātô–šellišlōmōh* (vs. 7a), *šiššîm–gibbōrîm* (vs.7b), *miggibbōrê–yiśrā'ēl* (vs. 7c), *'aḥuzê–ḥereb* (vs. 8a), *ḥarbô–yerēkô* (vs. 8c); word repetition: anaphora *min* + *kôl* (vs. 6d), *min* + *gibbōrê* (vs. 7c), *min* + *paḥad* (vs. 8d). Rhetorical devices: hyperbole "the column of smoke perfumed with all the fragrant powders of the merchant"; anthypophora, *subiectio* in the Latin, a figure of speech consisting of a question (vs. 6) followed by an answer (vs. 7); the portrait of the warriors.

Vocabulary Analysis (3:6-8)

Vs. 6: The first strophe is expressed as an interrogation, followed by a declaration in the second strophe. This construction, consisting in the juxtaposition of question and answer, is a literary device used for stressing a description or statement (3:6; 5:9; 6:1; 8:5). In the clause "what is that?" there occurs the interrogative pronoun *mî* (who?) used for persons (6:10;

8:5), and rarely also for things (JOÜON, *Gr* § 144h). As for the demonstrative pronoun "that" (*zōʾt*) in the feminine, it is also employed as a neuter (JOÜON, *Gr* § 152a), designating something indefinite, e.g. the royal cortege seen from the distance which could easily be mistaken for a merchant's caravan.

The approaching royal procession is "coming up" (*ʿōlāh*) on the road "from the desert" (*min hammidbār*). By *midbār* is meant the unsettled and unsown steppe-land as well as the desert. In the Bible, it is applied to regions specified by a geographical name or by the definite article, indicating an area whose location is to be inferred from the context. The desert referred to here is the Judean desert above the western shore of the Dead Sea. The road from Jericho to Jerusalem ascends some 4,300 feet, reaching the Judean plateau-edge and continuing on along the last stretch known as the "ascent of the Mount of Olives" (*maʿalēh hazzêtîm*) which leads across the hills toward Jerusalem (2 Sm 15:30). This desert road was one of the principal routes used by merchants' caravans in their overland journey from Arabia to the seaports of the Levantine coast. The expression "going up to Jerusalem," which frequently occurs in the Bible, is used in an idiomatic sense (ROBERT-TOURNAY, 140f). It is to be noted, however, that this expression has a religious connotation designating a pilgrim's journey to the Jerusalem temple, whereas here the Davidic heir's journey to Jerusalem is a political move with a view to his accession to the royal throne (8:5).

The inhabitants of the outskirts of Jerusalem observe the procession shrouded in a cloud of incense-like "columns of smoke" (*tîmarôt ʿāšān*) swirling up from censers; *tîmarôt* is a general plural with the sense of the singular as a "column" (JOÜON, *Gr* § 136j). Owing to the profusion of aromatic substances burnt in the censers, the litter is suffused with fragrance to the point of becoming "perfumed" (*mequṭṭeret*). None of the fragrant substances of either myrrh or frankincense were produced in Palestine, but were imported from Arabia, Ethiopia, and Somalia. Myrrh (*môr*) is an aromatic resin extracted from *Commiphora abessinica.* It was highly valued as perfume used on special occasions in royal courts, in temples, and in social meetings, and was one of the spices burned ceremoniously at processions (see the explanation above in 1:13). Frankincense (*lebônâ*) is an aromatic gum obtained from three species of trees of the genus *Boswellia,* chiefly *B. carterii, B. papyrifera,* and *B. thurifera.* Among other ingredients used for incense, frankincense was always, and still is, the most important one employed in religious services. In antiquity it was highly valued by the Egyptians for embalming and fumigating (MOLDENKE, 56–59). These aromatic ingredients procured by the people of Judah through trade are mentioned in connection with frankincense together "with all the fragrant powders of the merchant" (*mikkōl ʾabqat rôkēl*); the word *ʾabqâ* is a *hapax legomenon* signifying "resin, perfume, fragrant powder."

The detailed description of the scene exhibits the gorgeous cortege in order to distinguish it from a merchant's caravan. The cloud of incense given off by the censers lends a solemn aspect to the procession, rarely seen elsewhere except in religious ceremonies and never outside the cities. While the sumptuous splendor attracts the attention to this unique procession, the fragrant perfumes are a suggestive allusion to the presence of the future king.

Vs. 7: The second strophe presents "Solomon's litter" (*miṭṭātô šellišlōmōh*). The pleonastic Hebrew construction for indicating the possessive is used here to stress the owner of the litter (*GK* § 129h; JOÜON, *Gr* § 146f). The name Solomon does not refer to the historical Solomon, but is a title applied to the descendant of the Davidic dynasty and the representative of the monarchic state of Judah.

By "litter" (*miṭṭâ*), lit. "bed," is meant either a framework for transporting disabled persons, a bier on which a coffin is taken to a grave, or a portable couch for carrying dignitaries. According to the purpose for which the litter was designed, it would have to be decorated in different styles. Thus, the royal litter would have had to be so splendidly ornamented that it prompted the onlookers to exclaim with admiration: "Behold, the litter of Solomon!"

Ordinarily a herald would precede the procession and proclaim the approach of the dignitary. But on this occasion there is no one around to inform about the occupant of the litter so as to avoid royal honors being paid to him while the country is under Persian occupation. Yet the presence of an armed escort leaves no doubt as to the identity of the important person whom they are protecting on his journey and not kidnaping, since the burning of incense is a sign of homage rendered to the monarch. The body of armed men accompanying the heir to the throne has the same function as that of the former royal guard which served as the king's protectors during the monarchic period of the history of Israel. This contingent formed of "warriors" (*gibbōrîm*) is specified in the text by the adjunct *miggibōrê yiśrā'ēl*, which may be understood as a superlative "of the best warriors of Israel," but here it is to be taken as a specification of nationality "of the warriors of Israel." The number "sixty" (*šiššîm*) indicates probably a round sum of the sexagesimal system (RUDOLPH, 139).

The scene of the royal cortege is interpreted differently by commentators favoring diverging hypotheses concerning the identity of the occupant of the litter. To some it is the bride (DELITZSCH, 62; GERLEMAN, 137; GORDIS, *JBL* 1944, 269; KEEL, 120; POPE, 424; WINANDY, 118; ZAPLETAL, 94); to others it is the swain on his way to the wedding ceremony (ASENSIO, 601; COLOMBO, 72; KRINETZKI, 148; POUGET-GUITTON, 160), or the historical Solomon (BUZY, 520; PIATTI, 118; SEGAL, *VT* 1962, 472), or else the eschatological messiah (ROBERT-TOURNAY, 145; TOURNAY-NICOLAŸ, 81). It has also been suggested that this passage might refer to the mysterious presence of Yahweh in the ark of the covenant (Targum; Midrash Rabbah; JOÜON, *Ct*, 180; RICCIOTTI, 227); other hypotheses which lack textual support are not mentioned here. However, all of these interpretations are to be discarded, because they are based on presuppositions which are extrinsic to the thematic content of the book and do not take into account the basic theme which throws light on each song.

Vs. 8: The third strophe is a poetic amplification of the preceding scene intended for emphasis on the function and qualification of the warriors as well as on the pacific purpose of the future king. The bodyguards skilled in war are specified by technical terms taken from military vocabulary, such as "girt with swords" (*ʾaḥuzê ḥered*). The passive participle *ʾaḥuzê* is to be taken in the active sense, "those holding swords," as *ʾasûr* below in 7:6, because some participles of the *qatul* form have an active sense or one close to it (*GK* § 50f; Joüon, *Gr* § 50e). Another technical expression used here is "expert in war" (*melummedê milḥāmâ*). In other words, these warriors to whom the Song refers are the same "men of war" (*ʾanšê hammilḥāmâ*) as those mentioned elsewhere (2 Kgs 25:4). From the fact that the soldiers of the royal escort do not hold their swords drawn as if they were a phalanx lined up for battle, but rather each keeps it sheathed and fastened "on his waist" (*ʿal yerēkô*), one concludes that they are accompanying the king for safety and for honor. They will use the sword for defensive purpose only "against dangers by night" (*mippaḥad ballêlôt*). The word *paḥad* means "fear" as well as "danger" for which a separate Hebrew word does not exist (*THAT* II, 412). By means of this explicative clause, referring to the defensive function of the escort, the pacific purpose of the Jewish king is indicated. His arrival in the country will bring about the restoration of the monarchy without a resort to force in order to overthrow Persian domination.

Commentary: The Theme of the Repatriation of the King (3:6-8)

The theme of this song is the repatriation of the heir to the throne of David after the Babylonian exile with a view to the restoration of the monarchy in Judah. On the king's assumption of the reins of government, the inhabitants expected him to make use of his executive power to organize the community into a body politic. At the beginning of the Persian period, the edict promulgated by Cyrus granted the Jewish population the right to constitute a social and cultic community although without administrative autonomy over the Judean territory, which continued under the jurisdiction of the provincial governor of Samaria (Galling, *BR*, 267). Now the aspiration for independence and restoration of the monarchy was not a sterile hope nurtured by the local inhabitants, since the Persian overlord had granted other city-states the privilege of self-government under the rule of their local kings (BENGTSON, *FWG* V, 372). Among the city-states to be mentioned were Tyre and Sidon, which were integrated as kingdoms into the same Persian satrapy as the territory of Judah and other provinces located in Syria and Palestine.

The accession to the throne of Judah had to follow prescribed procedures laid down by the institution of the Davidic monarchy. The first concerns the dynastic principle according to which the legitimate successor had to be a scion of the house of David. Now, the most famous Davidic descendant in the OT is undoubtedly King Solomon. On account of his preeminence over all other succeeding monarchs of the Davidic line, the name Solomon is applied to the future king of the restored Jewish nation to whom mention is made in all songs of the book except in the editorial heading (1:1).

The arrival of the future king is such a memorable event that it had to be represented, in a striking scene, as a festal procession with an escort marching alongside a sumptuously decorated litter above which a towering column of incense could be seen from afar. The heir to the royal throne travels in a litter because, prior to his coronation and official enthronement, he is not entitled to make use of carriage or mule which are the means of transportation reserved to the king.

The starting point of the journey is the Jordan valley, whence the road leads across the Judean desert to the upland plateau toward Jerusalem. The same road had formerly been taken in the opposite direction by Zedekiah, the last king of Judah, on his escape from Jerusalem under siege at the eve of its conquest by the Babylonians in 587 B.C. Thus the escape route becomes now the return route for the heir to the throne, left vacant during the exilic period.

The royal bodyguard accompanying the cortege makes visible the support given by the armed forces to the future king. In accordance with another constitutive principle of the Davidic monarchy, regarding the stability of the royal throne, the king had to provide for his personal safety by means of a bodyguard which was attached to him by virtue of the oath of loyalty. As protectors of the future king, the soldiers formed a specially trained elite guard. The reason for specifying the Israelite nationality of these warriors is seen in the contrast between their bravery and the cowardice of the troops at the command of King Zedekiah who were put to flight by a detachment of Babylonian soldiers, into whose hands they let the king fall captive (2 Kgs 25:5).

Other themes related to the thematic content of this song are the coronation (3:9-11), the enthronement (5:9-16), and the king's taking possession of the country (6:1-3).

3. ✦ *The Royal Insignia (3:9-11)*

9 King Solomon made himself a coronation chair *Chorus*
from the wood of Lebanon.
10 He made its columns of silver,
its back of gold,
its seat of purple;
its centerpiece was inlaid for the sake of love.
Go forth, O daughters of Jerusalem,
11 and you, daughters of Zion, behold
King Solomon with the crown
with which his mother crowned him
on the day of his marriage,
on the day of the gladness of his heart.

Accented Transliteration (3:9-11)

9 *’appiryốn ‘āśāh lố hammélek*
šelōmṓh mē‘aṣế hallebānốn
10 *‘ammûdấw ‘āśā́h késef*
refîdātố zāhā́b
merkābố ’argāmā́n
tôkố rāṣû́f ’ahabấ
mibbenốt yerûšālā́im : ṣe’éynāh
11 *ûre’éynāh benốt ṣiyyốn*
bammélek šelōmṓh bā‘aṭārấ
še‘iṭṭerâ-lố ’immố
beyốm ḥatunnātố
ûbeyốm śimḥát libbố

Literary Analysis (3:9-11)

The scene of the coronation rites presents the heir apparent invested with royal authority. The song is composed of two strophes preceded by an introductory distich (vs. 9) which points to the owner of the coronation chair. In the first strophe (vs. 10), phrased in narrative style, the particular features of this chair are described; the second strophe (vs. 11) is an entreating request addressed to the daughters of Jerusalem and Zion inviting them to attend the coronation ceremony.

Poetic and rhetorical devices used in the song are sound repetition: recurrence of homophonous word endings -*ô*, e.g. *r*^{e}*fîdātô–merkābô–tôkô* (vs. 10), *'immô–ḥ*^{a}*tunnātô–libbô* (vs. 11); word repetition, e.g. "King Solomon," "daughters"; anaphora "on the day—on the day" (vs. 11de); repetition of structural patterns: synonymous parallelism "daughters of Jerusalem—daughters of Zion"; chiasmus *b*^{e}*nôt y*^{e}*rûšālāim ṣ*^{e}*'eynāh* // *ûr*^{e}*'eynāh b*^{e}*nôt ṣiyyôn* (vss. 10e, 11a), *š*^{e}*lōmōh bā'*^{a}*ṭārâ* // *še'iṭṭ*^{e}*râ-lô 'immô* (vs. 11bc). Rhetorical devices: etymological figure "to crown with a crown," the graphic description of the coronation chair.

Vocabulary Analysis (3:9-11)

Vs. 9: The kind of furniture designated by the word *'appiryôn* is easier to be determined by its constructional and decorative features and by the special purpose it was used for than by the explanation of its etymology. Its rendering as a "coronation chair" fits the description of the piece of furniture whose construction is outlined in the following verse. The meaning of *'appiryôn, a hapax legomenon,* is uncertain and its etymology is unknown. Several explanations of this word have been proposed by associating it with four different terms. The first proposal was offered by the LXX which interpreted it as a loanword from Greek *phoreion,* equivalent to the Latin *ferculum* of the Vulgate. The second assumes a morphological analogy with *aparyana,* a hypothetical word from Old Persian (Widengren, 355). The third proposes its derivation from Egyptian *pr-'3* "great house," later "pharaoh," with Hebrew affixes (*a* + *yôn*) added (Gerleman, 141). The fourth suggests its being a Hebrew word derived from *pry* (to cut, make, frame), with reference to the manufacture of a bed, hence "bed of state" (Delitzsch, 66). In addition to these etymological analogies there were proposed some variants: *'appeden* "palace" (Ricciotti, 230); *pûryômā'* "litter" (Midrash Rabbah on Ct 3:10) derived from the Greek *phorēma.* However, none of these proposals explains satisfactorily the origin of *'appiryôn,* nor are they in a condition to do so, because it happens to be a technical term designating a special kind of chair, like similar terms of unknown etymology referring to distinctive chair forms such as *ašti, nimattu* (*ANET,* 275), and *nîmedu* (*ANET,* 288), manufactured in Syria and Palestine. The analogy between *'appiryôn* and palanquin, a word derived from Sanskrit *paryanka,* through New-Aryan *palki* (Pope, 441), is based on the hypothesis that the text concerns the "litter" (*miṭṭâ*) mentioned in the preceding song, for which it would be a synonym. Yet the description in vs. 10 does not contain any reference to a baldacchino nor to carrying poles which are essential to a litter.

The fabrication of the "coronation chair," ascribed to the king, can only have been performed at his direction by another person; the verbal sentence "he made himself" (*'āśāh lô*) means implicitly "he commanded to be made for himself" (*GK* § 144n). The subject of the verb is King Solomon. Some commentators wish to delete this from the text for metric reasons, on the assumption that it is a later addition. However, the word "king" (*melek*) has an important function in the text for it qualifies the coronation chair as sign of royal authority. On account of this the Syriac version of the Bible (Peshitta) rendered *'appiryôn* "throne, seat" (*kursyā*). The name Solomon is applied to the Davidic successor for whom the coronation chair and crown are held for special use as royal insignia. By imported timber from Lebanon (*mē'aṣê hallebānôn*) is meant cedar wood used for high-quality furniture such as the ceremonial chair because of the grain and aromatic scent.

Vs. 10: The first strophe presents, in five verse-lines, the characteristic features of the coronation chair and mentions the role of the elite of the Jewish priesthood in relation to kingship. All furniture decoration is concentrated here on the legs and back of the chair; the legs are stylized as "columns" (*'ammûdîm*) either shaped while turning on a lathe or embellished with decorative carvings sheathed in silver foil. Its "back" (*refîdâ*) is overlaid with gold foil typical of the royal throne; the word *refîdâ*, a *hapax legomenon*, is derived from *rpd* signifying "to support" (cf. 2:5). Yet, by rendering this word by *anákliton* (LXX) and *reclinatorium* (Vulgate), all the metal overlay of the chairback would be covered up by upholstery and covers. Its "seat" (*merkāb*) is padded with a cushion in a purple cover; cloth dyed with "purple" (*'argāmān*) was used in antiquity for royal garments, hence purple came to symbolize royalty. Ivory plaques and precious stones inlaid in the gilded backrest enhance "its centerpiece" (*tôkô*). Since this decorative feature is only indicated by the passive participle *rāṣûf*, a *hapax legomenon*, its meaning has to be derived from the noun *riṣpâ* which designates panels with ivory and metal inlay shaped in various ornamental patterns and designs. In view of this generic allusion to ornamentation, many commentators try to specify it by means of the material to which they believe it to refer. Thus they propose either to replace "leather" for "love" since both are homonyms of the same form *'ahabâ*, or to emend *'ahabâ* (love) to *'abānîm* (stones) or *hobnîm* (ebony). Yet such an interpretation of the passage is not only an arbitrary procedure but also deviates from the basic meaning of this song by changing the key word which indicates the reason for the chair's decoration. According to its syntactic function in the sentence, *'ahabâ* is used as an *accusativus causae*, to be rendered "for the sake of love." Since the word "love" is a technical term—expressing the alliance between the house of David and the people of Judah—used here in the accusative it states the reason for the coronation chair having been so lavishly decorated in view of its use as a ceremonial seat for the king at the pact-enacting rite.

In a formal invitation to attend the coronation ceremony the elite of the Jewish priesthood are addressed as "daughters of Jerusalem" (*mibbenôt yerûšālāim*). Owing to their leading position in the Jewish community it was indispensable for the future king to secure their support in his endeavor to ascend to the throne. The prefix *min* attached to *benôt* is used partitively to designate an undetermined number of individuals, i.e. "some of the daughters" (*GK* § 119wN). On the other hand, *min* has mostly been taken by commentators in the sense of the preposition "by," equivalent to the Greek *apó*, introducing the personal agent of the passive participle *rāṣûf*, "inlaid." The passage in question is thus commonly rendered "it was lovingly wrought within by the daughters of Jerusalem," a statement which is inconsistent with those expressed in other texts referring to the same persons who are not on friendly terms with King Solomon, whereas here they are supposed to have adorned his coronation chair.

As regards the structure of the sentence, the "daughters of Jerusalem" is the subject, while its verb *ṣe'eynāh* (go forth!), though separated from vs. 10 by a pause, indicated in the MT, is placed at the beginning of the following verse. The presence of these dignitaries at the official ceremony for enacting an alliance between king and people is essential to the ratification of the mutually assumed obligations. The scene of the king seated on the coronation chair, proclaiming his relationship with the people gathered in front of him, implies the enactment of a covenant whose solemn commitment is confirmed by invoking the deity to witness and safeguard the covenant thus ratified by the priests.

Vs. 11: The second strophe gives an account of the coronation ceremony held in the presence of dignitaries and court officials. It is assumed that the representatives of the different groups mentioned in the preceding songs are already present, such as the representative of the autochthonous Jews (3:4) and the royal guardsmen (3:7-8). A special call goes out to the "daughters of Jerusalem and Zion," whose absence at the ceremony would deprive the social groups, represented by them, of its relationship with the royal house and would disrupt its association with those integrated into the community. The leaders designated as "daughters of Zion" (*benôt ṣiyyôn*) are the representatives of the urban population which previously, during the monarchy, had occupied a leading position in the administration of the affairs of state and in the socio-political organization of the inhabitants of Jerusalem. The leaders of both the urban and the rural population had formerly held strong ties with the Davidic monarchy, established by a formal pact of fealty to the king which entailed the constitutional prerogative for them to ratify the accession of a Davidid to the throne and to grant him the executive power and the right to use it (ALT, *Kl.S.* II, 126–134). By associating the leaders of the urban population with the name "Zion," which designated the old section of the city of Jerusalem (2 Sm 5:7, 9), it was probably intended to allude to the constitutional right that this group of repatriate Jews inherited from their forebears who had been deported from Jerusalem to Babylon in 587 B.C.

In the apostrophe addressed to the "daughters of Jerusalem" there occurs *ṣᵉʾeynāh* (go forth!), whose verbal form is unique and abnormal, apparently influenced by assonance with the parallel imperative form *rᵉʾeynāh* (behold!). To judge from this entreating request to "go forth," the ceremony is held outdoors, in a public square or in a spacious area, where a multitude would be able to gather. The function of *bᵉ* with the verb rʾ*h* (to see) intensifies the verbal idea (JOÜON, *Gr* § 133c), thus rendered "to behold." The name Solomon is applied to the Davidic heir to the throne, specified by the complement "with the crown" (*bāʿᵃṭārâ*), which is the royal emblem par excellence. The rite of investing the king with the regal crown is expressed by the sentence "his mother crowned him" (*ʿiṭṭᵉrâ lô ʾimmô*), whose direct object is subordinated to the verb by means of a *lamed* influenced by the Aramaic (JOÜON, *Ct,* 191).

The coronation of the heir to the throne of David is performed by "his mother" (*ʾimmô*) who represents the house of David (cf. 8:5). Since the royal succession in Judah was linked to the house of David, it was the prerogative of the royal house to pass on the regal crown to the legitimate successor of the Davidic dynasty on the occasion of his accession to the throne. The investiture of the just-crowned king with the royal insignia implies a renewal of God's covenant with David, through whom divine blessings are bestowed upon the nation. The legal bond between the house of David and the nation is expressed in terms of a marriage bond, called *ḥᵃtunnâ* (marriage, betrothal), a *hapax legomenon* designating a relationship based on legal rights traced back to the act of betrothal (TOSATO, 109n). The expression "on the day of his marriage" (*bᵉyôm ḥᵃtunnātô*) is in parallel to "on the day of the gladness of his heart" (*bᵉyôm śimḥat libbô*). It is to be noted that something else is involved here than an indication of a mere feast day (*yôm śimḥâ*) among other such festivals listed in the Israelite calendar, because it happens to be a memorable event celebrated for a personal reason as the source of "the gladness of his heart" (*śimḥat libbô*). Indeed no other event is quite so memorable as that of the restoration of the monarchy, which had been suppressed in 587 B.C., and the accession of the royal heir to the throne of David, which had been left vacant during the period of exile while the royal family lived as expatriates in Babylon.

Commentary: The Theme of the Coronation (3:9-11)

The theme of this song is that of the coronation of the king of Judah with special emphasis on the rite of his investiture with the insignia of dignity and royal authority by which executive power is conferred upon the descendant of the house of David on the occasion of his accession to the throne.

Religious rites connected with the civil ceremony are not mentioned here since they were probably performed in the sanctuary, such as anointing, the renewal of God's covenant formerly established with David, the proclamation of the protocol, and possibly also the imposition of the coronation name (DE VAUX, *AI*, 102–108). Nothing is said either of the rites of public acclamation and the homage of high officials, which used to be rendered at the time of the succession. This is so as to avoid any repressive measures which the Persian authorities might take in order to stifle any signs of public support to a movement of national independence. Further information on additional rites performed at the coronation will be given in the description of the enthronement (5:9-16) and of the king's taking possession of the country (6:1-3).

One of the characteristic insignia of kingship is the royal throne which, during the monarchic period of Israelite history, had stood in the king's palace located in the capital of the country. Since Jerusalem, formerly the capital of the kingdom of Judah, had not yet been rebuilt after its destruction in 587 B.C. and the royal palace still lay in ruins, the future king did not have, as yet, an official residence where the royal throne could be installed. While the Davidic descendant exercised the function of governor of Judah, he resided in Mizpah (thirteen kilometers north of Jerusalem), a small town where the Persians had established the seat of government and a garrison. Under these circumstances it should not be surprising that for the coronation rites a lavishly decorated chair would be used instead of a fixed throne. This chair had specially been made to serve as the ceremonial seat at the coronation and had the advantage that it could easily be placed on a precise spot in the outdoor area where the ceremony would be held. The choice of special material to be used in the manufacture and ornamentation of this chair followed the same directives laid down for the construction of the royal throne, viz. cedar wood from Lebanon, overlay with gold and silver foil, purple cloth for the cushion, and inlays embedded in the backrest. These ornamental details did not have a merely decorative function, but were specially designed for enhancing the ceremonial seat for the king at his coronation and on the occasion of his investiture with the insignia representing the royal authority bestowed upon him.

Among the dignitaries, high officials, and leaders gathered for the coronation ceremony are the members of the house of David ("mother"), the royal guard ("warriors"), the elite of the Jewish priesthood ("daughters of Jerusalem"), the leaders of the urban population ("daughters of Zion"), and the leading figure representative of the rural population ("Shulamite"). To each of them a special role is assigned at the ceremony: thus, the royal house bestows the crown on the successor of the Davidic dynasty, the royal guard take the oath of loyalty to the sovereign pledging to protect him and the royal institution, the elite of the Jewish priesthood ratify the covenant between king and people and renew God's covenant as it had been established with David, the leaders of the urban and rural populations offer their allegiance to the king sealing it by a formal pact of fealty and grant him the executive power and the right to use it.

A special call goes out to two social groups inviting their leaders to attend the coronation rites, viz. the elite of the Jewish priesthood ("daughters of Jerusalem") and the leaders of the urban population ("the daughters of Zion"). For political reasons both would rather stay away so as to abstain from giving their support to the project of restoring the monarchy. In fact, the "daughters of Jerusalem" are more concerned with fostering their own welfare than the interests of the Jewish nation. In order to achieve this goal they try to extend their sphere of influence to all the inhabitants of the country, and are thus reluctant to consent to the restoration of the monarchy in Judah. They propose an alternative political system for the post-exilic community: the theocratic system. As for the "daughters of Zion," they also are not inclined to join forces with those engaged in the restoration of the monarchy, since they have doubts whether this project will stand a chance of being approved by the Persian government. The political organization which they believe will be implanted, in spite of all efforts being made to bring about a change, is the provincial administration under control of the Persian satrapy.

The reason for convoking all the leaders of the different social groups to the coronation ceremony is, first, to comply with the constitutional right by which they are entitled to take part in the decisions that affect the interests of the entire Jewish population. Second, this would involve all the representatives in a common effort to unify their different groups into a political community, organized as a national monarchy in the molds of the former southern kingdom which was to be restored after the exilic period.

With the coronation of the heir to the throne, the monarchy is officially instituted in the country and the king is rightfully confirmed as sovereign of the nation, with the different social groups bound to him by their profession of loyalty. This bond is compared to the marriage bond in order to illustrate the link between king and people implying the common destiny they share from now on. The theme of the coronation will be related to that of the enthronement, dealt with in another song (5:9-16).

Poem IV *The Beauty of the Bride* (4:1–5:1)

1 ✦ *The Comely Bride (4:1-7)*

1 Behold, you are beautiful, my friend, *Bridegroom*
behold, you are beautiful!
Your eyes are doves
behind your veil.
Your hair is like a flock of goats,
moving down Mount Gilead.
2 Your teeth are like a flock of shorn ewes
that have come up from the washing,
all of which bear twins,
none bereft among them.
3 Your lips are like a scarlet thread,
and your mouth is lovely.
Your cheeks are like halves of a pomegranate
behind your veil.
4 Your neck is like the tower of David,
built with loop-holes
whereon hang a thousand bucklers,
all the quivers of warriors.
5 Your two breasts are like two fawns,
twins of a gazelle,
that feed among the lilies.
6 Until the day expires
and the shadows flee,
I will hie me to the mountains of myrrh
and the hills of frankincense.

7 You are all beautiful, my friend,
and no blemish is in you.

Accented Transliteration (4:1-7)

1 *hinnā́k yāfā́h raʿyātî́ hinnā́k yāfā́h*
ʿênáyik yônî́m mibbáʿad leṣammātḗk
śáʿrēk keʿḗder hāʿizzî́m
šeggālešû́ mēhár gilʿā́d
2 *šinnáyik keʿḗder haqqeṣûbṓt*
šeʿālû́ min-hāraḥṣā́
šekkullā́m matʾîmôt
wešakkulā́ ʾên bāhém
3 *keḥû́ṭ haššānî́ śiftōtáyik*
ûmidbārḗk nāʾwéh
kefélaḥ hārimmốn raqqātḗk
mibbáʿad leṣammātḗk
4 *kemigdál dāwî́d ṣawwāʾrḗk*
bānû́y letalpiyyṓt
ʾélef hammāgḗn tālû́y ʿālā́w
kṓl šilṭḗ haggibbôrî́m
5 *šenḗ šādáyik kišnḗ ʿofārî́m*
teʾômḗ ṣebiyyā́
hārôʿî́m baššôšannî́m
6 *ʿad šeyyāfû́aḥ hayyôm wenā́su haṣṣelālî́m*
ʾēlek lî́ ʾel-hár hammốr
weʾel-gibʿát hallebônā́
7 *kullā́k yāfā́h raʿyātî́*
ûmûm ʾên bā́k

Literary Analysis (4:1-7)

Poem IV on the beauty of the bride (4:1–5:1), divided into four songs, describes the attractive figure of a woman who personifies the Jewish nation. The corresponding poem (6:4–7:10) develops the same thematic content.

This song is composed of three strophes in which the imagery is drawn from the landscape of Palestine as well as from the local flora and fauna, thus portraying the woman with the distinctive features that appeal to the native population of Judah. Topographical references to Palestine are Mount Gilead (vs. 1), the tower of David (vs. 4), the mountains of myrrh and the hill of frankincense (vs. 6). The portrait of the woman exhibits the upper front of the person, from head down to the chest. The first strophe (vss. 1-2) describes the eyes, the hair, and the teeth, contrasting the black and white colors of their features and illustrating them with images drawn from the rural environment. The second strophe (vss. 3-4) depicts the lips, the cheeks, and the neck, with scarlet, reddish, and yellow colors compared to objects typical of urban life. The third strophe (vss. 5-6) mentions the breasts in a comparison with fawns whose coats are brown on the back and white on the abdomen; their mountain habitat is pictured with sharp contrasts between light and darkness at nightfall. The initial statement (vs. 1a) is repeated at the end of the pictorial representation (vs. 7a), thus forming an inclusion which serves as a frame for the portrait of the woman. In the description of the physical traits and their related imagery, attention is drawn to the combination of colors and the coordination of elements so as to form pairs. This produces an harmonious picture of the person whose beauty is enhanced by comparison with the surrounding landscape.

Poetic and rhetorical devices used in this song are sound repetition: assonance *i-a* (vss. 1a, 7a); word repetition: anaphora "behold, you are beautiful–behold, you are beautiful"; paronomasia *šekkullām–šakkulâ* (vs. 2cd). Figures of resemblance: the metaphor "your eyes are doves"; the simile "your hair is like a flock of goats"; "your teeth are like a flock of shorn ewes"; "your lips are like a scarlet thread"; "your cheeks are like halves of a pomegranate; "your neck is like the tower of David"; "your two breasts are like two fawns."

Vocabulary Analysis (4:1-7)

Vs. 1: The opening verse, identical with 1:15, is a formal introduction, in poetic phraseology, which presents a prospective ally to be admitted to the covenant relationship. The interjection "behold!" (*hinnê*) has formal significance in the pact-enacting rite (KALLUVEETTIL, 13n). Negotiations for a pact are opened with a calling forth of the ally, "behold, there you are!" (*hinnāk*). There follows a declaration of the new status attributed to the woman. By designating her as "my friend" (*ra'yātî*), the nature of the alliance is specified as that of friendship between allies. Admittance to this relationship is granted after approbation of the person qualified to become an ally, whose merits are highly valued; "beautiful" (*yāfāh*) has the sense of "right, appropriate."

The association of two things of different categories, "your eyes are doves" (*'ênayik yônîm*), describes specific qualities of the ally, i.e. candor and gentleness, which are required for a covenant relationship, while the opposite attitudes, i.e. duplicity and hostility, discourage collaboration and partnership. Another aspect of resemblance to doves' eyes is shown by their lack of brilliance which is compared to the woman's faint shining eyes owing to her visage covered with a transparent veil. In another text (1:7) she is identified as a "veiled" (*ʿōṭᵉyâ*) shepherdess, like a Bedouin woman whose face is covered with a non-transparent veil. Her external appearance is quite different here as she wears a transparent veil (*mibbaʿad lᵉṣammātēk*) as an elegant accessory of a woman's attire in refined circles, or proper to the time of betrothal and the wedding ceremony (4:1, 3; 6:7).

The black color of the hair (*śᵉʿār*) is the reason for its comparison with a "flock of goats" (*ʿēder hāʿizzîm*). Moreover, the tendency of goats to get separated from the flock, as opposed to sheep which stay together, occasioned its use as an image for the woman's hair falling to her shoulders. The meaning of the verb *glš* becomes clear from its context dealing with strands of disheveled hair tumbling down over the shoulder blades, thus referring to the motion of a flock of straying goats descending the slopes of a mountain. The uplands of Gilead, located to the east of the Jordan, were given over to sheep and goat farming. In the landscape with its broad valleys, basalt ridges or volcanic cones stand out, some of which reach three thousand feet in height. Mount Gilead need not be the highest mountain but rather one whose slopes are covered with lush pastures.

Vs. 2: After contemplating the high mountains the observer looks down to the valleys, catching sight of a flock of "shorn ewes" (*qᵉṣûbôt*). The passive participle of the verb *qṣb* (to shear) is a poetic synonym for "ewes" (*rᵉḥēlîm*) which occurs in the corresponding text (6:6). The downward motion of the goats, previously described, is related to the upward motion of the sheep "coming up" (*šeʿālû*) the bank of the watershed. The whiteness of the fleece of sheep which have been bathed in the "washing" (*raḥṣâ*) is the point of comparison with the woman's teeth. Her complete set of teeth is compared to the flock of ewes, each accompanied by a pair of lambs or "twins" (*matʾîmôt*), with none of the ewes "bereft of offspring" (*šakkulâ*).

Vs. 3: The second strophe begins with the description of the woman's thin lips compared to a "scarlet thread" (*ḥûṭ haššānî*), as opposed to thick-lipped features typical of people of foreign extraction. It is to be noted that *śiftōtayik* (your lips) is the plural instead of the dual form commonly used to designate those objects which naturally occur in pairs. As regards the Hebrew word for mouth, some commentators take *midbārēk* (your mouth)—as read with the Qere of MT—as the organ of speech, whereas others suggest that it refers to the action of speech, even though no mention is made of any words pronounced by the woman. The description of the cheeks uses the word "temples" (*raqqâ* in the singular) to designate either side of the face as a figure of speech which posits a part for the whole. In the comparison between temples and halves of a pomegranate (*rimmôn*) the pale red color of the fruit's rind resembles the hue of the cheeks' skin. Since a ripe pomegranate breaks in two, the color of its halves (*pelaḥ*) serves as a comparison for the woman's countenance. The facial features are not in full view but are seen through a diaphanous veil which in the text functions as an inclusion of the descriptive elements of the woman's head.

Vs. 4: The neck is likened to the "tower of David" (*migdal dāwîd*), jutting up amongst the enclosing walls of the city of David. It was built as a stronghold fitted with "loop-holes" (*talpiyyôt*), which are narrow vertical slits in the wall above the gate for shooting arrows at attacking enemies. The unique term *talpiyyôt* is explained by analogy with Akkadian *tilpanu* (arrow). To set forth the defensive position of the tower, the verb *bnh* (to build) is employed with *lamed* so as to introduce the object. This brings the nuance "to fortify" into the original meaning of the verb. On special occasions, bucklers and quivers were suspended on these loop-holes for ornamentation and enhancement of the city's splendor (cf. Ez 27:11; 1 Mc 4:57). The reference to "warriors" (*gibbôrîm*) explains the fact that these weapons were standard equipment of the royal guard and not some obsolete armament or war trophies stored in the armory. The "buckler" (*māgēn*) is made of bronze and the "quiver" (*šeleṭ*), of leather; however, the exact meaning of Hebrew *šeleṭ* is uncertain, but from its correlation with *šalṭu* (quiver), an Akkadian cognate, we assume that *šeleṭ* designates the same military equipment. Rows of bucklers and quivers attached to chains hanging in curves between loop-holes are a suggestive image of the woman's necklace of a single or double strand of medals strung together with pendants attached at intervals. Both the shape and the material of these weapons are used for comparison with colored ornaments: thus, bucklers of bronze represent gold medals, while quivers of leather would indicate cylindrical pendants of brown amber, cornelian, etc.

Vs. 5: The third strophe draws on comparisons from the countryside in the description of the woman's breasts. It was customary in antiquity to mention a girl's breasts in order to indicate that she had reached the age of marriage. As for the phraseology of the text, attention is called by a striking feature of the comparison which is the apparently needless repetition in succession of numerals which could easily be replaced by the dual form of the nouns. However, redundancy is used here as a figure of speech to attain emphasis. Indeed, "your two breasts" (*šᵉnê šādayik*) are such an attractive sight as that of "two fawns" (*šᵉnê ʿᵒfārîm*). For closer specification of these graceful members of the antelope family, they are referred to as "twins of a gazelle" (*tᵉʾômê ṣᵉbiyyâ*). The term of comparison between breasts and fawns is the symmetry as a pair and their color. Fawns always stay together and are identical in the light-brown coloring of the coat on the back in contrast with the white abdomen. The woman likened to this picture would be clad in a low-cut white dress, leaving part of the bronze colored skin of shoulder and breast exposed. The vegetation of the countryside provides further information about the fawns' habitat: "they are grazing" (*hārô'îm*) among "lilies" (*šôšannîm*). This flower, indigenous to the mountains of Palestine, is the figure used for the autochthonous Jewish population. A distinction must be made, though, between lilies, in the plural, representing several rural settlements (2:16; 4:5; 6:2-3), and lily, in the singular, which figuratively designates the bride in regard to her role as leader of the native population (2:1-2). Just as the local flora and fauna has its habitat in the Judean countryside, so, too, the woman here described as an autochthonous inhabitant of Judah has her permanent settlement there.

Vs. 6: The first part of this verse is identical with 2:17. Some commentators place vs. 6 after vs. 7 on the assumption that it is a later addition, inserted here for the sake of comparison with the breasts. However, the passage has nothing to do with the portrait of the woman, but with the king's intended journey to the mountainous region. The subordinate clause introduced by the conjunction "until" (*'ad še*) tells of some circumstances related to this journey. The time of the day is indicated by two idiomatic expressions referring to the breeze arising at sunrise and sunset, "the day breathes" (*yāfûaḥ hayyôm*), and to the shadows that vanish at sunrise or stretch out, as if fleeing away, at sunset, "the shadows flee" (*nāsû haṣṣelālîm*). Since these expressions denote typical features of that region, one has to infer from the context what part of the day is meant here. Now, the people's expectation that the king will return to Judah grows day by day. They hope that his arrival will not be too late, nor the opportunity for restoring the monarchy lost. This is condensed in the image of a moment for which they are waiting and which will come about before nightfall.

The journey of the king resembles that previously described in the scene of the approaching royal procession (3:6-8), except for the bodyguard and the litter which are not mentioned in this passage. By following the road known as the "ascent of the Mount of Olives" (*ma'aleh hazzêtîm*) which leads toward Jerusalem (2 Sm 15:30), he will have to cross the Judean uplands. Owing to conspicuous topographical features of this region, the city of David was designated Mount Zion, while its surrounding countryside was referred to as hills (Is 2:2; Mi 4:1). However, both expressions "mountain of myrrh" (*har hammôr*) and "hill of frankincense" (*gib'at hallebônâ*) do not refer to the whole mountainous region of Judah, but to a delimited geographical sub-region in a manner sufficiently detailed to indicate the real complexity and variety of that particular area. Stylistical approach classifies the couple of terms "mountain and hill" as components of a totality which is a figure of speech called merismus. As for the meaning of myrrh and frankincense specifying mountain and hill, we have to bear in mind that none of these aromatic substances were extracted from plants growing in Palestine, but were imported.

As the main ingredients of fragrant spices used for incense, they were burnt ceremonially at processions such as had been described in a previous song. Thus, all along the route, clouds of smoke swirling from censers would spread in the air pervading every mountain and hill which the royal procession passes. In order to reach the rural settlements located on terraced hillsides, the procession will have to ascend on winding paths leading up the slopes. The local population will be awaiting his arrival which the cloud of incense, as a silent harbinger of the approaching king, will announce.

Vs. 7: This verse repeats, as an abbreviated refrain, the idea expressed at the beginning of the song formulating it in terms of polarity. The first line extols the relationship of friendship between allies by virtue of which the bride is granted the status of "my friend" (*raʿyātî*). Her honored status commends the merits which are praised publicly, "you are all beautiful" (*kullāk yāfāh*).

The second verse-line tells of the bride's integrity, "no blemish is in you" (*mûm ʾên bāk*). Most commentators interpret the sentence as evoking corporeal beauty, whereas others explain it in terms of moral uprightness. However, these interpretations are inadequate, since they do not take into account the specific meaning of the idiomatic expression "there is blemish in him" (*ʾᵃšer mûm bô*), which is the opposite of "free of blemish" (*tāmîm*). Both of these expressions qualify attributes of relationship. In cultic usage, victims singled out for sacrifice ought to be "free of blemish" so as to represent the believer's integrity in his relationship with God (*THAT* II, 1048). In political usage of covenant enactment rites, an ally is "free of blemish" if he is found to be trustworthy in his covenant relationship (cf. Jgs 9:16, 19; Ct 5:2; 6:9).

Commentary: The Theme of the Integrated Nation (4:1-7)

The theme of this song deals with the nation, integrating social groups from both the rural and urban area, harmoniously incorporated so as to constitute a political community. Characteristic traits distinguishing inhabitants of the countryside from the townspeople are not suppressed by their integration into the body politic, but are assimilated and elevated to the sphere of social equality.

The nation is portrayed as a youthful woman, whose figure from head down to the chest is rendered with elegance and clever simplicity. A collar of gold jewelry and graceful pendants of semi-precious stones is the only decorative element shown on her neck, while scenes from the countryside are drawn for comparison with her externals. This expressive portrait showing the female figure surrounded by picturesque landscapes concentrates on the identity of the corporate personality and on the variety of her striking features. Comparative elements from the rural area illustrate different social groups by means of animals, both domestic (goats and sheep) and non-domestic (doves and gazelles). Yet both have in common the gregarious instinct which keeps them together. Other social groups are represented in the scenes which exhibit objects manufactured by townspeople, such as scarlet thread for embroidery, red dye extracted from the rind of unripened pomegranates, and personal ornaments consisting of medals and pendants, likened to bucklers and quivers hanging on the tower jutting up amongst the walls of the city of David.

The nation's exalted self-esteem is expressed by the topographical features of Palestine, standing out in the landscape described in the scenes, as e.g. Mount Gilead, known for its height, the tower of David, an imposing structure of the fortification network of the city of Jerusalem, and the Judean uplands with mountains and hills seen from afar. The multicolored picture with tints of black and white, dark shades and bright light, provides a visual impression of the heterogeneous groups integrated into the nation.

The integrating factor of the different social groups will be the institution of the monarchy when it is restored in Judah. Thereupon, the political structure of the Jewish community will be organized by the king, to whom the people will offer their allegiance, sealing it by a pact of fealty. Simultaneously, an integrated nation will be formed by a pact of association between autochthonous and repatriate Jews. The theme of this song will be developed in connection with that of the unified nation (6:4-7).

2. ✦ *The Privileged Bride (4:8)*

8 With me from Lebanon, my bride, *Bridegroom*
  coming with me from Lebanon,
you will travel from the peak of Amana,
  from the peak of Senir and Hermon,
from the dens of lions,
  from the mountains of leopards.

Accented Transliteration (4:8)

8 *ʾittî́ mill^{e}bānôn kallấ*
  ʾittî́ mill^{e}bānôn tābốʾî
tāšû́rî mērṓʾš ʾ^{a}mānấ
  mērṓʾš ś^{e}nî́r w^{e}ḥermốn
mimm^{e}ʿōnốt ʾ^{a}rāyốt
  mēhar^{e}rế n^{e}mērî́m

Literary Analysis (4:8)

This passage points to the highly promising prospects of engaging in foreign trade that the Jewish nation will have after regaining political independence. The bride is an image for the country's population, an image which illustrates both the covenant relationship with the bridegroom, who represents the Davidic king, and Judah's political organization as a national state. So as to carry on foreign trade the government of Judah reaches across its national boundary to tap Phoenicia's flourishing centers of commerce, whose trade routes are indicated by the mountain peaks and their heavily forested slopes infested by wild animals.

Poetic and rhetorical devices that occur in the song are sound repetition: homoeotelleuton *tābô'î–tāšûrî;* word repetition, e.g. "with me," "from Lebanon," "from the peak"; anaphora *'ittî millebānôn–'ittî millebānôn.* Rhetorical devices: staircase parallelism (vs. 8a-d); gender-matched parallelism (vs. 8e + f) *mimme'ōnôt* (fem.) *'arāyôt* (fem.)–*mēharerê* (masc.) *nemērîm* (masc.); and the accumulation of proper names denoting geographical features.

Vocabulary Analysis (4:8)

Vs. 8: In this periodic sentence, the main clause is placed after the opening clause, so as to gain emphasis. The ancient versions overlooked the peculiar structure of the sentence and thus emended the preposition *'ittî* (with me) of MT to read *'etî* (come!). But this emendation is inadmissible, because it changes the declaration into a command.

"Bride" (*kallâ*) is a title applied to the Shulamite indicating a relationship established on legal basis between bride and bridegroom, a comparison of the covenant relationship between king and people. According to Israelite marriage custom, the bride belonged to the bridegroom from the moment of his drawing up the marriage contract before cohabitation. Both finite verbs *tābô'î* (you will come) and *tāšûrî* (you will travel) are in the indicative mood, because they are used in declarative phrases which mention different routes from the Phoenician coast to the neighboring countries. Since these phrases are coordinated without conjunction, the first is rendered as a participial phrase, "coming with me from Lebanon." As for the meaning of *tāšûrî,* there are two homonymous verbs both of which offer an acceptable sense: *šwr* I "to travel" and *šwr* II "to look." The option for either one depends on the point of view adopted in the interpretation of the passage: "to travel" is the sense required from the context dealing with foreign trade, while "to look" refers to sightseeing to be enjoyed by tourists on trips to the mountain massifs of Lebanon.

The itinerary mapped out in this passage sets forth four routes indicated by the highest mountain round whose lowest slopes wind the road which leads from the seaports of Phoenicia to the neighboring countries. The first route follows the coastal plain running parallel to the Lebanon Mountains whose maximum elevation is at Qurnet es Sauda (3088 m.), lying east-southeast of Tripoli. From the springs draining the slopes of these mountains the Litani river is born. Its lower reaches flow westward to empty into the Mediterranean near Tyre. The second route leaves the coast at Tripoli, turning inland toward Kadesh, where it crosses the Orontes, the largest river in the Levant, on whose northbound stretch were located important cities such as Hamath, Qarqar, Alalakh, and Antioch, linked to each other by a major road. At Kadesh the road branches out, with one branch leading eastward to Mesopotamia and the other southward to Damascus, running alongside the Anti-Lebanon range with Talat Musa (2659 m.) and Halimet el Qabu (2462 m.) as its highest points. One of these is probably the "peak of Amana" (*rō'š 'ᵃmānâ*). The third route crosses the Lebanon range from Beirut to the Bekaa valley, continuing eastward across the central section of the Anti-Lebanon, whose highest mountain, Jebel ez Zebedani (1350 m.), we assume to be the "peak of Senir" (*rō'š śᵉnîr*). From its streams there arises the Barada river, flowing to Damascus in the east. The fourth route turns off from the east-west road junction in the Bekaa valley, leading southward to Hazor in Galilee through rugged terrain at the foot of Mount Hermon (*ḥermôn*), in Arabic Jebel esh Sheik, whose highest peak is Kasr Antar (2814 m.). Mount Hermon was called Saniron by the Assyrians, Senir by the Amorites, and Sirion by the Phoenicians. From the foot of Mount Hermon the river Jordan flows south to empty into the Dead Sea.

All of these mountains were bare of human settlements, except for the foothills, accessible by narrow paths or winding roads following rivers and streams entrenched in the valleys. The mountainous region was heavily forested and infested by "lions" (*'ᵃrāyôt*) and "leopards" (*nᵉmērîm*), which endangered travelers who ventured to cross it without an escort of armed men. An ancient Egyptian text, dating from the end of the thirteenth century B.C., describes the densely forested mountains of Lebanon and calls attention to lions, leopards, and hyenas abounding in this region. No less dangerous than these wild animals were the bands of outlaws who assaulted the wayfarers as soon as they reached the upper slopes, passed through deep-sided valleys, and crossed the streams (*ANET*, 477). Until recently, all but the lowest slopes were uninhabited, save by wild bears and hyenas (FISHER, 398).

Commentary: The Theme of Foreign Trade (4:8)

The theme of this passage is Judah's economic opportunity, to be fostered by government-sponsored development of foreign trade. This will go into operation as soon as the Jewish community achieves political independence. Since economic treaties were entered into with foreign countries by government leaders for the development of commerce, territories deprived of political autonomy did not have any means of economic expansion. The overlord state had a monopoly of the circulation of commodities. During the mandate of Samaria, the people of Judah were not in control of the economic policy of their territory. But this situation would have to change owing to the repatriation of large number of exiled Jews, whose resourcefulness would be put to use in trade and brisk enterprises. In order to achieve this it was indispensable for them to wrest the administration of the Judean territory from the jurisdiction of the provincial governor of Samaria by achieving political autonomy for Judah, which would thus be elevated to the rank of an independent province. Moreover, the autochthonous Jews aspired to the restoration of a monarchy with a status similar to that of the city-states of Tyre and Sidon, which were integrated as allied kingdoms into the Persian satrapy of Babylon and Beyond the River. Once political autonomy was achieved, the restored Jewish nation would seize an opportunity to establish the monarchy, whose subjects would be bound to the king by a pact of fealty which is compared to the marriage contract between bride and bridegroom.

The trade relations between Judah and Phoenicia's mercantile cities would both provide an outlet for agricultural products and give access to the thriving markets of imported goods from Mediterranean countries, such as implements of iron and bronze, precious metals, semi-precious stones, and products from the Orient: silk fabrics, spices, and rice. Workshops in Phoenician cities supplied the local and foreign markets with purple cloth, glassware, and furniture with ivory inlay. Timber from Lebanon's forests, such as cedar and pine, was exported to eastern countries for the construction of palaces and temples, and was used in the Phoenician furniture industry and in ship-building at local dockyards.

The journey from Phoenicia to Judah could be undertaken either by land or by sea. From the reference to the shipment of timber for the rebuilding of the Jerusalem temple (Ezr 3:7) we infer that passengers embarked as well on the ships sailing from the Phoenician seaports to Jaffa. For traveling by land there were four routes leading from Phoenicia to Judah. The *Via Maris* went southward along the Levantine coast. The main route proceeded from Tripoli to Kadesh and thence southward running along the foot of the Anti-Lebanon to Damascus until it joined the "King's Highway" which passed through the territories east of the Jordan to Heshbon where a road branched off to Jericho (7:5). The east-west mountain route from Beirut to the Bekaa valley crossed the Lebanon massif and continued eastward across the Anti-Lebanon to Damascus where it met the "King's Highway." The inland route turned off from the east-west mountain route in the Bekaa valley leading southward along the foothills of Mount Hermon to Hazor in Galilee where it fed into crossroads. Because of the mountainous region of Phoenicia, it was hazardous to travel on either one of the roads owing to the irregular topography, the streams and rivers obstructing the passage, and the heavily forested slopes infested by wild animals. Thus, alternative routes are indicated which would have to be taken when snowdrifts blocked the mountain roads in winter or flood-waters covered the fords in spring. Each route is identified by the highest peak or massif of the mountain range at whose foothills runs the road which fed into an overland highway. The peaks or massifs are listed clockwise according to their geographical location: the Lebanon Mountains in the west, the Anti-Lebanon massif (Amana) in the north, Jebel ez Zebedani (Senir) in the east, and Mount Hermon in the south.

From the slopes of these mountain ranges drain the fountainheads and streams that feed four rivers flowing in four different directions: the Litani in its lower stretches runs to the west, the Orontes to the north, the Barada to the east, and the Jordan to the south. As the streams from the Lebanese mountains feed the rivers flowing in four directions, so Phoenicia's trade supplies the countries near and far with an endless stream of manufactured goods in exchange for local products, thus fostering the economic development of the inland towns. The theme of this passage will be developed in another song whose thematic content is an account of political alliances advantageous to the Jewish nation (6:8-12).

3. ✦ *The Wealthy Bride (4:9-11)*

9 You have ravished my heart, my sister, *Bridegroom*
my bride,
you have ravished my heart with a glance
of your eyes,
with one jewel of your necklace.
10 How attractive is your friendship, my sister, my bride!
how much better is your friendship than wine,
and the fragrance of your oils
than any spice!
11 Your lips distill nectar, my bride;
honey and milk are under your tongue;
the scent of your garments
is like the scent of Lebanon.

Accented Transliteration (4:9-11)

9 *libbabtínî ʾaḥōtî́ kallấ*
libbabtî́nî beʾaḥád mēʿênáyik
beʾaḥád ʿanā́q miṣṣawwerōnáyik
10 *mah-yyāfû́ dōdáyik ʾaḥōtî́ kallấ*
mah-ṭṭṓbû dōdáyik miyyáyin
werếaḥ šemānáyik mikkol-beśāmî́m
11 *nṓfet tiṭṭṓfnâ śiftôtáyik kallấ*
debáš weḥālā́b táḥat lešônḗk
werếaḥ śalmōtáyik kerếaḥ lebānṓn

Literary Analysis (4:9-11)

In this song of three strophes, the growing prosperity of the Jewish nation, following in the train of economic and political independence, is illustrated by comparisons drawn from an improved lifestyle of the country people: ornaments appealing to the sight (vs. 9), perfumes pleasant to the smell (vs. 10), food and drink delightful to the taste (vs. 11).

Poetic and rhetorical devices occurring in the song are sound repetition: end rhyme *-ayik* in seven words; word repetition, e.g. *rêaḥ* (thrice), "bride" (thrice), "friendship" (twice), "sister" (twice), anaphora (vss. 9ab, 10ab). Rhetorical devices: simile, e.g. "your friendship is better than wine and the fragrance of your oils than any spice," "the scent of your garments is like the scent of Lebanon"; the etymological figure of speech *nōfet tiṭṭōfnâ* (vs. 11a); and the hyperbole "the fragrance of your oils is better than any spice," "the scent of your garments is like the scent of Lebanon."

Vocabulary Analysis (4:9-11)

Vs. 9: The verb *libbabtinî*, in *Piel*, denotes the fascinating effect of beauty: "you have ravished my heart." The reason for designating the woman as "my sister" (*ʾaḥōtî*) here and elsewhere (4:9, 12; 5:1, 2) is to indicate not a blood-relationship between the Shulamite and Solomon, but a title whose masculine form "my brother" occurs as a technical term in ancient treaty literature designating a partner of a covenant fellowship (KALLUVEETTIL, 198–210). This relationship is compared with the marriage bond between bridegroom and "bride" (4:8, 9, 10, 11; 5:1); *kallâ* used in the vocative is translated as "my bride."

The unusual gender agreement of a feminine noun *'ênayik* (your eyes) with a masculine numeral *'aḥad* (one) is explained by the fact that several names of body members of men or beasts, although usually feminine, are employed occasionally as masculine in Hebrew (GINSBURG, cited after POPE, 481). The noun *'anāq* (jewel) designates a single unit of a necklace whose plural form *ṣawwerōnāyik* (your necklace) refers to a type of necklace made up of more than a single strand of beads or jewels strung together.

Vs. 10: "Your friendship" (*dōdèkā*) is an expression for indicating a socio-political alliance between the heir of the Davidic throne and the Jewish community (1:2, 4; 4:10). Such an alliance is based on a legal bond as well as on a personal relationship. Hence the words of praise addressed to the covenant partners are meant to extol their status as allies or the bond of alliance, described as "beautiful, attractive" (*yāfeh*) and "good, pleasant" (*ṭôb*) (1:2, 15; 4:1; 7:7), or by equivalent verbal forms "they are beautiful, attractive" (*yāfû*) and "they are good, pleasant" (*ṭōbû*). The purpose of comparing friendship with fragrant wine is to set forth the pleasure that is born of friendship. Both provide a pleasurable experience, though this one is of a different nature and has a lasting effect, thus being "better than wine" (*miyyain*).

The growing prosperity of the Jewish community is illustrated by the steady supply of various kinds of spices and perfumes both imported from the Orient and produced locally which are traded throughout the country. The term "spice" (*beśāmîm*) is applied to various scented plants (4:10, 14, 16; 8:14) or spice-bearing trees and shrubs from which "aromatic substances or oils" (*šemānîm*) are extracted.

Vs. 11: In this strophe the prosperity of the population, settled in the uplands, is described by comparisons drawn from pastoral life which contributes considerably to raising the standard of living of the people engaged in stock-rearing. "Honey and milk" (*debaš weḥālāb*) symbolize nature's bounty. The same words occur in an inverted order with a different meaning, viz. "milk and honey," as an idiomatic expression used in the Bible to designate the only products of a rural economy that has no recourse to agriculture. This was owed either to the people's nomadic way of life (Ex 3:8, 17; 33:3; Dt 6:3; 11:9; 26:15 etc.) or to a reversion of cultivated land to steppes as a result of the devastation of the country's rural districts by war and the deportation of the farmers, except for a few survivors left in that area (Is 7:22-25). Unlike the precarious living conditions mentioned in these texts, the socio-economic aspects of the community described in this song are those indicating economic growth.

Nōfet is virgin honey though translated as "nectar" in order to set forth its liquid state. Lips "dripping, distilling" (*tiṭṭōfnâ*) nectar symbolize abundance of an exquisite beverage. Likewise, a large mouthful is shown by liquids "under your tongue" (*taḥat lešônēk*). Most commentators interpret it, however, as an allusion to the kiss, breath, or speech. Since these products are gathered in open air and are consumed while still fresh, they do not emit a sour or stale smell which impregnates the garments of those handling perishable foodstuffs stored in a musty cellar. The comparison of "the scent of your garments" (*rêaḥ śalmōtayik*) with "the scent of Lebanon" (*rêaḥ lebānôn*) is a figure of speech called hyperbole which brings the fragrance emitted by the forest covering the hills of Judah into relation with that of the forested mountains of Lebanon. The reference to Lebanon indicates the connection between the thematic content of this song and that of the preceding (4:8) and the subsequent literary unit (4:12-15).

Commentary: The Theme of the Nation's Prosperity (4:9-11)

The theme of this song is that of the nation's growing prosperity following Judah's political emancipation and economic independence from the administrative control exercised by the governor of Samaria. The prerequisite of the Jewish nation's economic growth is the elevation of its territory to the rank of an independent province on equal terms with other provinces and whose change of status would have to be approved by the Persian overlord who held sway over Palestine at that time. As long as Judah continued to be subject to the administrative control of the Samaritan province, all of its economic resources were drained by a rapacious tributary system instead of being retained for reinvestment in the country's development. Thus, the project put forward here concerns the restoration of a political regime with administrative self-government like that in force in the Phoenician city-states. Like these states, which had become independent kingdoms and were treated as allies of the Persians, so the Jews aspired to being granted the right of restoring the monarchy in their country—and a monarch who would have the necessary means to promote the economic growth of the nation. This policy entailed that proportionate rights and bargaining power be granted to all social groups engaged in this national endeavor. On account of this the leadership of the Jewish population is called "sister," signifying an interrelation based on equality and brotherhood among those in charge of the management of the country's internal affairs.

The nation's prosperity is illustrated by comparisons drawn from urban, rural, and pastoral surroundings. The necklace of jewels suggests an urban environment where women wearing expensive ornaments are seen walking about streets and city squares attracting admiring glances from passersby (vs. 9). The rural setting is the background of the reference to wine and scented plants from which are extracted oils and perfumes (vs. 10). The pastoral regions are referred to in the description of the people's natural food supply (vs. 11). There are no signs of economic imbalance among the inhabitants of the country. Both townspeople and the rural population are organized as a body politic under its own leadership represented by the "bride," whose relationship with the bridegroom implies a covenant of the people with the king in view of the restoration of the monarchy in Judah. The theme of this song will be taken up in the context of the country's leadership described in another song (7:1-6).

4. ✦ *The Assets of the Bride (4:12-15)*

12 A garden locked is my sister, *Bridegroom*
my bride,
a garden locked, with a sealed fountain.
13 Your shoots are an orchard of pomegranates
with all choicest fruits,
henna with nard,
14 nard and saffron, calamus and cinnamon,
with all trees of frankincense,
myrrh and aloes,
with all chief spices.
15 The fountain of the gardens is a well of living water
and torrents from Lebanon.

Accented Transliteration (4:12-15)

12 *gán nāʿûl ʾaḥōtî kallâ*
gál nāʿûl maʿyā́n ḥātûm
13 *šelāḥáyik pardḗs rimmônîm*
ʿim perî́ megādî́m
kefārî́m ʿim-nerādî́m
14 *nḗrd wekarkṓm qānéh weqinnāmốn*
ʿim kol-ʿaṣḗ lebônấ
mṓr waʾahālốt
ʿim kol-rāʾšḗ beśāmî́m
15 *maʿyán gannî́m beʾḗr mayim ḥayyî́m*
wenōzelî́m min-lebānôn

Literary Analysis (4:12-15)

This song, divided into four strophes, compares the woman to a garden of exclusive personal possession. Both the first (vs. 12) and the fourth strophes (vs. 15) deal with the Jewish nation represented as a garden, provided with an abundant water supply, and whose entrance is barred to outsiders. The second (vs. 13) and third strophes (vs. 14) mention various rare plants found to be growing there. These serve as an image of the nation's economic resources available to satisfy the needs of its citizens and the development of the country.

Poetic and rhetorical devices that occur in the song are sound repetition: assonance *a-e,* e.g. *ʿaṣê–rāʾšê* (vs. 14b + d), alliteration *k–q* (vs. 14a), end rhyme *-îm* (vs. 13); word repetition: anaphora *ʿim kol–ʿim kol* (vs. 14b + d). Rhetorical devices: the metaphor "my bride is a garden locked, with a sealed fountain"; and the technique of accumulation which lumps together all sorts of plants cultivated in the garden.

Vocabulary Analysis (4:12-15)

Vs. 12: The Jewish nation is compared to a "locked garden" (*gan nāʿûl*) which represents the status of political autonomy without foreign interference in its internal affairs. Its population is personified as "sister" and "bride" because of its relationship with the king by virtue of the bond of fealty. The word *gan* (garden) in the second hemistich is taken over from other Hebrew manuscripts for MT *gal* which designates a "heap of stone," whereas *gallîm* in the plural means "waves." Some commentators derive from this noun the hypothetical word *gal* in the singular signifying "source, spring." Since the repetition of key words is a stylistic feature used for the sake of emphasis at the beginning of three songs of this poem (4:1, 8, 9), we presume that the same feature occurs in the opening verse of this song. The change of *gan* to *gal* is to be explained as a scribal error due to alliteration between *g–l* and *ʿ–l* of the words *gal* and *nāʿûl.*

The nation's economic independence is compared to a "sealed fountain" (*maʿyān ḥātûm*) whose access is restricted to its owner and whose water supply is made available for his garden plants. In terms of the grammatical function, the "sealed fountain" is an adnominal adjunct of the "locked garden." Since the relation which the objects bear toward each other is not expressed in Hebrew, it was suggested that the preposition *ʿim* (with) be inserted into the MT (RUDOLPH, 151), in spite of its being implied in the case of an adnominal adjunct as expressed in Hebrew (JOÜON, *Gr* § 131c). However, most commentators interpret the "sealed fountain" in terms of a nominal predicate which they assume to be an illustration of the bride who is compared both to a garden and the fountain within it, thus producing a confusion with a mixed metaphor.

Vs. 13: The unique flora of the garden consists of rare plants and shrubs from which aromatic substances are extracted to be used as ingredients in the production of perfumes, spices, medicaments, and dyes. Some species of the following plants grew in Palestine while most of the others are known from aromatic resins and powders imported from the Orient.

The term *šᵉlāḥayik* (your shoots) is taken by some interpreters in the sense of "your channels" (Buzy, 329; Joüon, *Ct,* 219ff; Krinetzki, 171; Pope, 490). From the verb *šlḥ,* in *Piel,* with the meaning "to germinate, sprout," two plural nouns are derived, e.g. "tendrils" (*šᵉluḥôt*), mentioned in Is 16:8, and "shoots" (*šᵉlāḥîm*), referred to in this text (*THAT* II, 910).

The noun *pardēs* (orchard), taken over from the Old Persian, occurs in the late biblical Hebrew (4:13; Eccl 2:5; Neh 2:8) as well as in the Greek *parádeisos* and in the Latin *paradisus.* The garden described in the song is likened to a royal park of Persian monarchs not only by reference to its abundant water supply and rare plants, but also by its attributes proper to a royal domain whose access is restricted to the king and his bride accompanied by the guests of honor (5:1).

In the midst of a great variety of exotic vegetation there stands out a "pomegranate" (*rimmôn*), known as *Punica granatum,* because it is the only tree bearing edible fruit. Although it was native to Asia, the pomegranate was found to be extensively cultivated in Palestine as well. It is not surprising that the LXX and Vetus Latina versions deleted this name from the text, since the authors of these versions believed this common tree to be out of context with the vegetation. The purpose of this tree being cultivated in the garden was probably to offer protective shade, thus serving as a canopy for the plants sensitive to the rays of the sun. The commercial value of the pomegranate consisted in the dyes extracted from the rinds of its fruit and the medicinal properties of its roots and stem which were highly valued. On account of the great number of kernels found in each fruit, from which a refreshing juice was obtained, the pomegranate became a symbol of fertility in ancient times. The exquisite quality of this particular fruit is referred to by the word *mᵉgādîm* (choicest), a plural of abstraction, which qualifies natural products (4:13, 16; 7:14). The expression "with all choicest fruits" designates the quality of pomegranates, in parallel with the expression from the following strophe "with all chief spices" qualifying the aromatic plants.

The plant "henna," whose name is related to Arabic *al-ḥinna,* identified as *Lawsonia inermis,* corresponds to the shrub designated by the name *kōfer,* pl. *kᵉfārîm.* During ancient times, this plant native to northern India was found also to be growing in the Middle East and parts of Africa, particularly in zones of tropical climate. The white and yellow flowers of this plant were dehydrated and pounded and mixed with water producing a paste which was used as a dye. This dye of various colors (yellow, orange, and red) was used by women to color their nails, the palms of their hands, and the bottom of their feet. Men also used this dye to color their beards and the manes of their horses (MOLDENKE, 124f).

The "nard" (*nērd*, pl. *n^erādîm*) is a plant known as *Nardostachys jatamansi*, native to the mountainous districts of the Himalayan ranges, whence it was introduced into the upland regions of western Asia, and is typical of a cold and dry climate. This plant was not cultivated in Palestine but a powdered substance extracted from its roots and stem was imported for the production of perfume (1:12). It was of great commercial value up to the Roman period, appreciated as a favored perfume by ladies of the Roman aristocracy (MOLDENKE, 148).

Vs. 14: The names of the plants cited in this strophe are in the singular, with the exception of *ʾ^ahālôt* (aloes), a *plurale tantum*. Since these plants were not found to be growing in Palestine, their names are not mentioned as designating the existing flora of the garden, but stand for the most precious perfumes imported from the Orient. The perfume most highly appreciated by the ancients at this time was "nard" (*nērd*). "Saffron" (*karkōm*) is the name of two distinct plants, viz. the *Crocus sativus* found all over Palestine; its stigmas have medicinal purpose as well as use as condiment for food seasoning. Here the *Curcuma longa* is meant, which grows in India; from the rizoma of this plant the *curcumina* was obtained, a yellow dye which was commercialized in ancient Palestine (GERLEMAN, 160).

"Calamus" (*qāneh*) is known by the name *Acorus calamus*, a herbaceous medicinal plant growing in central Asia. The rizoma provides the oil of calamus, used in perfumery. "Cinnamon" (*qinnāmôn*) is the name of a common tree called *Cinnamomum zeylanicum*, native to the Asiatic region after which it is named. The same name designates both the powder produced by the pounded inner rind of the twigs, and an aromatic essence which was obtained from the fruit and the rind and was used in the production of perfume and of a special oil destined for ritual unctions (MOLDENKE, 76).

The "trees of incense" (*ʿ^aṣê l^ebônâ*) are of the family *Boswellia* which includes different species: *B. carterii*, *B. papyrifera*, and *B. thurifera*, found in parts of India, eastern Asia, and Africa. From its stem and branches is extracted an aromatic resin, which, when heated, produces a fragrant perfume. It was the most important aromatic substance for perfumes used in the Orient for religious purposes and court ceremonies, and by the ancient Egyptians for the embalming of the dead (3:6).

"Myrrh" (*môr*) is an aromatic gum collected from the shrub called *Commiphora abessinica*, growing in eastern Arabia, Ethiopia, and Somalia. It was in great demand as a fragrant substance with considerable commercial value for use as perfume, and for medicine, as well as being a main ingredient in the production of an oil used at religious ceremonials and for embalming (1:13; 3:6). "Aloe" (*'ahālôt, 'ahālîm*) is a tree known by the name *Aquilaria agallocha,* native to southeast Asia. Because partially decomposed pieces of its wood emit a pungent odor it became suitable as an aromatic ingredient added to other resins burnt as incense or mixed with preservative powders and herbs in ancient embalming practices (MOLDENKE, 47). The complement "with all chief spices" (*'im kol-rā'šê beśāmîm*) sums up in one every sort of imported spicery.

Vs. 15: This strophe amplifies the range of meanings of two words, i.e. "garden" and "fountain" which are mentioned in the first strophe (vs. 12). The "garden" provides an image for the Jewish nation, under the aspect of its entire population, whereas "gardens" in the plural represents the social groups integrated into the national body. However, some commentators interpret the word "gardens" as a generalizing plural with the meaning in the singular (DELITZSCH, 86; GERLEMAN, 161; KRINETZKI, 171; POPE, 495; WINANDY, 83). Others suggest that the term "gardens" be emended to "my garden" (*gannî*) by deleting a letter (WÜRTHWEIN, 54) or by transferring it to the following word (RUDOLPH, 151). It was also suggested that the term "gardens" be replaced by "waves" (*gallîm*), which was applied to the phrase with the meaning of "bubbling waters," in parallel with vs. 12b (JOÜON, *Ct, 224;* BUZY, 329).

The word "fountain" as used in the text symbolizes the internal product of the nation resulting from the economy of the country from different sectors. The distribution of the proceeds amongst the various social groups is represented by the words "well of living waters" (*be'ēr mayim ḥayyîm*), denoting the source of water available in each city and village of Judah. The "torrents of Lebanon" (*nōzelîm min-lebānôn*) serve as an illustration of foreign trade with the Phoenician maritime cities from which many products were imported. As for the meaning of "living waters," it specifies the good quality of flowing water unlike that of stagnant water stored in water supply cisterns. The reference to "Lebanon" (4:8, 11, 15) indicates the nexus between three related songs which deal with the same theme, that of economics.

Commentary: The Theme of the Nation's Economic Independence (4:12-15)

The theme of this song deals with the economic independence of the Jewish nation resulting from the political sovereignty of the territory of Judah. Together with the collective endeavor of the Judean community to be constituted as a state within the political constellation of countries under Persian rule, a growing aspiration for economic self-sufficiency emerged among repatriate and autochthonous Jews. While the territory of Judah was under the administrative control of the Samaritan province, the local population was reduced to a multitude of individuals kept within territorial boundaries by an external force. In order to eliminate all foreign interference in the internal affairs of the country, the Jews revindicated the right to constitute an independent state of equal status with other provinces integrated into a Persian satrapy.

As expressed in figurative language, the Jewish nation is compared to a garden in which are found to be growing all sorts of rare plants, both native and foreign. Owing to favorable conditions, the vegetation was able to take root and maintain its course of growth up to the stage of its full development thanks to an adequate irrigation system.

In order to protect the garden from trespassing by foreigners who attempted to rob its produce, it was necessary to surround the property by a fence to prevent their access. The garden described with paradisiacal features consisting of exotic plants, most of which are not to be found growing in Palestine, is interpreted as a metaphor of a prosperous nation endowed with sufficient financial resources to be able to acquire the costly products of the respective aromatic plants imported from the Orient. The purchase of these products is made possible by the population collecting the profit of its proceeds, free from the constant draining of its income through paying tributes to a foreign government that is more interested in gains for the state treasury than in the development of the subjugated territory. With the sound economic performance of Judah, all social groups benefit from its productive yield. This prevents certain groups benefiting from the economic yield at the cost of impoverishment amongst others.

The economic independence and the prosperity of the nation have as their prerequisites that the economic order be subordinated to the political order and maintained by the centralizing influence of the king. The theme of this song will be dealt with again in another song (7:7-10).

5. ✦ *The Delights of the Bride (4:16–5:1)*

16 Awake, O north wind, *Bride*
    and come, O south wind!
Blow upon my garden,
    let its fragrance be wafted abroad.
Let my beloved come to his garden,
    and eat its choicest fruits.
5:1 I come to my garden, my sister, my bride, *Bridegroom*
    I gather my myrrh with my spice,
I eat my honeycomb with my honey,
    I drink my wine with my milk.

Eat, O friends, and drink: *Chorus*
drink deeply, O lovers!

Accented Transliteration (4:16–5:1)

16 *‘ûrî ṣāfôn ûbô’î têmān*
hāfîḥî gannî yizz^{e}*lû b*^{e}*śāmâw*
yābō’ dôdî l^{e}*gannô*
w^{e}*yō’kal p*^{e}*rî m*^{e}*gādâw*
5:1 *bā’tî l*^{e}*gannî ’*^{a}*ḥōtî kallâ*
’ārîtî môrî ‘im-b^{e}*śāmî*
’ākaltî ya‘rî ‘im-dibšî
šātîtî yênî ‘im-ḥ^{a}*lābî*
’iklû rē‘îm š^{e}*tû*
w^{e}*šikrû dôdîm*

Literary Analysis (4:16–5:1)

This song, composed of two strophes, deals with the Jewish nation compared to a very productive garden. The first strophe (vs. 16) is formulated as an apostrophe to the winds, that they waft the plants' fragrance abroad, and as an invitation to the bridegroom to share in the produce of the garden. The second strophe (5:1) states his acceptance of the bride's invitation and adds a call to the guests of honor to participate in the festive celebration.

Poetic and rhetorical devices that occur in the song are sound repetition: assonance *a–i* (vs. 16b; 5:1); figures of relationship: synthetic parallelism "eat"–"drink," chiasmus *rē‘îm š*^{e}*tû–šikrû dôdîm,* and merismus "north wind–south wind."

Vocabulary Analysis (4:16–5:1)

Vs. 16: The "north wind" (*ṣāfôn*) is associated with cold weather and the "south wind" (*têmān*) is characterized by its warmth and dryness. Since these winds strongly influence the climate during a particular season, their passage over Palestine affects local weather conditions and its vegetation. Wind currents close to the ground may be very light, as if "awakening" (*‘wr*) from a calm; they may either "arrive" (*bw’*) as a breeze or "blow" (*pwḥ*) in sudden rushes. Under favorable weather conditions the fragrant gum "flows" (*nzl*) from incisions made on the stem and the branches of aromatic plants whose scents the winds carry abroad. The verb "blow!" (*hāfîḥî*), though in the singular, refers to both north and south wind. The object governed by this verb is "my garden" (*gannî*) in the accusative case in Hebrew, which is expressed in the translation by the use of a preposition "upon my garden."

Commentators differ in determining the identity of the person referred to by the possessive pronoun attached to the noun *gannî* (my garden). In the opinion of some it is the bridegroom, while according to others it is the bride. Since the entreating call is expressed by the verb in the masculine form *yābō'* (let him come), there is no doubt that the bride is the one addressing the bridegroom. By referring to him as "my beloved" (*dôdî*), she reminds him of the ties of friendship that bind them to each other by virtue of the covenant between the house of David and the Jewish nation. The national territory is described as "his garden" (*gannô*) which is an image of the country represented as a royal domain.

The bride's entreaty for the bridegroom to enter the garden symbolizes the yearning of the Jewish people for the long awaited restoration of the monarchy in Judah. With political autonomy soon to be regained, the prosperity of the nation is expected to set in as the country's annual yield comes to provide the "choicest fruits" for the people's well-being.

Vs. 5:1: In response to the bride's call the bridegroom gives his assent expressed by four verbs, whose past tense is used idiomatically to denote the present. This idiomatic use of the past, typical of the Hebrew language, occurs in types of sentences denoting a proleptic meaning of an action soon to take place (JOÜON, *Gr* § 112h). It is expected that the arriving bridegroom will be invested with royal authority and endowed with the power to rule the country. Its citizens are subject to the king to whom they are bound by ties of fealty as a result of the covenant between the house of David and the Jewish nation. On account of this relationship the king addresses the nation's leader as "my sister and my bride" which are terms used as titles equivalent to those applied to allies in ancient treaty literature.

The political unity established in the country also affects the economic means of production (vs. 1b) and consumption of goods (vs. 1cd) in Judah. As regards the country's means of production, the perfume industry is by far its major source of wealth. The production of aromatic resins and essences is mentioned by the phrase "I gather my myrrh with my spice" (*'ārîtî môrî 'im beśāmî*). One should observe, however, that myrrh itself is not found nor produced in Palestine (4:14), yet reference to this particular plant is made by FLAVIUS JOSEPHUS in the Greek name *myrobálanos* which is a derivative of myrrh and which was used for medicinal purposes and dyes (*BJ* IV, 8,3).

"Spice" is expressed in Hebrew by two words: *bōśem* and *beśem;* but the noun with an additional ending, i.e. *beśāmî* (my spice), can only be derived from the word *bāśām*, if such a word was used during that time. The tree known as *Balsamodendrum opobalsamum* is native to eastern Arabia from where it was introduced in Ethiopia and Somalia, and according to FLAVIUS JOSEPHUS it was found to be cultivated in the gardens of Jericho and En-gedi (*AJ* VIII, 6,6; IX, 1,2; XIV, 4,1; XV, 4,2; *BJ* I, 6,6 etc.). The garden of Jericho extended over an area of five hectares which was used for the cultivation of spice-trees, while that of En-gedi was a little bit smaller; the annual yield of both was approximately twenty-five liters of aromatic resins. Later during Roman administration of that area the productive yield increased considerably to attend the growing demands for perfume which was greatly appreciated throughout the empire (*DB* I, col. 1520).

The patterns of consumption of agricultural goods in Judah were reflected in the economic prosperity of the nation. In the verse we find the verbs "I eat" (*'ākaltî*) and "I drink" (*šātîtî*) which indicate the basic patterns of human sustenance and also designate the meal shared in common which, in a figurative sense, denotes the joy of companionship at table. The words used in this phrase provide us with an imagery that the meals partaken and shared were the finest, as denoted by "my honeycomb with my honey" (*ya'rî 'im dibšî*). Daily consumption according to the customs of the time contained both wine and milk. The function of the possessive pronoun "my" stresses two particular points: one being the king's centralizing figure at the head of the nation (my garden); number two, the economic control of the nation is administered by the king (my myrrh, my spice, my honeycomb, my honey, my wine, and my milk). As long as the political autonomy is not self-contained in Judah, the Jewish population continues to be totally dependent on the Samaritan province, and the economy of the country is subject to continuous exploitation by the Samaritans.

In the last stanza (vs. 1e-f) the chorus invites the guests of the bride to participate in the festive celebration in honor of the nation which will be restored. This viewpoint is not held indisputedly by all commentators. According to some, the speaker could be the author himself who expresses his personal opinion (GERLEMAN, 162; WÜRTHWEIN, 55) as if other parts of the Song were not the author's own ideas. A great number of commentators, on the other hand, interpret this same stanza to be an invitation which the bridegroom extends to his guests, rather than coming from the bride. This hypothesis is hard to accept based on the fact that the bridegroom never addresses anyone other than his bride. Furthermore, this hypothesis is unacceptable from a political point of view due to the fact that any public manifestation of patriotism sponsored by the Jewish governor would result in his removal by the Persian authorities and bring about repressive measures against a burgeoning Jewish nationalism in Judah.

Who are the persons designated by the terms "friends" (*rē'îm*) and "lovers" (*dôdîm*)? Some commentators believe them to be the two protagonists of the Song on the assumption that both are frequently addressed by terms of endearment (GERLEMAN, 162; LYS, 203; WINANDY, 131; WÜRTHWEIN, 55). One should observe, however, that no terms of endearment are ever used in this book but rather technical terms drawn from the treaty literature of the ancient Near East (KALLUVEETTIL, 101). Thus, the persons addressed as "friends" and "lovers" represent the parties of a covenant who are on friendly terms. This particular use of technical terms can be exemplified in another text, e.g. Lam 1:2, where allied nations of Judah are called "her lovers" (*'ōhabèhā*) and "her friends" (*rē'èhā*). As regards the usage of these terms in the Song, a distinction has to be made between the class of Hebrew nouns with an additional ending of personal pronouns, referring to either bridegroom or bride, and the nouns with no such ending which are used to designate the social groups associated with the bride. Thus the invitation of the bride is extended to these groups for the purpose of their participating in the feast held in commemoration of the restored Jewish nation.

In the MT there are two spellings of *dôdîm/dōdîm* to distinguish between two meanings: in *scriptio plena* occurs *dôdîm* designating "lovers, uncles, cousins"; in *scriptio defectiva,* the word *dōdîm* is used whose meaning in the abstract sense is "love" (Ez 16:8; 23:17; Prv 7:18), and "friendship" (Ct 1:2, 4; 4:10; 7:13). The ancient versions and most commentators took the word *dôdîm* in the sense of "lovers," in parallelism with "friends."

Commentary: The Theme of the Nation Firmly Established (4:16–5:1)

The theme of this song deals with the Jewish nation visualized as firmly established in Judah, its population organized as a political community, and its economic opportunity provided by the country's independence from foreign influence in its internal affairs. While some aspects of this theme have already been discussed in the context of social integration of different groups in the Jewish community, they are now viewed from the perspective of their relevance to the restoration of the monarchy in Judah. As soon as political autonomy is achieved, the country is raised to the rank of a province equal to those integrated into a Persian satrapy and is able to exercise administrative control over its territory, having been released from the mandate of Samaria. As a result of the restoration of national life, the country's economic activities, the means to welfare and aggrandizement of the state, will be increased by making its labor more effective and by extending specialization to the production of aromatic resins and accumulating revenue from the sale of products. In dealing with the community's economic life, as illustrated by the produce of the garden, its organization and direction are the tasks assigned to the king with the aim of fostering the country's prosperity and supplying the community's needs.

The organization of Judah as a political entity is a task attributed to the Davidic king as head of the monarchical state, whose restoration will take place upon approval by the Persian overlord, who held sway over Palestine during that time. Such approval is expected to be obtained from the Persian ruler, since the future king of Judah will seek to restore the traditional form of government of Judah whose population, integrated by repatriate and autochthonous Jews, had been established in the country of their forebears by imperial decree.

While some of the topics dealt with in this song are enlarged upon in the preceding and subsequent songs, the theme of this central passage displays the main object of the poem which will be illustrated further on by images drawn from nature (7:7-10).

POEM V

The Presence of the Bridegroom (5:2–6:3)

1 ✦ *The Call of the Bridegroom* (5:2-8)

2 I slept, but my heart was awake. *Bride*
Hark! my beloved is knocking.
"Open to me, my sister, my friend, *Bridegroom*
my dove, my perfect one;
for my head is wet with dew,
my locks with the drops of the night."
3 I had put off my garment, *Bride*
how could I put it on?
I had bathed my feet,
how could I soil them?
4 My beloved put his hand to the latch,
and my heart was moved for him.
5 I arose to open to my beloved,
and my hands dripped with myrrh,
my fingers with liquid myrrh,
upon the handles of the bolt.
6 I opened to my beloved,
but my beloved had turned and gone.
My soul failed me when he withdrew.
I sought him, but found him not;
I called him, but he gave no answer.
7 The watchmen found me,
as they went about in the city;
they beat me, they wounded me,
they took away my mantle,
those watchmen of the walls.

8 I adjure you, O daughters of Jerusalem,
if you find my beloved . . .
What shall you then say to him?
That I am faint with love.

Accented Transliteration (5:2-8)

2 *ʾ^{a}ní y^{e}šēnā́h w^{e}libbî́ ʿḗr*
qṓl dôdî́ dôfḗq
pitḥî-lî́ ʾ^{a}ḥōtî́ raʿyātî́
yônātî́ tammātî́
šerrōʾšî́ nimlāʾ-ṭā́l
q^{e}wuṣṣôtáy r^{e}sî́sê lā́y^{e}lâ
3 *pā́šaṭtî ʾet-kuttontî́*
ʾêkā́kâ ʾelbāšénnāh
rāḥáṣtî ʾet-ragláy
ʾêkā́kâ ʾ^{a}ṭann^{e}fḗm
4 *dôdî́ šāláḥ yādố min-haḥṓr*
ûmēʿáy hāmû́ ʿālā́w
5 *qámtî ʾ^{a}ní liftṓ^{a}ḥ l^{e}dôdî́*
w^{e}yādáy nāṭ^{e}fû-mốr
w^{e}ʾeṣb^{e}ʿōtáy mốr ʿōbḗr
ʿal kappốt hammanʿû́l
6 *pātáḥtî ʾ^{a}nî l^{e}dôdî́*
w^{e}dôdî́ ḥāmáq ʿābā́r
nafšî́ yāṣʾā́ b^{e}dabb^{e}rố
biqqaštî́hû w^{e}lōʾ m^{e}ṣāʾtî́hû
q^{e}rāʾtî́w w^{e}lōʾ ʿānā́nî
7 *m^{e}ṣāʾúnî haššōm^{e}rî́m hassōb^{e}bî́m bāʿî́r*
hikkû́nî f^{e}ṣāʿû́nî
nā́śʾû ʾet-r^{e}dîdî́ mēʿāláy
šōm^{e}rế haḥōmôt
8 *hišbáʿtî ʾetkém b^{e}nôt y^{e}rûšālā́im*
ʾim-timṣ^{e}ʾû́ ʾet-dôdî́
mah-ttaggî́dû lố
šeḥôlat ʾah^{a}bấ ʾānî́

Literary Analysis (5:2-8)

Poem V on the presence of the bridegroom (5:2–6:3) is composed of three songs which relate the stages of his manifestation to the inhabitants of Judah. On the occasion of his arrival at night, the manner of his appearance is quite discreet; later on he appears during the day bearing the royal insignia, and finally he shows himself in public to all the inhabitants as head of the government.

This song, divided into two parts, relates a dream which describes the conditions under which the attitudes of the bride toward the bridegroom are formed and changed. The first part (vss. 2-3) consists of two strophes, introduced by an opening distich (vs. 2ab) indicating the circumstances under which the oneiric experience occurred. In the first strophe (vs. 2c-f), there is mentioned the bridegroom seeking admission to her. The second strophe (vs. 3) shows the bride in a state of hesitation as to whether she should receive him at once or rather after certain conditions have been fulfilled. A verse of transition (vs. 4) introduces the second part, divided into four strophes. The first (vs. 5) deals with the woman's exultant state of mind at the forthcoming meeting with the bridegroom. The second (vs. 6) describes the transformation of the bride's heightened expectation into deep frustration at his sudden departure and at her fruitless search for the absent bridegroom. The third (vs. 7) illustrates the adverse circumstances she had to face as she went courageously about in the city inquiring as to his whereabouts. The fourth (vs. 8) presents the woman enlisting the cooperation of the daughters of Jerusalem to tell the bridegroom of her ardent love for him.

Poetic and rhetorical devices used in the song are sound repetition: assonance *a–i* (vss. 2cd, 6a), onomatopoeia which consists in the formation of words in imitation of natural sounds, viz. the knocking at the door indicated by the recurrence of the word ending *-tî* (vs. 2cd); word repetition: *dôdî* (five times), *'ᵃnî* (four times), anaphora *'êkākâ–'êkākâ* (vs. 3b + d), inclusion *'ᵃnî–'ᵃnî* (vss. 2a, 8d). Rhetorical devices: antithetic parallelism (vs. 6ab); synecdoche which consists in positing the whole for a part, viz. hand for finger (vs. 4); anthypophora, *subiectio* in the Latin, a figure of speech consisting of a question (vs. 8c) followed by an answer (vs. 8d); and hyperbole "my hands dripped with myrrh, my fingers with liquid myrrh" (vs. 5bc).

Vocabulary Analysis (5:2-8)

Vs. 2: The events described in considerable detail are to be classified as a dream, because they are reported as having been experienced during sleep. The tense of the stative verbs *y^ešēnâ* (asleep) and *'ēr* (awake) is that of the past, since the bride gives an account of that which she has experienced in her dream. Some commentators, however, render these verbs in the present tense as if the dreamer were actually cognizant of the fact of having a dream. That the bride is able to recall her dream upon awakening is due to her memory not having been impaired by exhaustion, as she says "my heart was awake" (*libbî 'ēr*).

The account of the dream is introduced by the interjection "hark!" (*qôl*), lit. "voice, sound," as explained above (2:8). This call to attention is a literary device used for the purpose of pointing at the person now entering the scene. Thus, it is neither a "voice" nor a "sound," made by somebody speaking or knocking at the door, which were the stimuli to a dream, because sensory experience is fully operative only in persons when in a state of alert consciousness. The events of the bride's past are reactivated in the dream and play a vivid role, as for instance her longing for the absent bridegroom whom she addresses six times as "my beloved" (*dôdî*), used in the Song as a title applied to the Davidic king on account of his covenant with the Jewish nation.

The sudden arrival of the bridegroom is to be concealed from the eyes of the Persian authorities, which accounts for his visit at night with the intent to confirm the covenant with the leading figure representative of the Jewish people. His knocking at the door and asking for admission to the house are significant gestures among allies, since a covenant relationship is established by spontaneous acceptance of the partner's stipulations as opposed to coercion by the superior exerted upon the inferior. Symbolic significance is attached to the use of titles by which the allies are addressed as a means to express their relationship based on friendly terms. "My sister" (*'ahōtî*) is a title applied to a covenant partner whose relationship is compared to that among members of a family (4:9). "My friend" (*ra'yātî*) is a designation of an ally who agrees to be on friendly terms with his partner. "My dove" (*yônātî*) is a metaphorical expression based on the resemblance which the bird's behavior bears to an ally's attitude. This metaphor appears in an extended form with two specifications added, as illustrated above (2:14), e.g. "let me see your comely face" denoting fidelity to covenant stipulations, and "let me hear your sweet voice" signifying consent to a binding agreement. "My perfect one" (*tammātî*) is an expression which qualifies a person as a trustworthy ally (4:7).

Circumstances related to the nocturnal visit are those mentioned as reasons for the bridegroom's seeking a shelter, viz. the dew falling at night and his hair getting wet. The conjunctive *še* (for) has causal meaning (JOÜON, *Gr* § 170c). "My head is wet with dew" (*rō'šî nimlā'-ṭāl*), lit. "my head is full with dew." The word *q^ewuṣṣôtay* (my locks) appears in MT in two variant spellings (5:2, 11). In the expression *r^esîsê lāy^elâ* (the drops of the night) occurs *r^e sîsê* as a *hapax legomenon* whose meaning is derived from that of the verb *rss* (to drizzle, sprinkle).

Vs. 3: In response to the request for a shelter two objections are raised against his visit at such an untimely hour. If the bride hesitates to admit the bridegroom to her house it is due not to selfishness on her part or a lack of interest, but for practical reasons, since she would need some time to get dressed and put on her shoes while she is feeling her way in the dark. The "tunic" (*kuttōnet*) is a garment worn both by men and women, differing though by its length and form. Another inconvenience she has to face is her groping barefoot on the naked floor until reaching the place where she had left her shoes. The verb *ṭnp* (to soil) is a *hapax legomenon* borrowed from Aramaic. For the personal pronoun of the 3rd person plural, added to a word as a suffix, the Hebrew frequently uses the masculine rather than the feminine form: *ʾaṭann^e fēm* (I soil them), referring to *raglay* (my feet) which is a feminine noun (Joüon, *Gr* § 149b).

Vs. 4: As the delay was being prolonged the bridegroom inserted his finger in the "keyhole" (*ḥōr*) in order to reach the bolt which could only be moved though by a key made specially to fit the bolt (Galling, 349). The reference to the "hand" (*yād*) in place of the finger is due to the use of a synecdoche, a figure of speech in which the whole stands for a part. The attempt at unlocking the door did not go unnoticed to the bride who felt sorry for his frustrated efforts, so that she says: "my heart was moved for him" (*mēʿay hāmû ʿālâw*). The sympathetic emotion is compared to a feeling of discomfort in the "entrails" (*mēʿîm*) which, in a figurative sense, are taken as the source of feelings. In place of MT *ʿālâw* (for him) there occurs a variant form *ʿālay* (in me) in some extant Hebrew manuscripts which was not adopted by any of the ancient versions. Among various interpretations of this passage the least probable that fits the context is the one which seeks to find a sexual symbolism underneath the meaning of some of the words here employed (Pope, 515–520).

Vs. 5: The scene here described deals with the bride's rising from bed. The pleonastic construction *qamtî ʾanî* (I arose) is not intended for emphasis on the subject of the sentence, but is peculiar to popular language (Robert-Tournay, 201). Liquid "myrrh" (*môr*), mentioned here and below in vs. 13, is a perfume prepared from pounded aromatic resin mixed with oil. This perfume was sprayed on the bedsheets (Prv 7:17), which, in turn, imparted the scent to the skin. From sheer excitement at the forthcoming meeting with the bridegroom, the bride's hands began to sweat. This phenomenon is described in hyperbolical terms "my hands dripped with myrrh" (*yāday nāṭ^e fû môr*). The fingers touching "the handles of the bolt" (*kappôt hammanʿûl*) transferred to them the scent of the myrrh. The plural noun "handles" is an indication of two or more sliding bolts being fixed on the inside of the door.

Vs. 6: The sudden departure of the bridegroom is expressed by two verbs in asyndetic coordination, e.g. "turned" (*ḥāmaq*) and "gone" (*ʿābār*). His absence led to a complete transformation of the bride's heightened expectation into deep frustration, as she says: "my soul failed me" (*nafšî yāṣʾâ*). The verbal form *bᵉdabbᵉrô* is ambiguous, because it can be derived either from *dbr* I (to withdraw, expel, persecute) or from *dbr* II (to speak). It is obvious that *bᵉdabbᵉrô* is not to be rendered "when he spoke" since the bridegroom withdrew silently from the house. Among the various meanings of the verb *dbr* I the one which is suitable to the text is translated as "when he withdrew."

The fruitless search for the absent bridegroom is described with terms identical to those used in the first "Nocturne" (3:1-5): *biqqaštîhû wᵉlōʾ mᵉṣāʾtîhû* (I sought him, but found him not); the only difference to be pointed out is the use of the pronominal suffix in its non-syncopated form. Furthermore, the search is not carried out in complete silence, as previously, but with a repeated calling of his name, e.g. *qᵉrāʾtîw* (I called him) "but he did not answer me" (*wᵉlōʾ ʿānānî*).

Vs. 7: The scene of this strophe is an urban environment; although no mention is made of streets and squares (3:2), the city is the same as that of the first "Nocturne" because of the presence of "watchmen who went about in the city" (*haššōmᵉrîm hassōbᵉbîm bāʿîr*). As explained above (3:3), the ostensive patrolling of the streets by detachments of soldiers is an indication of the city being placed under curfew as a repressive measure imposed by the occupying forces upon the local population so as to prevent an uprising against the foreign domination.

A significant item mentioned here is the reference to "walls" (*ḥōmôt*) which encircled a fortress or an urban center whose status was that of a fortified city. Before the exilic period, several fortified cities were to be found in Judah, e.g. Jerusalem, Lachish, and Azekah, all of which had their walls dismantled and the buildings leveled to the ground at the time of the Babylonian invasion in 587 B.C. During the Persian domination over Palestine, a garrison was stationed in the fortress of Beth-haccherem, located far from any other neighboring town (AHARONI, 418). Under Nehemiah's administration of Judah the city of Jerusalem regained the status of a fortified city when its walls were reconstructed so as to enclose the urban center, and, after completion, it was solemnly inaugurated in about 435 B.C. (Neh 12:27-43).

Unlike the peaceful atmosphere which pervades the search described in the first "Nocturne" (3:1-5), this scene shows the hostile attitude of the watchmen toward the inhabitants of the country. At the call of the bride for the bridegroom they approached her all of a sudden and struck and wounded her in order to reduce her to silence: "they beat me, they wounded me" (*hikkûnî pᵉṣāʿûnî*) and they "took away from me" (*nāśʾû . . . mēʿālay*) "my mantle" (*'et rᵉdîdî*). The "mantle" (*rᵉdîd*) is an article of dress worn by women on head and shoulders, whereas the "veil" (*ṣammâ*) is used for covering the face (4:1, 3; 6:7).

Vs. 8: The account of the events experienced in a dream ends with an appeal addressed by the bride to the "daughters of Jerusalem" that they speak for her to the bridegroom about her desire to enter into an alliance with him. It is significant that Jerusalem is mentioned in this context because it supplies the name for the city referred to in the preceding verse and identifies the elite of the Jewish priesthood as "daughters of Jerusalem," as explained above in 1:5. In the appeal to the "daughters" that they act as messengers of the bride's proposal to the bridegroom there is implicit a call for them to participate in the organization of the Jewish nation which the leader of the local population is trying to bring about.

The political structure of Judah's society has its principle of cohesion in the monarchical institution by virtue of the people's fealty pledged to the king—as expressed by the bride's "love" for her bridegroom—and by the pact of association between repatriate and autochthonous Jews.

The introductory phrase of the adjuration is the same as that employed in other passages (2:7; 3:5; 5:8; 8:4). But the clause which mentions "the gazelles or the hinds of the field," used elsewhere metaphorically to designate the rural population, does not occur in this text because the discrimination that formerly existed between repatriate and autochthonous Jews has already been overcome. The Hebrew particle *'im* introduces either a conditional sentence (5:8; 8:7, 9) or a negative clause (2:7; 3:5). The interrogative sentence "what shall you say to him?" (*mah-ttaggîdû lô*) is a rhetorical question, a figure of speech intended for making a statement rather than raising a question. Concerning the message to be transmitted to the bridegroom, its content is stated in the same words as those used in another passage (2:5) except for the conjunction *še* (that) instead of *kî* (because). In the concluding sentence occurs the participle *šeḥôlat . . . 'ānî* (that I am faint) as an attributive complement followed by a genitive of cause, *'ahᵃbâ* (on account of love). The word "love" is used in the Song as a technical term whose usage in ancient treaty literature dictates its political connotation, thus designating a "covenant."

Commentary: The Theme of the Restoration of the Monarchy (5:2-8)

The theme of this song is that of the restoration of the monarchy in Judah. The inhabitants had to proceed cautiously in this bold enterprise, maneuvering within the terms of the limited freedom which the Persian rulers had granted some of the nations conquered by them. Thus the author couches the theme in the disguise of a dream as a means of divulging the project of the political organization of the Jewish community in such a way that those who are acquainted with it know the meaning of the dream imagery, whereas those from whom this project should be concealed would regard the dream episode as some kind of reverie. If the Persian authorities suspected a concerted effort being made by the local leadership to get the people organized as a political community, they would take immediate action—under the pretext of quelling a burgeoning insurrection—and resort to repressive measures, such as the removal of the Jewish governor of Davidic descent from office, replacing him with a Persian official, and impose restrictions on social organizations under local leadership.

The chief characters that appear on the scene represent public figures of the Jewish community under Persian rule: the bridegroom personifies the Jewish governor and, as a descendant of the house of David, he is the legal heir to the throne; the bride is the leading figure representative of the autochthonous Jews; the "daughters of Jerusalem" represent the elite of the Jewish priesthood which the repatriated Jews had brought back to Jerusalem; the watchmen are the agents of Persia's foreign policy as enforced in occupied territories.

The visit at night is intended as a private meeting of the crown prince with the leader of the native population for the purpose of both reconfirming the covenant relationship, as expressed by the titles they apply to each other (my beloved, my sister, my friend, my dove, my perfect one). According to legal customs in vogue at that time, the very fact of a person paying a visit to someone and entering his house may have been symbolic of a covenant relationship being confirmed. Although the country's leader hoped that with the repatriation of the royal family one of its descendants would soon ascend to the throne, it was evident that the appropriate time for celebrating such a memorable event had not yet arrived. In fact, for as long as the country's leaders had to meet secretly and the occupying forces ordered curfews requiring citizens to remain indoors during hours of darkness, any attempt at changing the status quo in the country would surely be doomed to failure. These events are presented in the form of a dream in which the *dramatis personae* enact a pattern of happenings akin to those experienced in real life.

Since the leader of the Jewish population did not have enough political leverage to win the approval of the Persian authorities for the restoration of free institutions in Judah, he appealed to the elite of the Jewish priesthood to lend its support to the organization of national life under the auspices of the Davidic king. The theme of this song is an expansion of that dealt with in another song (3:1-5).

2. ✦ *The Attributes of the King (5:9-16)*

9 What is your beloved more than another beloved, *Chorus*
O fairest among women?
What is your beloved more than another beloved,
that you thus adjure us?
10 My beloved is all radiant and ruddy, *Bride*
distinguished among ten thousand.
11 His head is the finest gold;
his locks are date panicles,
black as a raven.
12 His eyes are like doves
beside springs of water,
bathed in milk,
sitting beside a pool.
13 His cheeks are like beds of spices
with tufts of aromatic herbs.
His lips are lilies,
distilling liquid myrrh.
14 His wrists are bracelets,
set with gems of Tarshish.
His body is ivory work,
encrusted with sapphires.
15 His legs are alabaster columns,
set upon bases of gold.
His appearance is like Lebanon,
choice as the cedars.
16 His mouth is most sweet,
and he is altogether desirable.
This is my beloved and this is my friend,
O daughters of Jerusalem.

Accented Transliteration (5:9-16)

9 *mah-ddôdēḱ middṓd*
hayyāfā́h bannāšī́m
mah-ddôdēḱ middṓd
šekkā́kâ hišbaʿtā́nû

10 *dôdî́ ṣaḥ weʾādôm*
dāgûl mērebābā́
11 *rōʾšṓ ketem pā́z*
qewuṣṣôtā́w taltallî́m
šeḥōrôt kāʿôrḗb
12 *ʿênā́w keyônî́m*
ʿal-ʾafiqḗ mā́yim
rōḥaṣṓt beḥālā́b
yōšebṓt ʿal-millḗʾt
13 *leḥāyā́w kaʿarûgát habbṓśem*
migdelṓt merqāḥî́m
śiftôtā́w šôšannî́m
nōṭefṓt mṓr ʿōbḗr
14 *yādā́w gelîlḗ zāhā́b*
memullāʾî́m battaršî́š
mēʿā́w ʿéšet šḗn
meʿulléfet sappîrî́m
15 *šôqā́w ʿammûdḗ šḗš*
meyussādî́m ʿal-ʾadnê-fā́z
marʾēhû kallebānṓn
bāḥûr kāʾarāzî́m
16 *ḥikkṓ mamtaqqî́m*
wekullṓ maḥamaddî́m
zeh dôdî́ wezeh rēʿî́
benṓt yerûšālā́im

Literary Analysis (5:9-16)

The song is divided into seven strophes which describe the king at the moment of enthronement and investiture with the royal insignia. The first strophe (vs. 9), formulated as a rhetorical question, mediates the transition between the previous song and this one and serves to introduce the graphic description of the person of the king. The second (vss. 10-11) refers to the color of the king's complexion and of the locks of his hair; the third (vs. 12) describes the eyes; the fourth (vs. 13) mentions his cheeks and lips; the fifth (vs. 14) specifies the ornaments worn on the wrist and royal robe; the sixth (vs. 15) refers to his legs and haughty appearance, and the seventh (vs. 16) alludes to his mouth and sums up the descriptive elements with the praise of the person. In conclusion, there follows an explanation which relates admiration for the king with the recognition of his authority and submission to his rule.

Poetic and rhetorical devices that occur in the song are sound repetition: alliteration *m-l* (vs. 14b + d); repetition of a sentence: refrain (vs. 9a + c). Figures of relationship: the synecdoche "his head is the finest gold" which denotes the artifact (i.e. the royal crown) by means of the material from which it is made (vs. 11a); the simile "his locks are black as a raven," "his eyes are like doves," "his cheeks are like beds of spices," "his appearance is like Lebanon," "choice as the cedars," and the metaphor "his head is the finest gold," "his locks are date panicles," "his lips are lilies," "his wrists are bracelets," "his body is ivory work," "his legs are alabaster columns."

Vocabulary Analysis (5:9-16)

Vs. 9: The introductory sentences, expressed as an interrogation and delivered by the chorus in lieu of the "daughters of Jerusalem," are employed as a figure of speech intended to arouse the reader's sympathy toward the king whose royal symbols and haughty expression are described in considerable detail in the following strophes. The figure of the king singled out for description outranks the rulers of the neighboring countries because he is endowed with attributes and powers that are associated with him alone. For comparisons founded either on likeness, difference, or superiority, the Hebrew uses the word *min* which functions as either a partitive or a comparative particle (*GK* § 119wN). Since degrees of comparison and dissimilarity are indicated in Hebrew by the comparative *min*, the sentence in question can be rendered in two ways: "what is your beloved different from any other beloved" or "what is your beloved more than another beloved." The preference for one of the two renderings depends upon the identification of the rank to which these persons belong and are set in contrast with each other. As regards their rank, all of them are governors under the auspices of the Persian overlord. What distinguishes the Jewish governor from all others is his royal descent from the house of David and the authority bestowed on him by divine ordinance and hereditary right.

As the king of Judah outranks the governors of other countries so too the Jewish nation—personified as a woman—surpasses its neighbors by her beauty as the "fairest among women" (*hayyāfāh bannāšîm*). The verb of adjuration is the same as that of the preceding verse "you adjure us" (*hišba'tānû*). The verbal form used here is the masculine instead of the feminine (*hišba'tînû*) which is quite unusual in the Hebrew language (JOÜON, *Gr* § 62f). The subordinating conjunction *še* (so that) is prefixed to the adverb *kākâ* (thus) whose emphatic form occurs in later Hebrew (ROBERT-TOURNAY, 210).

Vs. 10: The reference to the color of the king's complexion is meant as an indication of his noble lineage. "Radiant" (*ṣaḥ*) skin with a "ruddy" (*'ādôm*) color is typical of a nobleman's complexion to judge from a description of the externals of Judah's youthful princes whose white skin is compared to the whiteness of milk and the radiance of snow, while the healthily ruddy color of their complexion is likened to the color of coral (Lam 4:7). To illustrate this with a recently published text we refer to an Ethiopic popular song which mentions the white and ruddy skin as a sign of noble lineage (LEE, *VT* 21, 609). With these external features the figure of the king is easily to be identified among "ten thousand" (*r^ebābâ*) common citizens. The passive participle *dāgûl* (distinguished) is derived from the verb *dgl* I (to be conspicuous).

Vs. 11: The description of the king's figure displays the relevant features of his body from head to feet. "His head" (*rō'šô*) is adorned with "gold" (*ketem*) of the "finest" (*pāz*) quality, which symbolizes the royal crown by applying the figure of speech called synecdoche to denote the artifact by means of the metal from which it is made. "His locks" (*q^ewuṣṣôtâw*)—with a variant spelling above in 5:2—are likened to "date panicles" (*taltallîm*), a *hapax legomenon* whose meaning is uncertain. If this word is connected with the Akkadian *taltallū*, which designates the pollen of the date panicle, its meaning in Hebrew would be, by extension, the staminate inflorescence of the date palm. According to a custom in vogue in Mesopotamia, the pollination of date palms has been carried out artificially since antiquity by someone manually applying the pollen obtained from a male inflorescence to the female flower, because natural pollination by insects and wind is slow and unreliable, resulting in a low yield (HERODOTUS, *Hist.* I, 193). Since the date palm is representative of the fruit trees cultivated in Judah, the comparison between the locks of hair and the date panicle points to the royal task of caring for the country's fruit crop. In order to illustrate this we refer to Assyrian sculptures which represent winged figures, priests, farmers, and the king in the act of fertilizing date panicles manually. A relief of Ashurnasirpal II (883-859 B.C.) shows the king pollinating a date palm as he is clad in his royal garb which is embroidered with motifs representing the fecundation of a palm tree (PIJOÁN, *SA* II, 348). The attributive adjunct "black as a raven" (*š^eḥōrôt kā'ôrēb*) specifies the color of the hair.

Vs. 12: The eyes are regarded not as mere organs of sight, but as a mirror of the soul because they provide the physiognomy with a vivid expression. Comparisons drawn from idyllic scenery depicting doves sitting on the bank of a brook supply a number of images for the eye. Special emphasis is given to the radiance of the eye, because in Akkadian the "radiant eye" (*ênu namirtu*) is used to designate the benevolent attitude of a god or king toward his subject (DHORME, 76). The pupil is likened to a dove, the white of the eyeball to milk, the tear glands to springs of water, and the iris to a pool.

The word *millēʾt* is a *hapax legomenon* whose meaning is uncertain; if connected with the Akkadian *milû*, "flood" (MEEK, quoted by POPE, 539), *millēʾt* would denote the ring filled with pigment cells lying within the eye, i.e. the iris. In another text (7:5), the radiant eyes are compared to pools (*berēkôt*) on whose surface are reflected the rays of the sun.

Vs. 13: The cheeks framed by a dense beard are compared to "beds of spices" (*ʿarûgôt habbōśem*) of a garden, because on festive occasions the men used to impregnate their beards with sweet-smelling oils. Rather than MT *ʿarûgat* (bed) in the singular, we read *ʿarûgôt* in the plural with some Hebrew manuscripts and the LXX. Another comparison drawn from horticulture are the "tufts of aromatic herbs" (*migdelôt merqāḥîm*) which stand out among the scented plants cultivated in the garden beds. *Merqāḥîm* is a *hapax legomenon* signifying unguents or aromatic herbs; its underlying verb *rqḥ* (to mix) is used in reference to the preparation of perfumes. Some commentators adopt the LXX's emendation of *migdelôt* (towers, tufts) to *megaddelôt* (growing), thus changing a coordinate into a subordinate sentence (KRINETZKI, 191; POPE, 540; RUDOLPH, 159; WÜRTHWEIN, 57).

As a metaphor for "his lips" (*śiftôtâw*) are mentioned "lilies" (*šôšannîm*), whose bell-shaped flowers illustrate the shape of the lips rather than their crimson color which would only be feasible if the word *šôšannîm* be altered to *šānî* (crimson). The fluent speech delivered by the king on this occasion is compared to "liquid myrrh" (*môr ʿōbēr*) which the lips "distill" (*nōṭefôt*). The message and the emotional appeal of the king's words to the assembly deal with the setting out of his government policy. He lays down thereby as a norm of his dealing with his subjects the law which God bequeathed to the chosen people (Ps 101). On the other hand, MOWINCKEL inferred from Ps 2 that on the accession to royal office the king proclaimed the divine origin of kingship and admonished the leaders of the people to pay homage to him and to submit to his own and Yahweh's overlordship (*He That Cometh*, 64).

Vs. 14: "Hand" (*yād*) in biblical usage may imply also the wrist and the forearm. "Bracelets of gold" (*gelîlê zāhāb*) are worn by the king on the wrists as insignia of royal power (2 Sm 1:10). The term *gelîlîm* is used elsewhere in connection with curtains fastened on "rings" (Est 1:6). These valuable bracelets are wrought in gold and encrusted with precious stones. The participle *memullāʾîm* (encrusted) is associated with the goldsmith's work (GERLEMAN, 177). High quality items imported from afar are identified by their provenance; "Tarshish," which probably is the ancient city of Tartessos located at the mouth of the Guadalquivir in Spain (GALLING, 332), may stand for one of the more distant seaports of culturally advanced regions in the Mediterranean basin.

The word *mēʿîm* designates the entrails (5:4) as well as the abdomen (5:14) and by extension the body. The figure of the king clad in his royal robe is compared to "ivory work" (*'ešet šēn*) in reference to the ivory inlay on the back of the coronation chair. The term *'ešet* is a *hapax legomenon* whose meaning is uncertain; in Mishnaic Hebrew it is used in the sense of "wrought metal, bar, polished block." In connection with the decorative arts, this term designates ivory plaques inlaid in furniture and wall panels. The embroidery on the royal robe is compared to the sapphires "encrusted" (*me'ullefet*) on the frame of the coronation chair. "Sapphires" have a bright blue color like lapis lazuli.

Vs. 15: "His legs" (*šôqâw*) are like "alabaster columns" (*'ammûdê šēš*) which are characteristic of the Achaemenian palaces. Since the enthronement ceremony, described in this text, is held not in the throne room but in a public square, the "alabaster columns" are equivalent to the "columns of silver" to which the legs of the coronation chair have been compared above in 3:10. The "bases" (*'adānîm*) sheathed in gold, similar to the floor of Solomon's temple overlaid with gold (1 Kgs 6:30), represent the platform covered with a carpet under the coronation chair and provide an image for the king's brocade shoes stitched with gold thread.

"His appearance" (*mar'ēhû*) reflects a grandeur to be compared to nothing less than the summits of the Lebanon massif. Another image of the "choice" (*bāḥûr*) figure of the king, rising high above the common citizen, is the "cedars" (*'arāzîm*) standing out among the trees of Lebanon.

Vs. 16: The last feature mentioned in the description of the king is his mouth. The "palate" (*ḥēk*) denotes the organ of speech. By means of a grammatical construction which employs a noun in the plural of abstraction, i.e. *mamtaqqîm* (most sweet) as a predicate, the stress is placed on the subject of the sentence. Thus, the mouth is described as sweet by reason of the declaration and its effect on the listeners. From the account of the enthronement rites performed in Judah, during the monarchical period, we infer that the declaration here implied refers to the appointment of the ministers of state (DE VAUX, *AI*, 107). With the praise of the person in "its entirety" (*kullô*) the description lays stress on the "loveliness" (*maḥamaddîm*) of the sovereign enthroned, thus representing, in a proleptic view, the event whose decurrence in the near future the people ardently desire.

The final sentence of this song takes up the introductory verse (vs. 9) on the identity of the bridegroom and states the covenant relationship between king and people. The expressions "my beloved" (*dôdî*) and "my friend" (*rē'î*) are to be taken not as terms of endearment, but as a set of titles applied to allies.

Commentary: The Theme of the Enthronement (5:9-16)

The theme of this song is that of the enthronement of the Davidic king as sovereign of Judah restored as a monarchy. In a proleptic view, the author describes the enthronement rite which marks the assumption of power by the king. The data referring to the royal ritual serve as setting to the portrait. Yet the realistic representation of the human figure is strictly subordinated to its setting which was intended to be identified only by the members of the royalist party who enter the scene in the opening strophe as qualified interlocutors of the bride. In response to the question raised about the identity of the bridegroom, a detailed picture of the enthroned king is presented in the following strophes. Thus, he is pictured as endowed with power, symbolized by his royal insignia: the crown (vs. 11) and the bracelet (vs. 14). Specific features of the monarch's appearance indicate his noble lineage (vs. 10), his benevolence toward those under his rule (vs. 12), and his task of fostering the economic life of Judah (vs. 11b + c; 13a + b). In the description of his body analogies are provided, drawn both from the coronation chair and the royal robe in which he is clad during the state ceremony (vs. 14c + d). The coronation chair on which the king is seated during the enthronement ritual is indicated by the reference to the columns of alabaster (vs. 15a + b). The passages referring to the lips and the mouth of the sovereign are an allusion to the proclamation of his government policy (vs. 13c + d) and to the appointment of the ministers of state (vs. 16).

The nexus between the enthronement and coronation rites is indicated by the reference to Lebanon whence cedar wood is imported for the construction of the coronation chair (3:9). In analogy with the imposing height of the summits of the Lebanese mountains and the lofty cedars of Lebanon the exalted figure of the king is extolled as God's "chosen" leader of the people (vs. 15c + d). At the enthronement, the king takes possession of his throne and is empowered to perform his royal functions as God's representative and ruler of the people, following the law of the monarchy which had been laid down in Judah in olden times. The political organization of the community is based on the monarchical institution secured by a pact of fealty between people and king and a pact of association between autochthonous and repatriate Jews integrated into the nation. The theme of the enthronement is related to that of the coronation, dealt with in another song (3:9-11).

3. ✦ *The Favorite Resort (6:1-3)*

1 Whither has your beloved gone, *Chorus*
O fairest among women?
Whither has your beloved turned,
that we may seek him with you?

2 My beloved has gone down to his garden, *Bride*
to the beds of spices,
to pasture amongst the gardens,
and to gather lilies.
3 I am my beloved's and my beloved is mine;
he is a shepherd among the lilies.

Accented Transliteration (6:1-3)

1 *ʾā́nâ hālák dôdḗk*
hayyāfā́h bannāšî́m
ʾā́nâ pānā́h dôdḗk
ûnebaqšénnû ʿimmā́k
2 *dôdî́ yārád legannṓ*
laʿarûgṓt habbṓśem
lirʿṓt baggannî́m
welilqṓṭ šôšannî́m
3 *ʾanî́ ledôdî́ wedôdî lî́*
hārōʿéh baššôšannî́m

Literary Analysis (6:1-3)

This song about the bridegroom's "favorite resort" describes the country of Judah as a magnificent garden. The whole section consists of three strophes: in the first, the chorus inquires after the bridegroom's whereabouts (vs. 1); the second sets out the reply of the bride (vs. 2), and the third is formulated in two sentences which contain the covenant formula and information about the function of the bridegroom (vs. 3).

As regards the poetic and rhetorical devices that occur in the song we may mention sound repetition: assonance *i–o* (vs. 2cd), alliteration *l–š* (vs. 2cd), internal rhyme *-ôt* (vs. 2bc) and *-î* (vs. 3a), and end rhyme *-îm* (vs. 2bc); word repetition: "beloved" (five times), "lilies" (twice), "garden/s" (twice); anaphora *ʾānâ–ʾānâ* (vs. 1); repetition of a sentence: refrain (vs. 3a); repetition of structural patterns: chiasmus "garden–pasture–gardens" (vs. 2a-c), "lilies–shepherd–lilies" (vs. 2d-3b); anthypophora, *subiectio* in the Latin, a figure of speech consisting of a question followed by an answer (vs. 1-2). There is a figure of emphasis: the hyperbole "fairest among women," and a figure of resemblance: the use of images, e.g. "garden" for the country of Judah, "gardens" and "beds of spices" for the different Judean districts, "lilies" for the social groups, and "shepherd" for the king.

Vocabulary Analysis (6:1-3)

Vs. 1: The question directed by the "daughters of Jerusalem" to the bride is a literary device which gives occasion for the matter at hand to be developed highlighting the person identified under the title of "beloved" (*dôd*), repeated five times in this song. The same device occurs at the beginning of the preceding song (5:9) when it is asked who is the beloved. Here what is in question is the direction which he has taken. It is not a question then of expanding the fact of his absence, but of indicating the place of his presence. The questions "whither did he go?" (*'ānâ hālak*) and "whither has he turned?" (*'ānâ pānāh*) are replied to with an indication of the place to which he went down (vs. 2). The declarative sentence is linked to the second interrogative sentence by a conjunctive *waw* with a final or causal sense, i.e. "that we may seek him" (*ûnebaqšennû*).

The praise of the beautiful bride as "the fairest among women" (*hayyāfāh bannāšîm*) is an expression of courtesy of conventional gallant language (1:8; 5:9; 6:1).

Vs. 2: The rite of enthronement described in the preceding song is followed by the king's taking charge of the country. The road which leads from the city to the different points of the territory goes down (*yrd*) from the top of the hill to the valley, and from there it goes on to mountains and plains. The country of Judah is "his garden" (*gannô*), whose districts are denominated "beds of spices" (*'arûgôt habbōśem*) or simply "gardens" (*gannîm*). In the beds balsam trees are cultivated, in the gardens, fruit-bearing trees. By developing its family life in the same place as the activities of production and trade of aromatic resins and the fruits of the orchard, the population is organized in a rural community. With the official visit to this community the king has as his object to integrate its members into the political body of the nation.

In another context (4:12, 16; 5:1), the word "garden" designates the nation established in the territory of Judah, whose geographical characteristics serve as an image to describe the population. However, it is not only this word but the scene as such which the majority of commentators interpret in another sense. To describe the journey of the bridegroom as a visit to the orchard of his property, some substitute the phrase "so as to pasture amongst gardens" (*lir'ôt baggannîm*) by an emendation "so as to see the vineyards" (*lir'ôt baggefānîm*), because of the influence of a similar clause in another text (6:11).

The other area of the territory of Judah included on the route of the official visit of the king to the communities is the region of pastures which includes steppes, the slopes of hills, and valleys of unarable soil too arid and stony for agriculture. Because of the geographical configuration of the mountainous region of Judah, the orchards and the cultivated lands on the terraces of the hills are like "gardens" (*gannîm*) interspersed among the steppes where the flocks pasture. But into any of these gardens, lined by walls, the shepherd does not enter to pasture the animals; the preposition *b^e^* (amongst, close) as a prefix of "gardens" and "lilies" (6:3) denotes proximity (*BDB, b^e^* II, 1, 89).

The object of the official visit of the king to this region "so as to pasture" (*lir'ôt*) the population which lives from shepherding is to organize its integration into the political life of the nation, assuring it the same rights of citizenship as those of the agricultural population. The verb "to pasture" (*r'h*) applied to the activity of the king has the sense of "governing."

The description of the official visit ends with the phrase "so as to gather lilies" (*lil^e^qôṭ šôšannîm*). Now, the lily, a native plant of that region, is found to be growing in the fields and the valleys and serves as an image with which to designate, in the plural, the social groups of the autochthonous population of Judah (4:5; 6:2, 3). The same word, in the singular, refers to the leading figure representative of the native population (2:1-2). With the verb *lqṭ* (to pluck, gather) is designated, in a figurative sense, the king's action inserting that part of population into the national life, the population which had been kept until then at the margin of social and political organization.

This scene is interpreted in a different way by other commentators. Some explain it as a romantic gesture of the bridegroom gathering lilies to offer a bunch to his bride (Asensio, 610; Buzy, 341; Pope, 556). Others attribute to it a metaphoric sense as an expression of appreciation of the bridegroom for the bride: the lilies being an image of her exceeding virtues (Delitzsch, 108), of feminine charms (Colombo, 103; Gerleman, 180; Robert-Tournay, 228; Rudolph, 161; Würthwein, 59), the happy days of matrimonial life (Krinetzki, 197), or the idyllic life of the countryside (Piatti, 155).

Vs. 3: In this verse there appears the formula of the covenant between bride and bridegroom in the form set out by the pact which institutes it. Although the formula does not mention the commitment assumed because of the pact of alliance, it is a question of a pact of submission of the people in relation to the king, since the bridegroom is the literary figure of the king of Judah whose function is indicated in the same verse. At the same time the bride represents the leader of the native population of the country. According to the custom of the ancient Near East, on the occasion of the enthronement of a new king there was enacted the rite of his making a covenant with the people who swore an oath of fealty to the sovereign (Kalluveettil, 59–61).

The text does not say explicitly that the two allies had pronounced a covenant formula or had formulated the covenant by writing. However, from the characteristics of the language and because of its occurrence in another context it can be concluded that this formula, pronounced on another occasion, is repeated in different circumstances (2:16, 6:3; 7:11). The phrase is formulated in a declarative style which is characterized by the employment of the 1st and 3rd person of the personal pronoun, while in a dialogue style it is the 2nd person of the pronouns that is used.

If in the context there does not appear a reference to another rite, which establishes the covenant, the oral declaration of the formula constitutes the pact enacting rite (KALLUVEETTIL, 103f). But here it is only the bride who speaks while the bridegroom is making an official visit to the communities spread around the countryside. The reason for the allusion to the formal aspect of the covenant between king and people is the necessity of obtaining from the inhabitants of Judah their support for restoring the monarchy, the highest form of political organization to which the Jewish population could aspire in the post-exilic period.

What is the function of the covenant formula? According to its tenor this formula is classified in three categories: in the first, it *effects* a covenant relationship; in the second, it *reaffirms* an existing covenant; and in the third, it *refers* to the existence of the covenant. Thus, in the first case it *establishes* a covenant or *reestablishes* an abrogated covenant. In the second case it *renews* the existing union on the occasion of the enthronement of the king (KALLUVEETTIL, 103). This song expresses the renovation of the covenant since it seeks to restore the monarchy in the framework of the *ancien régime* previous to the exile.

With the phrase "he is a shepherd" (*hārōʿeh*), enunciated at the enactment of the pact, the inferior partner between the allies declares his submission to the superior (KALLUVEETTIL, 107). In the ancient Near East it was customary to designate the king by the title of "shepherd" instituted in the office of kingship by the tutelary deity of the nation. In Israel, however, this title was also applied to the leaders of the people starting from the exilic period (*THAT* II, 793f). The function of the bridegroom as "shepherd amongst the lilies" (*hārōʿeh baššôšannîm*) refers to his heading of the government as soon as he is endowed with royal authority to rule the people of Judah.

Commentary: The Theme of the King's Taking Charge of the Country (6:1-3)

The theme of this song is that of the king's taking charge of the country, recently instituted in his office by the rite of enthronement. In the perspective of the restored monarchy the king is presented in exercise of his function as head of government journeying through the country on official visit to the communities. The image of the royal garden applied to Judah evokes the ancient southern kingdom which for four centuries up to its conquest by the Babylonians was an independent state under the rule of the Davidic dynasty.

The various administrative districts of the country are not classified, according to the criteria of demographic density, by cities and villages, but, according to socio-economic criteria, by agricultural and pastoral regions. It is there that the communities of work are organized. While the demographic density remains stable, these sectors offer necessary conditions for the survival of the population. But the repatriation of exiles and their settlement in the cities and villages demanded a restructuring of the sectors of production and a planning of national life. The problem of absorbing these groups of newcomers, who appeared in successive waves, would not be solved by the hospitable commiseration and the communitarian sharing of the little that was possessed. It was necessary for the central government to create new productive and commercial mechanisms and also a communitarian context organized on the basis of the political equality of all the inhabitants.

The visit of the king to various local groups of the rural districts has as its object to organize an agrarian and pastoral society in communities which could be integrated into the political body of the nation, thus avoiding the marginalization and the breakdown of the relationship between autochthonous and repatriate Jews. While the repatriates have as their leaders the elite of the Jewish priesthood, represented by the "daughters of Jerusalem," the autochthonous Jews have as their leader the "bride" who, as a representation of the native population, presents the project of the restoration of the monarchy as a means of integration of all social groups through the pact of submission to the king and association between autochthonous and repatriate Jews.

The theme of the king's taking charge of the country complements that of the repatriation of the heir to the throne of Judah (3:6-8). It is to be noted that the pacific situation in the whole kingdom permits the king on his official visit to the various communities to dispense with the military escort which offered him security on his return to the country.

Poem VI *The Bride's Attractiveness* (6:4–7:10)

1 ✦ *The Charming Bride (6:4-7)*

4 You are beautiful as Tirzah, *Bridegroom*
my friend,
comely as Jerusalem,
splendid as the constellations.
5 Turn away your eyes from me,
for they disturb me.
Your hair is like a flock of goats,
moving down the slopes of Gilead.
6 Your teeth are like a flock of ewes,
that have come up from the washing,
all of them bear twins,
not one among them is bereaved.
7 Your cheeks are like halves of a pomegranate
behind your veil.

Accented Transliteration (6:4-7)

4 *yāfāh ʾát raʿyātî́ k*^{e}*ṭirṣā́h*
nāʾwấ kîrûšālā́im
ʾ^{a}*yummấ kannidgālốt*
5 *hāsēbbî́ ʿênáyik minnegdî́*
šehḗm hirhîbúnî
śaʿrḗk k^{e}*ʿḗder hāʿizzî́m*
šeggāl^{e}*šû́ min-haggilʿā́d*

6 *šinnáyik ke'ḗder hārᵉḥēlîm*
šeʿālû min-hāraḥṣâ
šekkullā̂m mat'îmôt
wᵉšakkulâ 'ên bāhém
7 *kᵉfélaḥ hārimmôn raqqātēk*
mibbáʿad lᵉṣammātēk

Literary Analysis (6:4-7)

Poem VI on the bride's attractiveness (6:4–7:10) comprises four songs which complement and amplify the thematic content dealt with previously in poem IV on the beauty of the bride (4:1–5:1).

This song in praise of the "charming bride" has two parts: the first presents the general aspect of the person (vs. 4); the second sets out specific particularities of the woman's facial features framed by black hair (vss. 5-7), repeating some descriptive elements which had been mentioned before (4:1-3).

The poetic and rhetorical devices that can be verified in the song are the end rhyme *-ēk* (vs. 7); the paronomasia *šekkullām–šakkulâ* (vs. 6cd); the antiphrasis, a figure of speech which consists in the use of a word in a sense opposite to the proper meaning, e.g. "splendid" for "terrific" (vs. 4c); the simile "beautiful as Tirzah, comely as Jerusalem, splendid as the constellations," "hair like a flock of goats," "teeth like a flock of ewes," "cheeks like halves of a pomegranate."

Vocabulary Analysis (6:4-7)

Vs. 4: The leader of the population of Judah is denominated by the title "friend" as in 4:1, indicating the relation of friendship between king and people. The pleasure of the king in this relationship is expressed by the qualification of the friend's beauty comparing her, in an ascending order, with Tirzah, the ancient capital of the northern kingdom, with Jerusalem, the capital of the southern kingdom, and then with the constellations which are groups of stars of the heavenly sphere. The reason for the constellations being mentioned here is the belief held in antiquity that special relations existed between celestial bodies and countries (*Kl.P.* I, 661). In order to find out which group of stars presided over a particular country, the astrologers superimposed the map of the world on the astronomical map, which was based on the presupposed geocentric universe, so as to locate the respective country against the background of the stars' position. The term of comparison is the beauty which qualifies the three, and the mode of comparison is the height both of cities set on the top of hills and the relation to the stars in the heights of the firmament.

Tirzah (*tirṣāh*) had been the capital of the northern kingdom, after Shechem and Penuel, under Jeroboam I or Baasha until the era of the rule of Omri (884–874 B.C.), when they were substituted by Samaria. The reference to Tirzah instead of Samaria gives value to its autochthonous population in relation to the Samaritans who were considered to be of a spurious origin, a mixture of Assyrian officials, Babylonians, and Persians, as well as other ethnic groups introduced by the Assyrians (ALT, *Kl.S.* II, 316–337). The mention of Tirzah is, according to the figure of speech called synecdoche, a literary device used for designating the inhabitants.

The adjectives qualifying the beauty of the bride are three: *yāfāh* translated as "beautiful" (1:15; 4:1, 7; 6:4) and "fair" (1:8; 5:9; 6:1, 10); *nā'wâ* translated as "comely" (6:4); *'ᵃyummâ* translated as "splendid" (6:4, 10), lit. "terrific"; the use of the word in a sense opposite to its proper meaning is a figure of speech called antiphrasis.

The meaning of the word *nidgālôt* (constellations) is generally interpreted in another sense based on its verbal form as a passive participle *Niphal* of *dgl:* "battalions" (BUZY, 343; JOÜON, *Ct,* 263; ROBERT-TOURNAY, 234; WINANDY, 137), "squadrons" (ASENSIO, 610; KEEL, 201; KRINETZKI, 125; WÜRTHWEIN, 59; ZAPLETAL, 125), "front of combat" (DELITZSCH, 108), "mirage" (GERLEMAN, 183), "unfolded banners" (COLOMBO, 105; RAVASI, 114), "standard bearers" (RICCIOTTI, 250), "squadrons with unfolded banners" (PIATTI, 161; POUGET-GUITTON, 169), and "impressive things" (LYS, 236).

Vs. 5: With this verse there begins the description of the four parts of the head, through comparisons referring to the respective colors: black hair, white teeth, colored cheeks, except for the eyes whose brilliance is specified by the fascination which they caused in the bridegroom. The aspect of fascination of the eyes of the bride, compared to the jewels of a necklace, results from their brilliance which constitutes the term of comparison between eyes and jewels (4:9). The brilliant eyes have the effect of "ravishing the heart" (*lbb*) of the bridegroom (4:9) and of "disturbing" (*rhb*) his innermost being. The sense of the verb *rhb* is "to perturb, agitate, importunate" (Is 3:5; Ps 90:10; 138:3; Prv 6:3; Ct 6:5) without any connotation of sexual excitation as has been suggested by LUTHER and WALDMAN (cf. POPE, 564f).

The majority of feminine Hebrew words which designate members or organs of the human body permit the occasional use of the masculine gender, whence the anomalous concordance between *'ênayik* (your eyes), which is a feminine noun, and the pronoun *hēm* (they) as well as the verbal form *hirhîbunî* (they disturb me) which are both masculine (cf. the interpretation of the text in 4:9).

The description of the hair is identical to that of 4:1, except for the variation *min haggil'ād* (from Gilead) instead of *mēhar gil'ād* (from Mount Gilead).

Vs. 6: This verse repeats word for word the text in 4:2, except for the word "the ewes" (*hārᵉḥēlîm*) instead for the passive participle "the shorn ones" (*haqqᵉṣûbôt*).

Vs. 7: In contrast with the two preceding verses which modify a word in the repeated text, this is a literal quote from 4:3. The repetition of words or phrases is a literary device used in various songs of this book. As to its end, it is necessary to distinguish two functions in various texts: the first is stylistic, characterized by a sense of beauty in its phraseology, verbal construction, and melody, e.g. repetition of sound, word, and phrase; the second is structural as a point of reference in songs which have corresponding themes.

It is to be noted, however, that the Greek terminology in the definition of the rhetorical and poetic devices does not correspond perfectly to the Hebrew. Thus, the biblical poets are not accustomed to repeat in the same form thoughts formulated in another context merely for stylistic reason. They do this rather to indicate the connection between related songs. Thus, the text in 4:3, repeated in 6:7, brings together the themes of the nation (4:1-7) and the unified nation (6:4-7). Another example of the repetition of a whole sentence can be found in 2:6 and 8:3, since both songs (2:4-7 and 8:1-4) deal with the same theme, i.e. the capital. Another example of the multiple repetition of a sentence is the text of the formula of adjuration in 2:7, repeated in 3:5, and taken up again in an abbreviated form in 8:4, and with another tenor added in 5:8. The repetition of this text in various songs has the function of serving as point of reference to the corresponding themes: the two songs (2:4-7 and 8:1-4) have in common the theme of the capital and the other two songs (3:1-5 and 5:2-8) deal with the theme of the restoration of the monarchy.

The use of word repetition at the beginning or end of the song serves also in many cases to indicate the division between poetic units. Thus, in this book, the division between the different parts is not indicated by means of headings denoting topics, scenes, or persons. Because they have not paid attention to the structural function of word repetition, many commentators join together in the same song poetic units which deal with different themes.

Commentary: The Theme of the Unified Nation (6:4-7)

The theme of this song is that of the nation united, constituted by the native population of Judah and the groups of repatriate Jews, organized into a center of convergence and irradiation for the Israelites of the province of Samaria and the Jews of the diaspora. Ever since Cyrus, in 538 B.C., promulgated the edict of repatriation of the exiled Jews, the population of Judah had been organized into a social community raising itself up to the level of a faith-community, its temple and priesthood having been restored and solemnly inaugurated in 515 B.C. (Ezr 6:16-18). The hope of the imminent restoration of the monarchy and of Jerusalem, as the capital of the country, awoke in the people of Judah the desire to organize their social groups into a political community.

The reference to Tirzah, the ancient capital of the kingdom of Israel, is not an appeal to the Jews to widen their sphere of political influence to the surrounding countries. There is no question of carrying out again the exploits of king Josiah (640-609 B.C.), since a dispute for the control of the territories of the former kingdom of Israel would imply a confrontation with the Persian empire, whose military power only the Greeks could match as they showed in their victory over Xerxes in 480 B.C. The change of Samaria for Tirzah is an implicit affirmation of the Jewish aversion to the Samaritans and an expression of their solidarity with the autochthonous population of the province, those Israelites who were faithful to the religious traditions of their ancestors.

Even more auspicious perspectives open up to the people of Judah. The sovereign nation would assume its function as a center of irradiation. Its capital, Jerusalem, would be a cultural and religious axis for all the Jewish communities of the diaspora and the point of convergence of the minorities who have the Yahwistic faith. This relationship between the Jewish nation and the communities faithful to Yahwism is compared to the system of interstellar movements represented by the symbology of the bonds which tie distant stars (cf. Jb 38:31). Just as the constellations of astral space have a center which is in the visual horizon of the observer, according to ancient astronomy, in the same form the Jewish communities of the diaspora have their reference point in the people of Judah. The theme of this song complements that of the native nation, a theme that had been developed previously in 4:1-7.

2. ✦ *The Distinguished Bride (6:8-12)*

8 There are sixty queens and eighty wives, *Bridegroom*
and maidens without number.
9 My dove, my perfect one, is only one,
unique to her mother,
favorite of her that bore her.
The daughters see her and call her happy;
the queens and wives also, and they praise her.

10 "Who is this that looks forth like the dawn, *Chorus*
fair as the moon, bright as the sun,
splendid as the constellations?"
11 I went down to the nut orchard, *Bride*
to look at the blossoms of the valley,
to see whether the vines had budded,
whether the pomegranates were in bloom.
12 Before I was aware, my fancy set me
in a chariot of a nobleman of my people.

Accented Transliteration (6:8-12)

8 *šiššîm hḗmmâ melākốt*
ûšemōnîm pîlagšîm
wa'alāmốt 'ên mispā́r
9 *'aḥat hî' yônātî tammātî*
'aḥat hî' le'immā́h
bārâ hî' leyôladtā́h
rā'ûhā bānốt waye'aššerûhā
melākốt ûfîlagšîm wayehalelûhā
10 *mî-zō't hannišqāfâ kemô-šā́ḥar*
yāfā́h kallebānâ
bārâ kaḥammâ
'ayummâ kannidgālốt
11 *'el-ginnát 'egốz yārádtî*
lir'ốt be'ibbê hannā́ḥal
lir'ốt hafāreḥâ haggéfen
hēnḗṣû hārimmōnîm
12 *lō' yādá'tî nafšî śāmátnî*
markebốt 'ammî-nādîb

Literary Analysis (6:8-12)

This song in praise of the distinguished bride is divided into two parts which are linked by a transitional strophe. The first part, in two strophes (vss. 8-9), situates the community of Judah in the political context of surrounding nations personified by women of different social rank. The transitional strophe following it presents this community as an emergent nation with images drawn from astral space (vs. 10). The second part, in two strophes (vss. 11-12), describes the geographical environment of the Judean territory (vs. 11), and presents the Shulamite at the head of a body of delegates traveling in carriages to other countries so as to establish diplomatic relations with these foreign nations (vs. 12).

Poetic and rhetorical devices used in the song are sound repetition: alliteration *š–m* (vs. 8ab), assonance *a–i* (vs. 12), internal rhyme *-î* (vss. 9a, 12a); word repetition: anaphora *'aḥat hî'–'aḥat hî'* (vs.9), *lir'ôt–lir'ôt* (vs. 11); figures of relationship: number parallelism "sixty–eighty–without number" (vs. 8), metaphor "she is my dove" (vs. 9), simile "who is this . . . like the dawn, like the moon, like the sun, like the constellations?" (vs. 10); figures of emphasis: hyperbole (vs. 10) and rhetorical question (vs. 10).

Vocabulary Analysis (6:8-12)

Vs. 8: This verse presents various political communities, classified in three categories according to their form of political life. It is from within the political constellation of the surrounding nations that the community of Judah will begin its historical journey. Under Persian domination a single political administrative system was imposed on all the countries of the ancient Near East. These were organized into satrapies, provinces, and annexed regions. The populations of the respective administrative territories are represented in the song by feminine figures which personify them.

The "queens" (*meläkôt*) represent the vassal kingdoms of Persia and the satrapies of the empire. In the Old Testament the title "queen" (*malkâ*) is never applied to any consort of the kings of Israel. The round number "sixty" (cf. 3:7) has probably in this context merely the meaning of a multitude, even though more than sixty kingdoms had existed before the Persian domination. With their integration into the empire many of them were deprived of their monarchic institutions and their territories were reduced to the rank of a satrapy or a province. In the time of the emperor Xerxes I (486–464 B.C.) there were one hundred and twenty-seven provinces from India to Ethiopia (Est 1:1). As for the number of satrapies in the Persian empire, the inscription of Behistan, carved by Darius I (522–486 B.C.) at the beginning of his reign, lists only twenty-three (*DB* I, 12–17). Even though the same emperor had later added three more, the historian HERODOTUS mentions only twenty satrapies (*Hist.* III, 89).

The personal pronoun *hēmmâ* has the function of establishing a connection between subject and predicate of the noun-clause. The grammatical peculiarity of substituting the feminine pronoun by the masculine *hēmmâ* (they), although frequent in later books of the Old Testament, is rare with separate pronouns (JOÜON, *Gr* § 149c). The declarative sentence has its verb in the indicative mood "they are." However, the meaning of the text is modified, if vs. 8 is formulated as a concessive phrase subordinated to the principal phrase of the following verse (BUZY, 344; KRINETZKI, 204).

The numeric upgrading of sixty to eighty amplifies a numerous collectivity. The "wives" (*pîlagšîm*), lit. "secondary wives," represent provinces subordinated to the jurisdiction of a governor. The reason for personifying kingdoms and provinces by means of married women is based on the marriage bond which constitutes the term of comparison for the relationship between governor and governed. The social rank of these women symbolizes the forms of political life as well as the prerogative of self-government in the administrative and economic sectors which the Persians conceded to some of those nations represented by "queens," in contrast to those which did not possess this prerogative which are personified by "wives."

In the context of marriage in antiquity it is useful to distinguish between the polygamy of governors and that of citizens. For the sovereign, marriage was a question of public law, while for the simple citizen it was a question of private law. The marriages of the king had a political character for *raison d'état,* as sealing national and international alliances. The national and foreign wives of the monarch were classified into principal wives, who were free and of noble birth, and secondary wives, who were servants or slaves. The first were called "queens" (*melākôt*) or "noblewomen" (*nāšîm śārôt,* 1 Kgs 11:3); the others were "secondary wives" (*pîlagšîm*). To designate the wives of this inferior rank with the term "concubines" would be to impose the image of a contemporary phenomenon upon a quite different situation from the past (TOSATO, 176f).

The "maidens" (*ʿalāmôt*) represent regions annexed to the provinces, under the jurisdiction of a provincial governor. The term *ʿalmâ,* which has the generic meaning of "young woman," is used to designate maidens of very diverse socio-juridical conditions: unmarried women (e.g. Rebekah, Gn 24:43; the sister of Moses, Ex 2:8), or married women (Is 7:14; Prv 30:19), virgins (Gn 24:43; Ex 2:8), and non-virgins (Is 7:14; Prv 30:19), as well as amateur singers and dancers (Ex 15:20; Jgs 21:21).

In analogy with matrimonial laws, the social status of "queens" and "wives" is compared respectively to the political status of the kingdoms and of the provinces. The "maidens," who do not have a proper statute referring to their status in society, are an image of the regions annexed to the provinces. However, the communities localized in these regions did not fall prey to piecemeal absorption by the population of the respective territory, but preserved their ethnic and religious identity. For this reason the "maidens" designate, in a geographical and ethnic sense, the annexed regions (6:8, 9), and also, in a religious and ethnic sense, the Jewish communities of the diaspora (1:3).

The multitude of "maidens," although expressed in a vague form, viz. "without number" (*'ên mispār*), is without doubt more numerous than that of the "queens" and "wives," because of the ascending numbers: sixty–eighty–without number.

Vs. 9: In contrast with the Persian empire, which gloried in its domination over many nations, the kingdom of Judah is constituted by one single nation. In the sentence structure, the predicate "only one" (*'aḥat hî'*) is highlighted by its being placed at the beginning so as to emphasize the adversative relationship between the two phrases.

The expression "my dove" (*yônātî*) is a title based on metaphor, whose extrinsic elements illustrate qualities intrinsic to the person who assumes the commitment of the covenant (cf. 5:2). The metaphor is worked out in the text above (2:14) by means of two expressions: "to show a comely face," meaning adherence, and "to let a sweet voice be heard," indicating consent. This title alludes therefore to the adherence and to the consent to the covenant, formalized in terms of submission of the nation to the king (cf. 2:16-17). "My perfect one" (*tammātî*) refers to the person whose behavior is characterized by integrity in the relationship between allies, thus avoiding attitudes incompatible with their status (cf. 4:7).

"Her mother" (*'immāh*) is a poetic personification of the Israelite nation (1:6; 3:4; 6:9; 8:1, 2). The community of Judah had reason to be proud of its nationality, because of its historical roots as an independent kingdom for four centuries. The word "mother" designates the pre-exilic nation, while its offspring in the post-exilic period is the community of Judah under the leadership of the Shulamite.

Two qualities specify the community of Judah in the post-exilic period, i.e. "unique" (*'aḥat*) and "favorite" (*bārâ*). The first restricts the bounds of this community to the territory of Judah, in opposition to the Persian empire which includes many nations. The second sets out its status as a chosen community which in the biblical theology of the Old Testament expresses the relationship between God and the people of Israel (*THAT* I, 283–286). The *locus classicus* of the election of Israel in the Old Testament is found in Dt 7:6-8 in which the object of the divine election is designated by the expressions "holy people" (*'am qādôš*) and "people of exclusive property" (*'am s^e^gullâ*). The people of Israel were conscious of their divine election from origin until exile; in the same way, the community of Judah considered itself the chosen people, rooted in the land of its ancestors from whom it had received the heritage of religious traditions as a legacy of faith.

The adjective *bārâ* (favorite) comes from the verb *brr* (to segregate, purify); from this verb adjectives of two distinct meanings are derived: "segregated, chosen, favorite" (6:9) and "clear, brilliant" (6:10), according to Gerleman (*BK* XVIII, 184).

The declarative sentence which expresses the praise spoken by the women has the verbs "to see, call happy, and praise" in the indicative mood.

However, some commentators translate this sentence as if it were a statement of a contrary-to-fact condition: "if they saw her, they would call her happy, and they would praise her" (GERLEMAN, 186; KRINETZKI, 205; RUDOLPH, 164). Yet this is not the meaning of the sentence, since what is enunciated expresses a real fact: "the daughters see her" (*rā'ûhâ bānôt*). Now, the community of Judah is constituted by various social groups, personified by feminine figures: "daughters" (2:2; 6:9), "daughters of Jerusalem" (1:5; 2:7; 3:5; 5:8, 16; 8:4), "daughters of Zion" (3:11), and "noble daughter" (7:2). The praises sung by the daughters, queens, and wives are an eloquent expression of approval, on a national and international level, of the elevation of the Jewish community to nationhood.

Vs. 10: The strophe of transition between the first part of this song and the second is recited by the chorus. According to the figure of rhetorical question, the clause is not formulated with the intention of asking but of affirming, since the reply is evident. The interrogative clause "who is this?" (*mî zō't*) localizes the person who bends down from on high to look. The meaning of the verb *šqp,* in *Niphal* and *Hiphil,* has the connotation of the height and the superiority of the one looking. In analogy with the stars which appear in the firmament, the community appears in the political space of the nations as a new star among the constellations of astral space. The emergence of the Jewish nation is as conspicuous as the "dawn" (*šāḥar*), which announces a new day and the "constellations" (*nidgālôt*), which begin their orbit at the beginning of the night; it is visible in the whole world as the "moon" (*lᵉbānâ*), during the night, and the "sun" (*ḥammâ*) by day. For an explanation of *'ᵃyummâ* in its meaning as "splendid," see the vocabulary analysis of the text in 6:4.

Vs. 11: The strophes of the second part of the song are expressed in narrative style and spoken by the bride (BEA, 53; COLOMBO, 170; DELITZSCH, 114; GERLEMAN, 189; PIATTI, 168; POUGET-GUITTON, 170; SEGAL, *VT* 12, 476; WINANDY, 140). Other commentators attribute these strophes to the bridegroom who recounts his visit to the orchard (ASENSIO, 611; BUZY, 345; JOÜON, *Ct,* 271; KEEL, 207; KRINETZKI, 209; LYS, 243; POPE, 585; RAVASI, 119; RICCIOTTI, 256; ROBERT-TOURNAY, 242; RUDOLPH, 166; WÜRTHWEIN, 61; ZAPLETAL, 127).

After the question about the identity of the bride—a figure representing the Jewish population—there comes the information about the extent of her territorial domain (vs. 11) and the function she exercises there (vs. 12). The territory of Judah is compared to a "nut orchard" (*ginnat 'egôz*). The form *ginnat* of the feminine noun in the *construct state* in place of the masculine (4:12, 15, 16; 5:1; 6:2; 8:13) is a grammatical peculiarity of late Hebrew (cf. Est 1:5; 7:7, 8). The word *'egôz* is a *hapax legomenon* meaning nut-tree, identified by the name *Juglans regia.* A nut orchard is a highly valued rural property because of the demand for nuts in the internal and foreign markets; as an image applied to Judah, the orchard of fruit trees could represent the economic independence of the Jewish nation. In another context, the national territory is compared to a park (*pardēs*) in which are found to be growing aromatic plants of great commercial value (cf. 4:13).

The visit to the orchard has as its object to verify (*lir'ôt*) in the vegetation of the valley and in the vineyards on the hills the appearance of the buds and the blossoms as a sure sign of the beginning of spring. The "bud" (*'ēb*) is the first offshoot put out by the vegetation in spring. The meaning of *naḥal* is "torrent" and by extension "valley, brookside meadow." The asyndetic construction of the verbs "had budded" (*pārḥâ*) and "were in bloom" (*hēnēṣû*) is rendered by means of the repetition of the conjunction "whether."

Vs. 12: This verse is conceded by the commentators to be the most difficult in the Song and constitutes the *crux interpretum*. The problem resides in the explanation of the syntactic order of the words, in the interpretation of the meaning of the sentence, and in the understanding of its significance in the context of the Song. There is almost a general consensus about taking the expression *lō' yāda'tî* (I did not know) as an isolated clause, meaning "before I was aware." Because of this, there is rejected the proposal of including *nafšî* (my soul) in the same clause, whether as the subject of the verb "I myself did not know" or as the object of the verb "I did not know my soul." Neither is it pertinent to the text to interpret the clause in terms of an idiomatic expression "I was out of my mind" (*lō' yāda'tî nafšî*), according to the suggestion of PAUL (*Bib* 59, 545–547).

The following phrase has *nafšî* as the subject of the verb *śāmatnî:* "my fancy set me up." The word "soul" (*nefeš*) as seat of the sentiments, has various meanings: "impulse, desire, caprice, fancy." The verb *śîm* with a double accusative means "to place, install, lift up, promote" someone to a position. The first accusative is the objective complement of the person "me" (*nî*); the second is the objective complement of thing: "carriages" (*mark^{e}bôt*). The meaning of *markābôt* is "war chariots, carts, or carriages of state." There is no question here of war chariots or carts, but of carriages destined for transporting the dignitaries of the people. The act of placing someone in the carriage could mean to provide for him a vehicle for the journey (2 Chr 35:24), or to send him on a diplomatic mission to a governor (2 Kgs 5), or even to concede him public honors (Gn 41:43). The plural form of "carriages" indicates a plurality of vehicles occupied by the members of the delegation, or represents a plural of amplification designating a large or sumptuous carriage (JOÜON, *Gr* § 136f).

The three words of the second hemistich "carriages, my people, noble" are interdependent: the word "carriages" (*mark^{e}bôt*) depends on the two following words "my people" (*'ammî*) and "noble" (*nādîb*) which are taken as words of nearer definition. In some Hebrew manuscripts and in the Greek and Latin versions *'ammînādîb* occurs as one single word, interpreted in terms of the proper name Amminadab. In the Hebrew bibles there is not, however, uniformity in the writing of these words: *'ammî* and *nādîb* are written in separate form, without Maqqeph, in the Second Rabbinic Bible, called "Bombergiana" (Venice, 1524–25), as well as in the Hebrew bibles published by "The Koren Publishers" (Jerusalem, 1963) and by the British and Foreign Bible Society (London, 1958). In the *Biblia Hebraica Stuttgartensia* (Stuttgart, 1967–77) there can be found *'ammî-nādîb* connected by Maqqeph so as to indicate that in respect of tone and pointing the two words are regarded as one, and therefore have only one accent. From the point of view of morphology, *'ammî* is a word composed by the agglutination of the pronominal suffix *-î* (my) to the noun *'am* (people). Some commentators suppose that the suffix *-î* is a mere leftover from the construct state indicated by the *ḥireq compaginis.*

The word "noble" (*nādîb*) designates one of the leaders of the community by virtue of the social position which he occupies and by the influence which he exercises in society. The rank of "noblemen" (*n^e^dîbîm*) is in parallel to that of the "high officials" (*śārîm*) [Nm 21:18; Prv 6:18; 2 Chr 28:21], "powerful" (*'^a^fîqîm*) [Jb 12:21], "leaders" (*n^e^sîkîm*) [Ps 83:12], and "king" (*melek*) [Jb 34:18]. The "noblemen" occupied a place of honor in the assemblies (1 Sm 2:8; Ps 113:8) and were rich and powerful (Ps 118:9; 146:3; Prv 19:6). These influential men of high social standing could properly be called "noblemen" in the broad sense of the term even though they did not form part of the nobility in the sense of a restricted class to which one belongs by birth, which enjoys certain privileges and owns large landed properties (DE VAUX, *AI,* 69f).

Some commentators take *nādîb* in the sense of the adjective "magnanimous, noble" and connect it with the word *'ammî* as an attributive adjunct which qualifies it "my noble people." However, the text does not justify attributing to the people the quality of lofty character nor is there any reason for mentioning the use of the people's carts by the leadership of the community.

Both *'ammî* and *nādîb* are related to *mark^e^bôt.* According to the attributive relation of these Hebrew terms, *mark^e^bôt* is the *nomen regens* which precedes *'ammî* and *nādîb,* two nouns in the genitive (*nomina recta*). Now, a *nomen regens* can be related to various coordinated genitives (JOÜON, *Gr* § 129b). In the group of these three terms, the principal one is *nādîb,* while *'ammî* is an accessory term, since it is added to the other for nearer definition: it is an appositive of *nādîb* whose meaning it specifies. In the position of the terms *'ammî-nādîb,* the integrative categorical concept comes before the concept which it integrates: "my people" (*'ammî*) constitutes the sphere within which the "nobleman" (*nādîb*) exercises his function. According to Hebrew syntactical order, however, the appositive should be placed after the noun whose meaning it specifies, except for some cases of transposition (cf. *GK* § 131g). Because of this, the syntactical function of the terms is indicated by their position: "carriages of a nobleman of my people."

Commentary: The Theme of Diplomatic Relations (6:8-12)

The theme of this song is that of diplomatic relations between the Jewish nation and foreign nations. The establishment of international relations means the entry of the community of Judah into the political constellation of nations within which it will begin its historical journey. Complementary or identical interests of the different nations lead them to a concerted action and the rendering to each other of reciprocal services.

Under Persian domination a single political administrative system was imposed on all the countries of the ancient Near East: they were organized into satrapies, provinces, and annexed regions. Countries that had once been independent were reduced to dependent states or were treated as vassals. Some preserved their former government and enjoyed the prerogative of administrative and economic autonomy. However, this was in fact limited since the Persian authorities maintained control in the military area, the area of taxation, and that of foreign policy. Kingdoms that had spread over a large territory ended by losing their political independence, becoming instead satrapies of the Persian empire, their monarchs substituted by puppets (OLMSTEAD, 59). Smaller kingdoms, the size of city-states, as for instance the great mercantile centers of Phoenicia, became allies of the Persians.

The poetic personification of these countries by feminine figures is the symbolic expression of the population living there with hints of an attractive physiognomy. These women are classified into various ranks, according to the matrimonial law of a polygamy-based regime. They represent the political status of their respective countries integrated into the Persian empire and the bond of each one with the sovereign. The "queens" represent the kingdoms organized into satrapies as well as the local monarchies allied to the Persians. The "wives," indicating a position of inferiority with respect to the "queens," personify provinces administered by a governor, while the "maidens" without a matrimonial bond are the image of the regions annexed to the provinces under the jurisdiction of a provincial governor.

Unlike the countries organized according to the political structure introduced by the Persians, the community of Judah does not fit into the category of "maidens" even though it is situated in a region annexed to another province, but, because it had been an independent monarchy for four centuries, it claims for itself the status of a kingdom. The Jewish community of the post-exilic period considers itself by right to be the offspring of the kingdom of Judah whom it calls its "mother." As the legitimate heir of the political and religious institutions of that kingdom, this community urges its claim to the title of chosen people and to the status of a monarchy. The conditions of the making effective of a monarchical regime in Judah are the presence of the Davidic descendant in the country and his institution in the office of kingship. Now, the nomination of the heir to the royal throne of David to the post of governor of Judah would constitute an auspicious sign of the future restoration of the monarchy. Already the autochthonous population of the country professes its loyalty to the successor to the throne of David, and its bond with the monarch, through a pact of submission.

The project of the restoration of the monarchy has the support of other social groups integrated into the community of Judah who are personified by the "daughters." But also on the international scene there is a positive reaction to the restoration of this monarchy since this is a public demonstration of the central government's policy of tolerance toward its subject countries. Beyond this, the raising of a country to the rank of a kingdom, allied to the Persians, opens up the perspective of cooperation between states on the basis of commercial treaties. This is brought about by the prerogative of relative autonomy in the administrative and economic sectors conceded to them as states, but denied to the provinces and to the annexed regions. Since the tributary system of the Persian empire weighed heavily on some countries, it was a matter of survival to assure the collaboration of others in generating resources that guaranteed food supplies for the population and the annual payment of tribute.

The emergence of the Jewish community as a nation among nations is compared to the appearance of a new star in astral space. This image expresses a growing self-esteem among the people of the satrapy of Syria-Palestine at belonging to an empire with international hegemony (BENGTSON, *FWG* V, 373). Under Persian domination, the Phoenician city-states enjoyed an increasing prosperity which led to the benefit to other people owing to intensive trading relations (*DBS* VII, col. 1195–99).

The territory of Judah is described in terms of an orchard of fruit-bearing trees: an image of the countryside in reference to the horticulture practiced there. The purpose of this description is not, however, to give a general overview of the economic life of the community, but to represent the promising perspectives of the kingdom of Judah through the comparison with the flowering of the vegetation in spring.

The elevation of the Jewish community to the rank of a nation implies the passage of the society of individuals, kept in a system of domination, to a society of citizens who assume freedom of participation and are responsible for the decisions which affect the organization of the state, its social structure, its administration, and its economy. Under the centralizing activity of the king, the administration of the commonweal does not remain at the mercy of a contest of forces between the social groups who defend private interests, but is exercised by the people holding the confidence of the ruler in the service of the common good. The high officials of the state are the "noblemen" of the people, recruited among the leaders of the respective social groups of Judah, and not from among the class of nobility. In view of the economic interests of the state, it becomes vital to create the post of representatives of the government accredited to other states so as to establish diplomatic relations, leading thus to collaboration in the area of commerce. Since the diplomatic function is a post demanding a high level of confidence, to which it is important that the king name a high government official, the leader of the autochthonous population of Judah offers itself to take on this function by the fact of its having raised the question of international relations between the states. Confirmed in its nomination for this job, the leader and the members of the delegation get into carriages and begin a journey to the foreign countries. The theme of this song complements the corresponding theme about commercial relations dealt with previously in 4:8.

3. ✦ *The Attractive Bride (7:1-6)*

1 Return, return, O Shulamite, *Chorus*
return, return, that we may look upon you.
How are you able to look *Soloist*
upon the Shulamite
at a dance for two groups?
2 How graceful are your feet in sandals, *Chorus*
O noble daughter!
Your rounded thighs are like jewels,
the work of a master hand.
3 Your navel is a rounded bowl
that never lacks mixed wine.
Your belly is a heap of wheat,
encircled with lilies.
4 Your two breasts are like two fawns,
twins of a gazelle.
5 Your neck is like an ivory tower.
Your eyes are pools in Heshbon,
by the gate of Bath-rabbim.
Your nose is like a tower of Lebanon,
overlooking Damascus.
6 Your raised head is like Carmel,
and the locks of your head are like purple yarn,
which a king keeps fastened in the tanks.

Accented Transliteration (7:1-6)

1 *šû́bî šû́bî haššûlammî́t*
šû́bî šû́bî weneḥezeh-bā́k
mah-tteḥezû́ baššûlammî́t
kimḥōlát hammaḥanā́yim
2 *mah-yyāfû́ fe‘āmáyik banne‘ālî́m*
bát-nādî́b
ḥammûqế yerēkáyik kemố ḥalā’î́m
ma‘aśḗh yedế ’ommā́n
3 *šorrḗk ’aggán hassáhar*
’al-yeḥsár hammā́zeg
biṭnḗk ‘arēmát ḥiṭṭî́m
sûgấ baššôšannî́m
4 *šenê šādáyik kišnế ‘ofārî́m*
to’omế ṣebiyyấ
5 *ṣawwā’rḗk kemigdál haššḗn*
‘ênáyik berēkốt beḥešbốn
‘al-šá‘ar bat-rabbî́m
’appḗk kemigdál hallebānốn
ṣôféh penế dammā́śeq
6 *rō’šḗk ‘āláyik kakkarmél*
wedallát rō’šḗk kā’argāmā́n
mélek ’āsû́r bārehāṭî́m

Literary Analysis (7:1-6)

The detailed description of the bride's attributes, contained in this song of six strophes, displays the woman's beautiful limbs from feet to head. Her charming figure is seen through the eyes of enthralled onlookers watching her dancing as a soloist turning and leaping in the center of the circle. Each of her limbs is described and illustrated by comparisons drawn either from topographical features of Palestine or from products of rural economy and selected items of arts and crafts associated with urban centers. From the combination of two stylistic devices, viz. prosopography and amplification, there results a cumulative effect of two sumperimposed pictures: one of the Shulamite, personifying the Jewish community, and the other of topographical features of the territory of Judah.

The first strophe (vs. 1) begins with a call addressed by the spectators to the Shulamite for her to stage a swirling dance for public exhibition, while the chorus' leader reminds them that she is going to perform a folk dance with two opposing groups forming a circle around her. The following strophes are recited by the chorus so as to convey to the bystanders, held at a distance, a lively picture of the physical traits of the dancer.

The second strophe (vs. 2) alludes to the dancer's feet shod in dancing slippers unlike professional dancers who used to perform barefoot. Her rounded thighs are mentioned in connection with the sinuous movements of the hips. The third (vs. 3) refers to navel and belly fully exposed to view during the dance. The fourth (vss. 4-5a) describes breast and neck. The fifth (vs. 5b-e) illustrates her eyes and nose by the use of comparisons drawn from topographical features typical of the "King's Highway." The sixth (vs. 6) adds a finishing touch to the description of the Shulamite by comparing her head and hair respectively to a promontory situated on the *Via Maris* and to the purple industry established in the cities located on the Levantine coast.

Poetic and rhetorical devices that occur in the song are sound repetition: assonance *u–i* (vs. 2ab), end rhyme *-îm* (vs. 3c, 4a); word repetition: anaphora (vs. 1ab, 1c-2a); figure of emphasis: hyperbole "navel is a bowl," "belly is a heap of wheat," "neck is like a tower," "eyes are pools," "nose is like a tower of Lebanon"; figures of resemblance: simile "thighs like jewels," "breasts like two fawns," "neck like an ivory tower," "nose like a tower of Lebanon," "head like Carmel," "tresses like purple yarn," metaphor "your navel is a rounded bowl," "your belly is a heap of wheat," "your eyes are pools of Heshbon"; the prosopography of the Shulamite (vss. 2c-6c); the amplification consisting in the enlarging of the woman's description by alluding to particularities of her physical traits.

Vocabulary Analysis (7:1-6)

Vs. 1: The verb *šwb* means "to come, turn around, return." Formulated in the imperative "return!" (*šûbî*) the verb here is emphatically repeated by the chorus in the scene of the presentation of the dancing girl. It is to be noted that *šwb* cannot be translated "to whirl around" which would be expressed by *sbb* (RUDOLPH, 168).

The use of *b*^{e} to introduce the object is peculiar in this passage where the expression *ḥzh b*^{e} means "to look with delight, to look upon, esteem," whereas elsewhere it is rendered "to see something in," or "to contemplate."

The name of the Shulamite (*haššûlammît*), individualized by the definite article, is not a proper name of a person, which in Hebrew is never accompanied by an article (JOÜON, *Gr* § 137b). It is in fact a substantified adjective which designates "she who belongs to Solomon." Some commentators see an analogy between the Shunamite, associated with David, and the Shulamite, related to Solomon. Thus, Shulamite would be a name correlative to that of the Shunamite. However, it is not known from what place the word Shulamite might be derived. Others regard the word Shulamite as a secondary form of Shelomith (*šelōmît*) which represents a feminine form of the corresponding masculine name Solomon. But the difference in vocalization does not permit the permutation of Shelomith for Shulamite (cf. POPE, 516f). The meaning of the Shulamite was explained as "pacific" because of the ancient form of the passive participle of *šlm*, rendered as *eireneuousa* by the Greek versions Aquila and Quinta, analogous to the name of Solomon translated as *pacificus* by the Vulgate in 8:11, 12 (ROBERT-TOURNAY, 250). This meaning is attributed not only to the name but to the person herself, named later in 8:10 "the one who finds peace" (*môṣ'ēt šālôm*). The assonance between the two words, Shulamite and Solomon, could have been intentional to suggest an association between the Shulamite and the descendant of the Davidic dynasty.

The question formulated by the solo voice is introduced by the adverb "how?" (*mah*) to express astonishment in the face of a desire for something that is regarded as an impossibility (*BDB, mh* 2.a, 553). The verb *teḥezû* is in the form of *yiqtol* with a modal nuance (JOÜON, *Gr* § 113 l). The principal verb is "to look upon" and the auxiliary verb here is "to be able," not "to want" as it is sometimes translated, since what is indicated is the difficulty of the public in seeing the dancing girl surrounded by two choral groups.

The last line of the strophe constitutes a *crux interpretum* similar to that of 6:12 (BUZY, 348). The difficulty is precisely to find an explanation for the particle *ke* which prefixes the word *meḥōlat*, and in the working out the meaning of *maḥanāyim*. The Hebrew particle *ke* prefixed to a verbal noun has the value of a preposition to be rendered as "on the occasion of" (*BDB, ke* 3.b, 454). The feminine noun *meḥōlat* occurs in the singular only in the *construct state;* its meaning "dance" is the same as that of the masculine *māḥôl*. So as to ascertain the meaning of *maḥanāyim* some commentators tried to establish a nexus between this word and Mahanaim, the name of a village near the river Jabbok, a tributary of the Jordan. Two etymologies of the name Mahanaim can be found in the book of Genesis: that of "two camps"—one of the angels and the other of Jacob (Gn 32:3)—and that of "two camping grounds" of the family of Jacob (Gn 32:7-8). Inspired by these etymologies some commentators have attributed to the proper name of this place the qualifying function of a typical dance; thus the dance of Mahanaim would be a dance similar to the gracious movement of angels (DELITZSCH, 121), or a war dance (KRINETZKI, 213), or a country dance (COLOMBO, 116). Others emend the MT to interpret the expression as a sword dance executed in military camps (POUGET-GUITTON, 171; ZAPLETAL, 134), or so as to attribute to the Shulamite the role of a "camp dancer" (GERLEMAN, 188).

The Hebrew term *maḥ^aneh* means "military camp," the "army" on the march or in line of battle, or the "camp" of travelers, flocks or caravans, or simply a "group" of people. In the context of the dance, the word *maḥ^anāyim* has the meaning of "two choral groups" which accompany the dancer's movements by imitative patterns or by background rhythms. According to this interpretation, the role of these choral groups consists in the accompaniment by suitable background rhythms whether vocal or instrumental, or by hand clapping. Other commentators attribute to them a more active participation as dancing groups. From the interpretation of these choruses depends the syntax of the words *m^eḥōlat* (dance) and *hammaḥ^anāyim* (two choral groups). If they were translated as a "dance of two choral groups," the idea of an active participation of the choruses in the dance would be expressed; if however they are translated as "a dance for two choral groups," a more discreet participation is enounced. The relation of interdependence between the *nomen regens* (*m^eḥōlat*) and the *nomen rectum* (*hammaḥ^anāyim*) is used in this phrase to express purpose (*GK* § 128q).

It has also been suggested that the duality of the choral groups is an indication of an alternate recitation of vss. 2-6, where the first hemistich of each line, about the physical details of the dancing girl, would be recited by one chorus, and the second, which adds to it a topographical amplification, by the other (RICCIOTTI, 263). This suggestion explains the function of the choral groups in the dance about which only a few brief allusions are found in the Bible (Ex 32:18; 1 Sm 21:21; 29:5). However, vss. 2-6 *en bloc* are addressed to the Shulamite without a change of voice being indicated to hint at an alternate recitation of these verses by two choruses. It is possible though to attribute to one of the choral groups a recitative role and to the other the function of marking a beat so as to keep rhythm.

Vs. 2: The exclamatory sentence is introduced by the adverb "how!" (*mah*). The term *pa'am* designates mostly a man's step or foot of one marching or dancing. The allusion to dancing slippers (*n^e'ālîm*) points out the high social condition of the Shulamite in relation to professional dancers who danced barefoot, to judge from the pictographical representations of dance scenes from antiquity.

"O noble daughter!" (*bat-nādîb*), lit. "O daughter of a nobleman!" in the vocative does not mean that she is a descendant of a noble family, but holds a high social status because she belongs to the rank of high officials designated by the title of "noblemen" (cf. 6:12).

In the description of the thighs there occur four *hapax legomena* in Hebrew and any explanation of the meanings of the terms is approximate. The expression "your rounded thighs" (*ḥammûqê y^erēkayik*) corresponds to the two Hebrew nouns which are linked by subordination, i.e. "the curves of your thighs." The term *ḥammûqê* derived from the verb *ḥmq* means in the *Qal* "to deviate" and in *Hiphil* "to oscillate." There exist two possibilities in interpreting this term referring to the curves of the thighs, depending on the point of view adopted as to whether the body described is in movement or repose. In the first case, *ḥammûqê* means "sinuous movement," in the second, "curves, contour." Here it is a question of the second because of the decorative object with which it is compared; its term of comparison is the rounded form of thighs and jewels.

The meaning of *ḥ^{a}lā'îm* is probably "jewels" to judge by similar related nouns: *ḥ^{a}lî* "jewel" (Prv 25:12) and *ḥelyātāh* "her ornament" (Hos 2:15). The rounded shape of the jewels is the image of the contours of the thighs. The reference to the artistic work of the ornaments (*ma'^{a}śēh y^{e}dê 'ommān*), lit. "the work of the hands of an artist," specifies the value of the jewels in relation to where they came from: a well-known goldsmith. The term *'ommān* (artist) is a *hapax legomenon* whose meaning is identical to that of the variant form *'āmōn* (Jer 52:15; Prv 8:30). The artistic form of the jewels worked by a famous goldsmith is related to the rounded contours of the Shulamite's thighs. The reason for using this comparison is to point out the high social position of the Shulamite by means of the expensive ornaments with which she is decked out in contrast with the cheap fashion jewelry worn by professional dancing girls of more modest social condition.

Vs. 3: The terms "navel" and "belly" as well as the comparisons drawn from the Palestinian region have given rise to the most diverse interpretations. The description of the abdomen mentions first a detail, i.e. the navel, and then the totality, i.e. the belly. The navel of the Shulamite has the form of a small depression. The Hebrew term only occurs in the composite form *šor^{e}rēk* "your navel" or *šorrēk* (Ez 16:4) and *šorrekā* (Prv 3:8), both in the sense of "your umbilical cord." The suggestions presented by some commentators who interpret this term in another sense on the basis of cognate words in Arabic are not pertinent.

The cuplike cavity of the navel is compared by hyperbole with a bowl whose purpose is the watering down of wine. The form of the "bowl, crater" (*'aggan*) is indicated by the term *sahar*, a *hapax legomenon* whose meaning is furnished by the homonymous word in post-biblical Hebrew *sahar* "a round enclosure" for animals, and by another in Syriac *sahrā* "moon." The idea common to all of these terms is the bowl-shaped space which is open at the top and closed at the bottom. In this receptacle "mixed wine" is prepared, designated by the term *mezeg*, a *hapax legomenon* taken from the Aramaic *m^{e}zag*. The variant form in Hebrew *mesek* occurs in parallel with *yayin* "wine" (Ps 75:9; Prv 23:30) in such a way that *mezeg* is a poetical synonym of the common term for wine. According to the ancient mentality, "it is harmful to drink wine by itself, or again to drink water by itself, while wine mixed with water is delicious and enhances one's enjoyment" (2 Mc 15:39). Wine as a staple in the rural districts is plentiful and "is never lacking" (*'al-yeḥsar*) at meals. The particle *'al* has not the usual prohibitive force here, but serves as an emphatic negation (Joüon, *Gr* § 114k).

What is the relationship between the Shulamite and the wine, or between the navel and the bowl? Only in the context of the relationship to which they correspond can these terms be understood. They are, in an ascending order, three terms of comparison: first, that of anatomy, i.e. navel–belly; second, that of measure, i.e. bowl–heap; third, that of product, i.e. wine–wheat. The function of these terms is to serve as an image of the Shulamite who represents the native population of Judah in the exercise of agricultural activities.

The interpretation of the expression in relation to the cosmological theory of the "navel of the earth" (ROBERT-TOURNAY, 259) moves away from the meaning of the text. This geographical conception was used in antiquity to promote nationalistic pride. The prophet Ezekiel applies this idea to Jerusalem because of its religious importance in the salvific design of God in relation to the people of the whole world. However, the text does not refer to Jerusalem and even less does it allude to the topography of the city as the center of the earth, according to a universalistic view, but deals with the economic life of Judah.

The explanation of the "navel" as a symbol of the fertility of the country of Israel (JOÜON, *Ct,* 281) is not appropriate because it reduces one of the ten physical traits of the Shulamite to the function of an image without attending to the real meaning of the figure described in this song.

The "belly" (*beṭen*) of the Shulamite is compared to a "heap of wheat" (*ʿarēmat ḥiṭṭîm*) threshed and winnowed. In relation to the curvature of a heap of wheat it is interesting to note that the angle of inclination of a heap of wheat is from twenty-five to thirty degrees, while that of a heap of barley is between thirty and thirty-five degrees. Now, the curvature of the belly of a pregnant mother is superior to thirty-five degrees. Thus the heap of wheat does not symbolize the state of pregnancy of the Shulamite as has been suggested by some commentators (BUZY, 349; KRINETZKI, 215; PIATTI, 170). On the other hand, the majority see in this expression a similarity between the golden color of the grains of wheat and the skin of the belly, in contradiction with the information in 1:6 about the "swarthy" skin of the Shulamite.

The heap of wheat is "encircled" (*sûgâ*) by lilies. The verb *swg* II is a *hapax legomenon* of which there are related cognate verbs in Aramaic, in post-biblical Hebrew, and in Arabic with the meaning of "to encircle." As regards the function of the lilies around the heap of wheat there is no consensus among the commentators. The prevailing opinion is based on the hypothesis that we are dealing with the description of the belly, in opposition to the literary procedure of this song which consists in the mere listing of the physical traits of the Shulamite without any addition of descriptive details, except in vs. 2 and vs. 6. The amplifications only make explicit the objects mentioned so as to serve as comparisons. There arises, however, the question about the meaning of the "lilies" (*šôšannîm*). According to the widespread opinion that lilies were not to be found at the time of the wheat harvest, it was argued that these flowers would have just a metaphoric sense (RUDOLPH, 172). However, this opinion cannot be upheld because of the fact of the lily, the *Lilium candidum,* having been found growing in the mountains of upper Galilee in a pit between shrubs of maqui as late as May. Some specimens with brilliantly white flowers on a stalk one hundred and twenty-one centimeters tall were discovered in mid-May in recesses on the slopes of Mount Carmel sprouting from clefts of rocks and in the shade of shrubs (MOLDENKE, 279). Now, the harvest season for wheat was extended from May to June. Some of these lilies could have been brought to the threshing floor so as to serve as a marker between the heap of grain and the chaff with fragments of straw which accumulated on the side in the process of threshing and winnowing the grain. These residues were later fanned to separate the grain from the remaining refuse (DALMAN, *AuS* III, 128f).

Corn and wine are the most important products of Judah and represent by merismus the agricultural production of the country. The abundance of wheat and wine is indicated respectively by the heap of wheat and by the bowl full of the drink, meaning that each producer has just made a good harvest and has supplies guaranteed. The navel and the belly of the Shulamite are exposed during the dance not to exhibit her nudity, but so as to highlight the sinuous movements of the body. In a folkloric milieu she performs a dance among the rural population to celebrate the festival of harvest-tide. This population living in the territory of Judah is the backbone of the Jewish people, and as landowners established in the country of their ancestors they fulfill the conditions necessary to be constituted a nation.

Vs. 4: This verse repeats literally the text in 4:5, except that for *t^e'ômê* the more common form *to'^omê* (twins) is substituted and the attributive clause "that feed among the lilies" is omitted, because the lilies have been mentioned at the end of the preceding verse. The breasts and the fawns are here qualified by the number "two" (*š^enê*) rather than with the dual form with which Hebrew expresses a pair of equal objects. "Your two breasts" (*š^enê šādayik*) are compared to the "two fawns" (*š^enê ʻ^ofārîm*).

The term of comparison between the breasts of the Shulamite and the fawns is their symmetry as a pair (see the interpretation of the text in 4:5). Between the Shulamite and the gazelle there exists a relation of proximity in geographical terms which is expressed in the comparison between the habitat of the rural population and that of the native fauna. Both are rooted in the same part of the countryside: the latter feeds in the fields and the meadows by night, the former draws her sustenance from there by day.

Vs. 5: The "neck" (*ṣawwā'r*) of the Shulamite is compared to an "ivory tower" (*migdal haššēn*); in 4:4 it is to the "tower of David." The term of comparison is the slender form of the woman's neck corresponding to the canon of beauty in vogue among the ancients. With the word "ivory" (*šēn*) it is not intended, however, to qualify the color of the skin, as the majority of commentators suppose, but the tower decorated with ivory plaques inlaid into the wainscotting of the inner walls. Sumptuous buildings were in any case called "ivory houses" (1 Kgs 22:39; Am 3:15); the residences of the royal family or of high officials were called "ivory palaces" (Ps 45:9). The word "tower" without any qualifying adjective might signify a watch-tower, a turret, or even a granary. To avoid ambiguity, the elegance of the architectural construction is specified by the term "ivory" and this image is applied to the slender neck of the Shulamite.

The "eyes," in the dual form *'ēnayim,* are brilliant like glistening pools reflecting the sunshine. At the foot of the hill of the city of Heshbon there were open-air reservoirs for rainwater storage. To judge by the dimensions of one of these reservoirs, which, although it is only partially excavated, is fifteen meters long, twelve meters wide, and four and a half meters deep (*IDB.S,* "Heshbon," 410), we are dealing with large pools to supply the city and the caravans encamped there with water. The geographical location of these pools is indicated by the reference to the way of access to the city through the gate called Bath-rabbim (*bat-rabbîm*). If this name designates the direction for Rabbah, the capital of Ammon, the pools are located to the north of Heshbon. The importance of Heshbon resides in its strategic location at the "King's Highway" extending from Damascus to the Gulf of Akaba. It is also close to the junction where the local road for the territory of Judah branches off. This road was plied by caravans with their merchandise following the route in the direction of the ports of embarcation on the Levantine coast.

The pointed and prominent "nose" (*'ap*) rises out of the face like a turret jutting up among the walls of a city. By the "tower of Lebanon" (*migdal hallebānôn*) there is probably indicated a turret which formed part of the fortification network of the city of Damascus. Thanks to these fortifications the city resisted the siege of the Assyrians for two years until it was conquered in 732 B.C. Two centuries later, Jeremiah prophesied the destruction of the walls of Damascus by the Babylonians (Jer 49:27).

However, the most widely suggested explanation with respect to the "tower of Lebanon" does not imagine that one is dealing with a fortified construction, but with a promontory among the high peaks of the Anti-Lebanon Mountains. On the basis of this hypothesis, the attributive clause which explains the tower "overlooking Damascus" (*ṣôfeh penê dammāśeq*) would have the function of indicating the road in the direction of Damascus. The meaning, however, of the preposition *penê* used with the verb *ṣfh* II is not "in the direction of," but "before." In fact the houses of the city nestle around the tower of Lebanon like its inhabitants around the sentry, since *ṣôfeh* signifies both "overlooking" and "sentry."

With the two proper names of the places Heshbon and Damascus there are indicated two cities on the route of the "King's Highway" which appear on the itinerary of the Shulamite. The names of buildings include the gate of Bath-rabbim and the tower of Lebanon whose function is to mark the direction of the road to be followed on the respective junctions on the various roads. The gate of Bath-rabbim is an indication of the northbound direction on the principal north-south highway where the local road branches off to the west. The tower of Lebanon is the reference point at which to abandon the "King's Highway" which forks for Palmyra and Kadesh on the Orontes, and to follow instead the road which crosses the Anti-Lebanon and Lebanon Mountains in the direction of Beirut.

Vs. 6: This verse is one of the most difficult to interpret in the whole book and has given rise to the most diverse hypotheses and various attempts to emend the text. The expression "your raised head"' (*rō'šēk 'ālayik*), lit. "your head upon you," is distinguished from the rest of the physical parts of the person, mentioned in the preceding verses, by the addition of the qualifying term "raised" to the word "head," while the other parts of the body are quoted by only one word except for the reference to the feet which are "graceful" and to the thighs which are "rounded." It is the two extreme parts of the body, i.e. feet and head, which form an inclusion in relation to the other parts. While in the description of the shodden feet in vs. 2 there is stressed the elevated social position of the Shulamite, in the portrait of her head there is emphasized her attitude of haughtiness. This is the bearing of a person conscious both of her dignity as a free person and of the importance of her office.

One of the reasons for comparing the head to Mount Carmel is the analogy with the name "holy head" (*rš qdš*) attributed to Mount Carmel by the Pharaoh Thut-mose III (AHARONI, 161). The other is the strategic location of this promontory close by the *Via Maris* between the plains of Sharon and Esdraelon on the stretch along the Levantine coast from Phoenicia to Egypt.

The "locks" (*dallâ*) of her hair are compared to "purple yarn" (*'argāmān*) of wool or linen dyed in the pigment obtained from murex shells which were found on the Levantine coast. Owing to the great quantity of murex shells which were necessary to make one gram of this natural dye (8000), the purple cloth was very expensive (GALLING, 73). The term of comparison between the locks and the yarn is the color *red* since in antiquity women occasionally tinged their hair red with a vegetable dye extracted from safflower (*Carthamus tinctorius*), from the root of the *Rubia tinctoria* and of the henna plant (*Lawsonia alba*) which produce different varieties of the color red (GALLING, 72).

There have been discovered in the places where dyeing took place in that time cylindrical tanks made of stone or excavated in rock, seventy to ninety centimeters deep and seventy centimeters wide. In these "tanks" (*r^{e}hāṭîm*) the purple was dissolved in a solution of cold or lukewarm water; other receptacles were used to fix the color on the fibers by means of a solution of a vegetable substance and another to rinse the now dyed fibers (GALLING, 74). The dyer fastened the yarn into a skein before placing it in the tank so as to facilitate its management and to avoid the yarn becoming tangled up during this complex operation. The action of fastening is expressed by the passive participle *ʾasûr*, but the meaning is active, i.e. "keeping fastened," because some *qatul* participles have an active meaning or one proximate to it (*GK* § 50f; JOÜON, *Gr* § 50e). In the same way, the passive participle *ʾ^{a}ḥuzê* is translated "those who manage" with an active sense (3:8). The subject of the phrase is the "king" (*melek*) who keeps the purple yarn bound together in the tanks. This phrase sets out the fact that the purple industry was either under the king's control or was a royal monopoly in the Phoenician city-states.

The meaning of this verse which closes the description of the Shulamite can be worked out in the context of the journey from Judah to Phoenicia. The itinerary is indicated by two junctions on the road from Jerusalem: one at Heshbon, where the "King's Highway" passes to the north, and the other at Damascus, starting point of the road passing the Anti-Lebanon and Lebanon Mountains in the direction of the Phoenician coast, where the onward journey closes. The *Via Maris* passes all along the seacoast, heading south and turning around Mount Carmel from where there can be seen at a distance the mountainous region which extends to the territory of Judah. There arises, however, the question as to why these routes are being set out, routes which pass through both cities mentioned and a number which are left implicit. All those are roads which link Judah to foreign lands. The answer is given by the relation between the geographical indications and the Shulamite, whose figure is compared with the topographical characteristics of the respective places indicated on the journey. The geographical description constitutes the account of a journey whose preparations were mentioned previously (6:12). The purpose of the journey can be deduced from the fact that the Shulamite passes through important urban centers which were the seats of government or capitals of their respective countries, i.e. Rabbah and Damascus, or were city-states, i.e. Byblos, Sidon, and Tyre. Owing to the importance of these cities as commercial centers, the government of Judah proposes to establish diplomatic relations and trading treaties with the rulers of these flourishing centers of international commerce so as to foster the economic development of its own country.

Commentary: The Theme of the Judean Leadership (7:1-6)

The theme of this song deals with the role of the Shulamite who represents the leader of the autochthonous population of Judah. This population rooted in the territory of Judah is the backbone of the Jewish people and as landowners in the country of their forefathers they fulfill the conditions necessary for being constituted a nation. Social groups who join together to form a homogeneous society and to develop an exclusive depository of positive values, values that are also specific and permanent, can constitute a people, but not a nation unless they possess territorial dominion whose ownership both *de jure* and *de facto* is recognized by other countries. Now, the merit of the autochthonous population of Judah was exactly having held on to the ownership of its land during the period of exile, defending it against a massive infiltration of outsiders, against the annexation of its dominions to foreign countries, and against alienation of its land by sale to foreigners.

The personification of the Jewish population by the Shulamite presents the collectivity as a corporate personality. Through the description of this woman the reader perceives the aspirations of the population living in Judah, the customs that were once in vogue, the economic activities of the agrarian world, the structures of society, and the diplomatic and commercial relationships between countries. The Shulamite as an individual person and as a representative of the collectivity has all the characteristics of someone as real as the socio-economic aspects of life, and the geographical details mentioned in this song are real. It is not that, in order to describe the function of this representative person, one of the inhabitants of the country is over-idealized by being dressed up with imaginary qualities under the inspiration of the ideal of beauty according to the Semitic conception. She is identified as the Shulamite, because of her association with the descendant of the royal house of David called Solomon. Furthermore, the relationship between the two names, i.e. Shulamite and Solomon, on the basis of the same underlying lexeme *šlm*, hints at the covenant relationship between king and people which is established on the occasion of the restoration of the monarchy. We are dealing in fact with the people of Judah organized into a political community in which the citizens make themselves present in the political sphere through the leader who represents them in the centralized government of the monarchy. This leader exercises high public office and enjoys exalted social position, although not belonging to the nobility (vs. 2). On the occasion of the harvest festival, celebrated in folkloric style, the Shulamite executes a dance in the midst of the rural population. Two choral groups placed round about her delimit the space while they recite the verses to the rhythmic movement of the dance (vs. 1). The figure of the dancing girl furnishes the visual component which is amplified by the description of agricultural activities exercised in the rural districts (vs. 3) and of the itinerary indicated by the roads which lead to other countries (vss. 5-6).

The autochthonous population of Judah is not a rural proletariat which lives in a situation of dependency like a laborer on a farm whose owners, almost always absent from the land, dwell in the big cities or abroad. On the contrary, they were deeply rooted in the land whose areas constituted family lots where the man of the countryside dwelt as owner of his property (vs. 4).

The initiative of the government in establishing commercial relations with foreign countries aims at the fostering of the economic interests of the Jewish nation without depending on intermediaries for the trading of agricultural products and the acquisition of imported articles. This is because the tariffs charged for their services weighed very heavily on the final price paid by the consumer. According to the custom of antiquity, commercial treaties were signed between the governments of the respective countries when the supplier was a state company which maintained the monopoly. This had been the case with the importation of the products from the east and the west in the ports of Phoenicia with the export of timber from Lebanon, naval construction and purple industry in the Phoenician city-states and in Ashdod. To judge by the journey indicated in this song, the Shulamite entered into contract with the government of various countries situated along the "King's Highway" from Heshbon to Damascus, and along the *Via Maris* from the Phoenician coast to Ashdod. The journey of the Shulamite through these foreign countries had as its object to assure direct access to the flourishing centers of international commerce by means of treaties signed by the "king" of the respective country and by the diplomatic delegation of the government of Judah represented by the "noble daughter." The theme of this song complements the corresponding theme about the prosperity of the Jewish nation dealt with previously in 4:9-11.

4. ✦ *The Stately Bride (7:7-10)*

7 How fair and pleasant are you, *Bridegroom*
on account of love, O delectable daughter!
8 Your stature is like a palm tree,
and your breasts are like its bunches.
9 I say I will climb the palm tree
and lay hold of its branches.

Oh, may your breasts be like clusters of the vine,
and the scent of your nostrils like apples,
10 and that of your mouth like the best wine
that flows smoothly to the lovers,
gliding over the lips of the sleepers.

Accented Transliteration (7:7-10)

7 *mah-yyāfı̂́t ûmah-nnāʻámt*
ʼah^{a}bấ battaʻ^{a}nûgı̂́m
8 *zṓʼt qômātḗk dām^{e}tấ l^{e}tāmā́r*
w^{e}šādáyik l^{e}ʼaškōlṓt
9 *ʼāmártî ʼeʻ^{e}léh b^{e}tāmā́r*
ʼōḥ^{a}zā́h b^{e}sansinnấw
w^{e}yihyû-nā́ʼ šādáyik k^{e}ʼešk^{e}lṓt haggéfen
w^{e}rế^{a}ḥ ʼāppḗk kattappûḥı̂́m
10 *w^{e}ḥikkḗk k^{e}yên haṭṭṓb*
hôlḗk l^{e}dôdî́ l^{e}mêšārı̂́m
dôbḗb śiftế y^{e}šēnı̂́m

Literary Analysis (7:7-10)

This song is composed of three strophes formulated as an apostrophe addressed to the bride. The first strophe, an exclamatory sentence, indicates the personal reason for the bridegroom to praise the bride, i.e. their mutual friendship (vs. 7). The second strophe compares the slender figure of the woman to a date palm and alludes to the date harvest (vss. 8-9b). The third strophe establishes the relationship between the fruits of the orchard and the rural population, represented by the bride; these enjoy in peace the fruit of their labor in the era of the restored monarchy (vss. 9c-10).

Poetic and rhetorical devices that occur in the song are sound repetition: alliteration *m–t* (vs. 8a); figures of speech: metonymy which consists in the use of one word for another that it suggests, viz. bunches and breasts denote the maturity of both the date palm and the woman; simile "your stature is like a palm tree, and the scent of your nostrils is like apples," "your mouth is like the best wine"; and the amplification which adds descriptive elements to the particularities of the woman and of fruit-growing.

Vocabulary Analysis (7:7-10)

Vs. 7: The two exclamatory clauses, introduced by the adverb "how!" (*mah*), highlight the beauty of the bride: "you are graceful" (*yāfît*) and "you are pleasant" (*nāʿamt*). In the preceding song it was the chorus which extols the attributes of the Shulamite; in this it is the bridegroom who exalts her for a personal reason, i.e. their mutual friendship.

The word "love" (*ʾahabâ*) is used in Hebrew as an accusative of cause (*GK* § 118b); for this reason it is translated by an adverbial adjunct of cause "on account of love." The meaning of the word "love" is the result of its function in the language. In common language, "love" expresses the subjective sentiment of affection between persons. In the Song, however, this word is always used as a technical term of juridical terminology to express a political relationship, as ancient Near Eastern treaty documents amply attest (see the explanation of the text in 1:3).

In place of the interpretation of *ʾahabâ* as an adverbial adjunct there can be found in other commentaries various attempts to explain and emend the MT. Most interpreters attribute to it either an abstract meaning or a concrete one, or even change the phrase into an apostrophe to abstract love "O love!" Other commentators emend *ʾahabâ* to *ʾahubâ* "beloved," finding basis for this in the ancient versions (Aquila, Peshitta, Vulgate).

The expression "O delectable daughter" indicates the person as the principal subject of the sentence. However, in the MT both of these words are connected owing to haplography, *battaʿanûgîm*, meaning "in the delights," instead of maintaining them separate, i.e. *bat taʿanûgîm* "daughter of delights," as it is translated by two ancient versions (Aquila, Peshitta). The idea of the word *taʿanûgîm* is expressed by an abstract plural which occurs also in other idiomatic expressions, e.g. "your sons of delights" (Mi 1:16) and "their house of delights" (Mi 2:9).

The meaning of this verse is not the expression of an exuberant romantic sentiment between lovers, but the expression of the delight in the covenant which binds the leading figure representative of the Jewish population to the house of David.

Vs. 8: In the description of the slender figure of the woman her "stature" is compared to a "palm tree" (*tāmār*), the *Phoenix dactylifera*. To give the impression that the apostrophe is being directed to a person who is present the noun is accompanied by a demonstrative pronoun, i.e. "this your stature" (*zōʾt qômātēk*). The symmetrical position of the "bunches" (*ʾaškōlôt*) on the crown of the date palm is an image of the woman's breasts. Both bunches and breasts denote by metonymy the maturity of the date palm and of the woman: both are fully developed.

Vs. 9: This verse deals with the harvest of dates, grapes, and apples. The sentence, formulated in direct style, "I say: I will climb . . . I will lay hold" is introduced by a verb of saying (*'āmartî*) to express the combination of two main clauses by coordination, i.e. "I will climb and lay hold." If the verb of saying were left out, the sentence would have the following meaning: "I will climb so as to lay hold," since the second clause would be subordinated to the first and the proper relationship would be indicated by a subordinating conjunction. However, no one climbs the date palm so as to lay hold of its "branches" (*sansinnîm*), but rather so as to pluck dates while getting a hold in the crown of the tree. The term *sansinnîm* is a *hapax legomenon* translated as "branches" of the palm tree in view of its Akkadian cognate *sissinnu* which designates the topmost branches of the date palm (POPE, 636; *HAL* III, 718). The intention of participating in the harvest is expressed by the verb in the cohortative mood denoting the will to action, e.g. "I will climb" (*'e'eleh*) and "I will lay hold" (*'ōḥazāh*) (JOÜON, *Gr* § 114b).

In order to illustrate the peculiarities of the woman and of fruit-growing the literary device of amplification is used. Three aspects of the person are compared to three products so as to establish the relationship between the fruits of the orchard and the rural population, represented by the Shulamite. This relation does not yet exist since the sentence is not phrased in the indicative used for a declarative sentence, but is the object of an ardent desire formulated in an optative clause "and may they be!" (*weyihyû-nā'*).

The comparisons are drawn from products of orchards of the various Judean regions in which date palms, vines, or apple trees were cultivated. The order of precedence in the listing of these fruit trees indicates their respective harvest seasons, beginning with the dates, harvested in August, followed by the grapes, whose harvest extends from August to September, and ending with the apples whose in-gathering is in the autumn. The breasts are compared to bunches of dates and clusters of grapes which symbolize maturity. The air breathed out from the nostrils resembles the fragrance of apples. In the Hebrew phrase the "fragrance" is connected by subordination to the "nostrils," i.e. "the fragrance of your nostrils" (*rêaḥ 'appēk*), and for this reason some commentators have emended *rêaḥ* to *rûaḥ* (breath).

Vs. 10: The mouth which tastes the wine is the image of the people's enjoyment at the products of the vineyards. The term used to indicate "mouth" is *ḥēk* which designates the interior of the mouth, i.e. the palate or the gums, as well as the organ of speech and the sense of taste. Wine of superior quality (*yên haṭṭôb*) is "the best wine" because it flows smoothly (*hôlēk lemêšārîm*) down the throat while more astringent wine leaves a certain bitterness in the mouth. The *lamed* in *lemêšārîm* designates the norm according to which one determines the taste of wine, similar to the *bet* in *bemêšārîm* (Prv 23:31) which indicates the accompanying circumstance of wine tasting (DELITZSCH, 132).

The word *l^e^dôdî* (to my beloved), following the verb *hôlēk* (going), has caused a problem for the interpretation of the sentence and given occasion for various emendations of the MT. In all the passages of the Song of Songs, *l^e^dôdî* has been used to indicate the bridegroom. Now, how is it possible that in this verse the bridegroom should refer to himself in terms of "to my lover"? To avoid this incongruity in his speech some commentators have emended *l^e^dôdî* to *l^e^ḥikkî* "to my palate" (BEA, 56; BUDDE, DALMAN, and HOUBIGANT quoted by BUZY, 352), to *l^e^fî* "to my mouth" (BUZY, 352; COLOMBO, 122; JOÜON, *Ct*, 296), to *lî* "to me" (RUDOLPH, 174), to *l^e^dōday* "to my love" (KRINETZKI, 310; POPE, 639; RAVASI, 116), "under my caresses" (KEEL, 221; PIATTI, 173), or it has been proposed that the whole clause be eliminated (WÜRTHWEIN, 64).

Other commentators suppose that there is an abrupt interruption in the apostrophe with the insertion of words of the Shulamite to the bridegroom (DELITZSCH, 131; GERLEMAN, 302; LYS, 269; POUGET-GUITTON, 174; RICCIOTTI, 268; ROBERT-TOURNAY, 274; WINANDY, 90). In this form the meaning *l^e^dôdî* is clarified, but the parallelism between this term and *y^e^šēnîm* (sleepers) is lost.

The solution to the problem was proposed by GORDIS (quoted by POPE, 639) who explains *l^e^dôdî* in terms of an apocopated plural form of the word *dôdîm* (lovers). The use of the apocopated plural form is attested in other biblical texts (*GK* § 87f) as well as in Ct 8:2 which uses *rimmōnî* instead of the plural form *rimmônîm* (pomegranates) as it is written in many Hebrew manuscripts.

These "lovers" (*dôdîm*) have been previously mentioned as allies of the bride (5:1). On that occasion it was the chorus who invited them to participate in the festive celebration in honor of the consolidated nation. In this scene it is the bridegroom who calls those who gathered to taste the wine "lovers," a term which is applied to the partners of a covenant fellowship. They are the social groups of Judah who, owing to their relation with the local leaders through the pact of association, deserve to be called by the title of "lovers" of the king. The reason for the reunion of these "lovers" is not, however, some sort of festive celebration, but is the occasion of tasting wine produced from the grapes of the last harvest.

The quality of the wine is specified not only by its taste but also by its alcoholic strength. To judge by the effect produced in the "lovers," who became all "sleepy" (*y^e^šēnîm*) with tasting the wine "gliding over the lips" (*dôbēb śiftê*), the wine contained a high degree of alcohol. The verb *dbb* I is a *hapax legomenon* whose meaning is derived from cognate verbs, i.e. from Hebrew *zwb* "to run, glide, drip" and from Aramaic *dwb* "to flow" (*HAL* I, 200).

The expression "the lips of sleepers" is emended by the majority of commentators to "my lips and teeth" on the basis of the translation by the ancient versions. This emendation of the words of the MT supposes being able to offer an apparent improvement of the text by the reference to the teeth making it possible to form a parallelism with the lips. However, this parallelism only serves as an image of the consumption of the drink without specifying the quality of the wine which the text seeks to highlight. This is known by the effect which it produces. Thus, the drowsiness caused in the lovers is an indication of the high degree of alcohol of the wine of superior quality. The participle "sleeping" is an attributive adjunct which complements the noun "lovers" explaining its meaning. The fact is that wine producers are also the owners of the vineyards.

Commentary: The Theme of the Union between King and Nation (7:7-10)

The theme of this song is the union between king and nation in the land of Judah. Both the administrative system in the country, centralized in the Davidic king, and the organization of the political community constitute the objective of the collective aspirations of the Jewish population. With the establishment of a new political order in the country it is proposed to restore the monarchy to which the subjects will be bound by a pact of submission and whose commitment they assume out of loyalty to the king (vs. 7).

The representation of the Jewish nation by means of a palm tree became the characteristic emblem of Judah (vs. 8), minted into their coins in the era of Roman domination (GALLING, 233). In analogy with the image of the palm tree the function of the king in the government of the country is illustrated. His exercise of control over the public administration by means of a body of ministers benefits the economic development of the nation (vs. 9a + b).

The products of the orchards of the different regions of Judah in which date palms, vines, or apple trees were cultivated are harvested by the fruit-growers of the country, and not by outside collectors in the service of a foreign government which grabs most of the local production under the pretext of taxation in payment of annual tribute. The rural population which collects clusters of grapes and breathes the fragrance of the apples represents the economically active inhabitants of the country (vs. 9c-e).

The harvest of dates, grapes, and apples is abundant to judge by the reference to trees, weighed down by the bunches and clusters, and the fragrance of the fruits which impregnates the air. The description of the abundance of fruits seeks to offer a hopeful perspective to a population which have been living in an economically desperate situation. The land which ought to have been their horizon and their hope had not given them the conditions necessary for survival. The biblical texts from the period of the restoration mention the dramatic situation of the community of Judah. Frequent draughts destroyed the plantations (Hag 1:6, 10f) and plagues reduced production (Hag 2:16-17). To these natural causes economic factors were added which led to the impoverishment of the people, viz. lack of resources, the absorption of agricultural profit by commercial sectors, indebtedness of the small landowners whose land was then either mortgaged or confiscated, and finally the devastation of the agricultural sector by the state taxation system (Neh 5:1-5). In view of this situation of poverty the song sets out the benefits which would follow on in the train of a new political and economic order established in Judah in function of the necessities and the resources of the nation.

There is mentioned not only the quantity but also the quality of the products. Their prices can compensate the losses made in previous harvests. Thus, the stock of wine of high quality (vs. 10) is a guarantee of financial resources which help the man of the countryside to get over adverse economic situations. The theme of this song complements the themes which have been dealt with previously, i.e. that of the economic independence of the nation (4:12-15) and that of the consolidated nation (4:16–5:1).

POEM VII *The Bliss of Love* (7:11–8:5)

1 ✦ *The Bond of Friendship (7:11)*

11 I am my beloved's *Bride*
and his desire is for me.

Accented Transliteration (7:11)

11 *ʾanî́ ledôdî́*
weʾāláy tešûqātố

Literary Analysis (7:11)

Poem VII on the bliss of love (7:11–8:5) is divided into four poetic units which recall the mutual happiness that bride and bridegroom had enjoyed during their former meetings, dealt with in poem II (2:1-17). The thematic content of each song is taken up, in the inverse order, with a view to a permanent relationship being established between bride and bridegroom.

The opening lines of poem VII are a distich phrased as a covenant clause expressing reciprocal relationship between allies. In relation to the preceding and subsequent poetic units, this distich has a strictly structural function within its context, so as to set out the beginning of the poem and to serve as a point of reference to related songs with identical themes (2:16-17 and 7:11). On the other hand, some commentators join this distich to the preceding song of which it would be a concluding verse (DELITZSCH, 133; GERLEMAN, 201; RUDOLPH, 174). Others place it at the beginning of the succeeding song as if it were an introductory verse (ASENSIO, 614; BEA, 57; BUZY, 352; COLOMBO, 124; LYS, 270; POUGET-GUITTON, 174; RAVASI,

127; RICCIOTTI, 269; SEGAL, *VT* 12, 476; WÜRTHWEIN, 64; ZAPLETAL, 139). Others again keep it separate from the preceding and subsequent songs in keeping with the theory that the book is a collection of love songs with stray stanzas and fragments scattered in its various parts (KEEL, 232; KRINETZKI, 225; PIATTI, 173).

Vocabulary Analysis (7:11)

Vs. 11: The association between the king and the Jewish nation, represented by the Shulamite, is expressed by two clauses which specify the covenant relationship: "I am my beloved's" (*'anî ledôdî*) "and his desire is for me" (*we'ālay tešûqātô*). This relationship is set forth by means of a shorter formulation in 2:16 "my beloved is mine and I am his," and in 6:3 "I am my beloved's and my beloved is mine." Here there is mentioned the intention of the "beloved" (*dôd*) to associate himself with the Shulamite, making explicit "his desire" (*tešûqātô*) to establish this union. The word *tešûqâ* (desire, impulse) also occurs in Gn 3:16 which deals with the relationship between wife and husband in which union she finds her plenitude and her social status. This word is used furthermore in the story of Cain where the temptation to sin is described in terms of desire which is shown personified as threatening to take control of Cain (Gn 4:7). The prepositions used with *tešûqâ* are *'el* "for" (Gn 3:16; 4:7) and *'al* "on, onto" (Ct 7:11). JOÜON ascribes the use of *'al* to the influence of Aramaic (*Ct,* 297). It is possible, however, that the use of *'al* is a means of expression which indicates the status of the superior in relation to the inferior (cf. 2 Chr 32:9).

In comparison with the other texts which set out reciprocal relations and specify the function of the "beloved" by the title of "shepherd" (2:16; 6:3), this text is just a generic formulation of the union between king and nation. It does not constitute, thus, a covenant formula because the type of association is not indicated nor is the commitment that is taken on.

Commentary: The Theme of the Covenant (7:11)

This theme deals with the covenant between the king and the Jewish nation, represented by the Shulamite. The identity of the king, designated by the title of "beloved," and that of the Shulamite is so well known at this stage in the poem that the generic formulation of the reciprocal relationship between the two persons acquires its own specificity in the context of the aspirations of the population of Judah for the restoration of the monarchy. With the declaration of belonging to the king, the population, represented by its local leaders, accepts the pact of submission in relation to the Davidic ruler. And the representative of the house of David shows his intention of linking the destiny of the royal family to the future of the nation. Thus he accepts the commitment of collaborating in the protection and upholding of the population's interests in the ways prescribed by the covenant. The theme of the covenant has been dealt with previously in 2:16-17 in the perspective of the future restoration of the monarchy.

2. ✦ *The Return to the Countryside (7:12-14)*

12 Come, my beloved, *Bride*
    let us go forth into the fields,
    and lodge in the villages;
13 let us go out early to the vineyards,
    and see whether the vines have budded,
whether the grape blossoms have opened
    and the pomegranates are in bloom.
There I will give you my friendship.
14 The mandrakes give forth fragrance,
    and at our doors are all choice fruits,
new as well as old,
    which I have laid up for you, O my beloved.

Accented Transliteration (7:12-14)

12 *lekā́h dôdî́ nēṣḗ' haśśādéh*
    nālî́nāh bakkefārî́m
13 *naškî́māh lakkerāmî́m*
    nir'éh 'im pārehấ haggéfen
pittáḥ hassemādár hēnḗṣû hārimmônî́m
    šā́m 'ettḗn 'et-dōday lā́k
14 *haddûdā'î́m nātenû-rếaḥ*
    we'al-petāḥếnû kol-megādî́m
ḥadāšî́m gam-yešānî́m
    dôdî́ ṣāfántî lā́k

Literary Analysis (7:12-14)

This song presents in three scenes the itinerary proposed to the bridegroom for his visit to the rural districts of the country (vs. 12), to the orchards (vs. 13), and to the settlements of the local population (vs. 14). The action is carried out in rural surroundings during an excursion in spring. Thus there is applied to this song that which in Greek drama was called the rule of the three units: of action, of time, and of place. A comparison between the two songs about the excursion into the territory of Judah (2:8-15 and 7:12-14) highlights similar and different aspects: the invitation, the description of spring, the picture of the landscape, and the joint journey of the two are similar; however the authors of the invitation are different, viz. the bridegroom in 2:10, 13 and the bride in 7:12; also different is the journey, viz. the country in 2:12, the fields in 7:12, and the gift mentioned only in 7:14.

Poetic and rhetorical devices used here are sound repetition: assonance *a–i* (vss. 12b, 13a); word repetition: inclusion "my beloved–my beloved" (vss. 12a, 14d), paronomasia *dûdā'îm–dôdî* (vs. 14a + d); figures of relationship: merismus "new and old" (vs. 14c), indicating the annual yield of an orchard; synecdoche which consists in the use of a part for the whole, viz. doors for houses (vs. 14b).

Vocabulary Analysis (7:12-14)

Vs. 12: The invitation to undertake the journey through the rural districts of Judah is directed to the "beloved," a title which the bride confers on the Davidic descendant who has been instituted by the Persians in the office of governor of the country. The title "my beloved" (*dôdî*) is to be found in the first and the last verse of this song forming an inclusion. Since the two persons belong to different social ranks it does not befall the bride to give orders to the bridegroom, and thus the imperative mood of the verb "come!" (*lekāh*) does not express a command, but an appeal, equivalent to the interjection "come then!" (Joüon, *Gr* § 177f). The verbs referring to the itinerary set out the appeal in the cohortative mood in Hebrew *nēṣē'* (let us go forth!) and *nālînāh* (let us lodge!). In the spelling of the verb *nēṣē'* the cohortative ending is suppressed as it normally is in *lamed 'aleph* verbs (Joüon, *Gr* § 125n). The direction of the itinerary is indicated by the terminative complement "to the fields" (*haśśādeh*) expressed in Hebrew by the accusative of direction without a preposition (Joüon, *Gr* § 114n). The stops anticipated for rest during the journey are situated in "villages" (*kefārîm*) of the rural districts of Judah. Some commentators, however, take *kefārîm* in its meaning of henna bushes (1:14; 4:13), a homonymous word in Hebrew, and interpret the clause in terms of an invitation to bed in the henna bushes (Pope, 645; Rudolph, 175; Würthwein, 64; Zapletal, 139).

Vs. 13: The route which the journey takes is specified by the direction "to the vineyards" (*lakkerāmîm*) which designate by metonymy the rural districts and its inhabitants because the vineyards are to be found on the slopes of the hills near the settlements. The invitation is expressed in Hebrew by the cohortative mood *naškîmāh* "let us go out early!" and *nir'eh* "let us see!" In *lamed he* verbs the cohortative mood is expressed by the common form of the imperfect (*GK* § 75 l).

In the other account of the visit to the same region (6:11), by means of a comparison with the flowering of the vegetation in spring an allusion is made to the promising perspectives of the kingdom of Judah on its way to restoration. In this text the following ideas and expressions are repeated: the "vineyards" (7:13a) correspond to the "nut orchard" (6:11a), "to see whether the vines have budded" (6:11c and 7:13b), and "whether the pomegranates were in bloom" (6:11d and 7:13d). The reference to the blossoming (*s^e^mādar*) can be found in this verse and in 2:13, 15 indicating the link between the two descriptions of the countryside in spring and between the two songs which deal with the same theme (2:8-15 and 7:12-14).

The vine and the pomegranate tree are mentioned together in this verse because they coincide in the season in which they are in bloom. The following song refers to the juice extracted from their fruits, an allusion to the harvest season, thus establishing again a link between the two songs (7:12-14 and 8:1-4).

The adverb of place "there" (*šām*) indicates the place of meeting where the bride will personally express her friendship toward the bridegroom. This "friendship" (*dōdîm*) indicates the political relationship between the Davidic descendant and the leader of the inhabitants of the country represented by the bride. It is to be noted that in the MT two spellings of *dôdîm/dōdîm* are to be found so as to distinguish between two meanings: in *scriptio plena, dôdîm* is used to designate "loved ones, uncles, cousins," and in *scriptio defectiva* there can be found *dōdîm* in the abstract sense "love" (Ez 16:8; 23:17; Prv 7:18) and "friendship" (Ct 1:2, 4; 4:10; 7:13). The option for one of the several connotations of *dōdîm* "friendship, caresses, love" to translate this term in the Song of Songs depends on the focus adopted in the interpretation of the whole book.

The phenomenon of the borrowing of terms from the common language happened before the fixing of the terminology for treaties. Thus in the diplomatic correspondence of Mari the Akkadian terms *salim* (friend) and *salīmum* (friendship) used in the treaties have a political meaning (McCarthy, 141). In the same way in the Song of Songs the terms *dôd* (beloved) and *dōdîm* (friendship) have an analogous meaning owing to the context of the covenant.

The token of friendship is the gift handed over (*ntn*) to the ally, a gift that is specified in the following verse. This is a question of a symbolic gesture that brings about the covenant (Kalluveettil, 29).

Vs. 14: Springtime is indicated in this verse by the blossoming of the "mandrakes" (*dûdā'îm*) whose pungent and sweetish scent is quite distinctive among the fragrances emitted by other plants that are in flower. There are two species of mandrakes. We are dealing here with the *Mandragora officinarum* which flowers in spring, since the *Mandragora autumnalis* flourishes in the autumn. There is only mentioned in this text the typical fragrance of its flowers and not its fruit which in ancient times was considered an aphrodisiac and was thought to promote pregnancy (Gn 30:14-16). In the clause "it gives forth fragrance" (*nātan rêaḥ*) the verb *ntn* (to give) is used in the sense proper to an idiomatic expression (1:12; 2:13).

The transition from the description of the countryside in spring to that of the village scene is indicated by the reference to the doors which give access to the dwelling places of the rural population. The doors represent by synecdoche the houses by positing a part for the whole. In the orchards close by are to be found fig-trees whose early figs (*paggîm*) are collected at the beginning of spring (2:13). These are the "new" (*ḥadāšîm*) fruits. Within the houses "old" (*yešānîm*) and dehydrated fruits are kept, e.g. raisins, figs, and dates. The correlation between old and new fruits in the figure of merismus represents the annual production of the orchards. The delicious taste of these fruits is expressed by the word *megādîm* (choice) an abstract plural which qualifies natural fruits (4:13, 16).

Some commentators take the preposition *ʿal* as an indication of the superior position "over" instead of proximity "next, close" (1:7, 8; 5:12; 7:5, 14), and interpret the phrase "over our doors" as an allusion to the niche or the shelf above the doors where fruits might be stored (DELITZSCH, 137; KRINETZKI, 234, et al.). The phrase "at our doors" (*ʿal petāḥênû*) has a broader meaning: there results from it an indication not only of the place but also of the abundance and variety of "the fruits of all sorts" which the rural population has for its consumption.

At the end of the invitation the bride expresses her expectation that she will be able to show her adherence to the bridegroom through the handing over of natural fruits. By this symbolic gesture the inhabitants of the country demonstrate their fealty to the sovereign so as to bring about the covenant between the house of David and the population of Judah.

Commentary: The Theme of the Country (7:12-14)

The theme of this song is the country of Judah whose inhabitants live expectantly, waiting for the monarchy to be restored in the near future. The condition for this monarchy to be reestablished in the country is the coming of the Davidic descendant invested with royal authority so as to exercise the government over the people in the territory of Judah (vs. 12). This coming, so anxiously awaited, will give rise to a new era in the history of Israel compared to the morning, beginning of the day, and to the spring, beginning of the year (vs. 13). In the agrarian world where the population dwells in villages and lives in contact with nature it is not surprising that the expectancies of the community be compared with images drawn from their surroundings. This is not done so as to make country life more romantic or to preach ruralism as a perennial source of national and authentic values. The author of the Song, while describing the land of Judah in terms which are attractive to the eyes of the Jews whether they be autochthonous or repatriated, wants them to conceive it as their homeland in which they can realize themselves as free citizens dedicated to the tasks of the reorganization of their political community. Although the measures which affect the administration of the provinces of the Persian empire are taken by the central government, the movement in favor of the restoration of the monarchy in Judah has at least a chance of being tolerated by the imperial authorities if it has the support of all the citizens. In order to obtain a consensus among all the inhabitants of Judah on the system of government to be installed there, the covenant between the house of David and the population, following the pattern of the old regime, is mentioned (vs. 14). The theme of the country dealt with in this song complements the same theme that had been developed previously (2:8-15).

3. ✦ *The Return Home (8:1-4)*

1 Oh that you were like a brother to me, *Bride*
   who nursed at my mother's breast!
If I met you outside, I would kiss you,
   and none would despise me.
2 I would lead you so as to bring you
   into the house of my mother, as she taught me.
I would give you spiced wine to drink,
   the juice of pomegranates.
3 His left arm would be under my head,
   and his right arm would embrace me.
4 I adjure you, O daughters of Jerusalem,
   that you stir not up nor awaken love
   until it be propitious.

Accented Transliteration (8:1-4)

1 *mî́ yittenkā́ keʾāḥ lî́*
   yônḗq šedế ʾimmî́

'emṣā'akā́ baḥûṣ 'eššāqᵉkā́
gám lō'-yābûzû lî́
2 *'enhāgᵃkā́ 'ᵃbî'ᵃkā́*
'el-bết 'immî́ tᵉlammᵉdḗnî
'ašqᵉkā́ miyyáyin hārḗqaḥ
mē'ᵃsî́s rimmōnî́
3 *śᵉmō'lṓ táḥat rō'šî́*
wîmînṓ tᵉḥabbᵉqḗnî
4 *hišbá'tî 'etkém*
bᵉnṓt yᵉrûšāláim
mah-ttā'îrû ûmah-ttᵉ'ōrᵉrû́
'et-hā'ahᵃbā́ 'ad šetteḥpā́ṣ

Literary Analysis (8:1-4)

This song composed of two strophes and a double refrain expresses the longing of the Judean population for the renewal of the covenant with the descendant of the Davidic dynasty (vs. 1) and manifests the people's expectancy for the restoration of Judah's capital (vs. 2). The first refrain mentions the embrace as a symbolic gesture of the enactment of the covenant between bridegroom and bride (vs. 3). The second refrain contains a warning to the representatives of the inhabitants of Jerusalem not yet to establish relations with other people (vs. 4).

Poetic and rhetorical devices that occur in the song are sound repetition: end rhyme *-î* (vss. 2d, 3ab); word repetition: paronomasia *'eššāqᵉkā–'ašqᵉkā* (vss. 1c, 2c), epistrophe which consists in the termination of two clauses with the same word *lî* (vs. 1a + d); repetition of a sentence: refrains (vss. 3 and 4). Rhetorical devices: antithetic parallelism "his left arm–his right arm"; asyndeton (vss. 1c-2c), synecdoche "the house of my mother" so as to indicate the capital of Judah (vs. 2b), and the simile "you are like a brother to me."

Vocabulary Analysis (8:1-4)

Vs. 1: The desiderative clause, introduced by the idiom "would that!" (*mî yittēn*), expresses the desire that the bridegroom become like a brother. The Hebrew term *'āḥ* means blood brother and also a member of the same family or tribe. The basic bond among the Semites was in fact kinship based on relations of consanguinity and affinity. By a fictitious extension of kinship strangers were adopted by the family or the tribe and came to be designated "brothers" who were entitled to membership of a discrete group. Through this bond of brotherhood they became thus full members of the family or tribe and partners of equal status. In the political field this terminology of social relationship was applied to the allies of the nation or the people to indicate the type of association existing between them in virtue of the covenant union between the partners (KALLUVEETTIL, 99f, 204f).

The comparison between bridegroom and brother is based on the analogy between family relationship and a relationship of a political nature. It is this sort of relationship which it was intended to establish between bridegroom and bride through the covenant. The commentators who emend the text on the basis of the Greek and Latin versions, deleting the particle *kᵉ* (like) as dittography of the object suffix of the preceding verb, deprive the clause of its comparative meaning (RUDOLPH, 178; ZAPLETAL, 144).

The insertion "nursed at my mother's breasts" (*yônēk šᵉdê ʾimmî*) is an amplification of "brother." The mother of the bride is a poetic personification representing, as a corporative personality, the pre-exilic Israelite nation (1:6; 3:4; 6:9; 8:1, 2) whose post-exilic successor is the community of Judah under the leadership of the bride.

The coordination of the clauses without a conjunction here indicates the conditioning relationship (JOÜON, *Gr* § 167a), e.g. "If I met you" (*ʾemṣāʾᵃkā*), "I would kiss you" (*ʾeššāqᵉkā*). The circumstantial adjunct "outside" (*baḥûṣ*) designates the space outside the house or the city, i.e. the street, the fields, or the desert in opposition to "house" in the following verse.

The kiss could be a gesture of greeting (1:2), or an expression of erotic passion (Prv 7:13), or again an act of cultic reverence (1 Kgs 19:18; Hos 13:2). Although oriental customs did not permit spouses to manifest their affection in public, they tolerated them, however, in the case of greetings between brothers and allies. The following intensive clause, introduced by the particle *gam* (even), has its indefinite personal subject expressed in Hebrew by the 3rd plural masculine of the verbal form *yābûzû* (someone despises).

Vs. 2: In this verse the verbs of the principal clauses are in the subjunctive mood: "I would lead you" (*ʾenhāgᵃkā*), "I would bring you" (*ʾᵃbîʾᵃkā*), "I would give you to drink" (*ʾašqᵉkā*). The succession of two almost synonymous verbs, e.g. "to lead" and "to bring," is a literary device employed here so as to highlight the point of arrival, i.e. "the house of my mother" (*bêt ʾimmî*), meaning the capital of the country. Since in the pre-exilic period the city of Jerusalem was the capital and the religious center of the Israelite nation, personified by the "mother," in the same form in the post-exilic period the community of Judah longs for the restoration of the Davidic monarchy with its seat in Jerusalem, once again the capital of the country.

The insertion "she taught me" (*tᵉlammᵉdēnî*) specifies the role of the "mother." The verb *lmd* in *Piel* means "to teach, instruct" and does not have the generic connotation "to bring up" as it has been translated elsewhere

(PIATTI, 175). This inserted clause, which cuts the flow of the clauses interrupting their meaning, is placed in the complex sentence containing several clauses (vs. 2). Now, asyndetic coordination is a literary device employed in poetry which consists in the leaving out of conjunctions. The translation can, however, demand the use of conjunctions so as to indicate the relationship between the Hebrew clauses. Thus the link between the juxtaposed clauses "I would lead you . . . I would bring you" is indicated by the final conjunction "so as to." As to the relation of the insertion "she taught me" with its preceding clause, the type of conjunction which corresponds to the logic of the ideas is that of conformity "as." For this reason the coordination of Hebrew clauses by juxtaposition is translated by subordinating conjunctions "so as to bring you . . . as she taught me."

The title "mother," who taught the daughter, does not concern the function of providing sustenance, but that of transmitting the norms of life and mores that had been in force in the Israelite communities at first under tribal rule and thereafter under the absolute control of a king. Now, the "mother" represents the pre-exilic community from which its post-exilic successor learned the meaning of the participation of social groups in political life. Furthermore, she was taught that the Davidic monarchy embodies the national consciousness of the Jewish people, and because of this it was her task to bring the descendant of the house of David to the seat of government in Jerusalem.

The tense of the verb *t^e^lamm^e^dēnî* is not future, because the *yiqtol* is used here to express an action repeated in the past (JOÜON, *Gr* § 113e). This interpretation was adopted by other expositors (BEA, 57; KRINETZKI, 312). The ancient versions, however, suppressed this verb so as to put in its place the clause "and into the chamber of her that conceived me" (3:4). Some commentators have copied this emendation of MT from those versions (BUZY, 356; RICCIOTTI, 271; WINANDY, 90; ZAPLETAL, 144). Others substitute this verb by another of a different root, i.e. *tēl^e^dēnî* (she bore me), a verb similar to that in 3:4 (POPE, 659; RUDOLPH, 178; WÜRTHWEIN, 66). However, the majority of the commentators of the Song translate *t^e^lamm^e^dēnî* "you will teach me," based on the morphological similarity between the 2nd singular masculine and the 3rd singular feminine of the verbal form of the *yiqtol*. According to this translation, the subject of the verb is the bridegroom who will give instruction to the bride about loving relationship.

The mention of two types of drink, e.g. one alcoholic (wine) and the other non-alcoholic (pomegranate juice), constitutes the connecting link with the previous song, where the vine and the pomegranate tree are referred to (7:13). The verb *šqh* (to give to drink) in *Hiphil* normally takes the accusative both of person and of thing, but in this text there is a modification of the use of the verb construed with the partitive *min* to introduce the second object, a possible indication of later usage (JOÜON, *Ct*, 306). The "wine" (*yayin*) is specified by *hāreqaḥ* (the spice), in apposition, a *hapax legomenon* related to the cognate word *merqāḥîm* which means "aromatic herb," as is explained in 5:13. The "spiced wine" is prepared with a mixture of aromatic essences so as to increase its flavor and avoid deterioration. In the expression "pomegranate juice" (*ʿᵃsîs rimmōnî*) the apocopated plural form *rimmōnî* is used instead of the regular form *rimmōnîm* (pomegranates), as it is written in many Hebrew manuscripts and in the Targum. The use of apocopated plural nouns is attested in other biblical texts (*GK* § 87f) as also in Ct 7:10. It is not then a question of a word composed by the agglutination of the pronominal suffix *-î* (my) to the noun *rimmōn* (pomegranate), and thus the translation "my juice of pomegranate" or "the juice of my pomegranate" is to be discarded.

To serve drinks is no mere expression of hospitality or of friendship, but a symbolic rite which precedes the ceremony of the covenant enactment. A similar rite can be found in the covenant ceremonial of the Assyrians who drank water from a jug while they pronounced the formula of the commitment that has been assumed (McCarthy, 150). However, the rite as such, even without verbal communication, has a special meaning by the fact that the leading figure representative of the Jewish population and the heir to the throne are participating in it, as also because of the importance of the place where it is carried out, i.e. the capital of the country.

Vs. 3: This verse is a literal quotation of the text in 2:6 except for the suppression of the preposition *lᵉ* with *taḥat* (under) without, however, altering its meaning. There is no unanimity among commentators concerning the interpretation of the mood in which the verbs of the sentence are expressed. The majority of them transcribe the text in 2:6 in the form of a declarative sentence with the verbs in the present tense; some translate it as a conditional sentence (Bruno, 51; Rudolph, 178), or as a desiderative sentence (Bea, 59; Lys, 281; Pouget-Guitton, 176; Zapletal, 150). The absence of the bridegroom in this scene does not permit the verbs to be translated in the indicative mood with the action expressed in the present tense. The translation by a conditional sentence ties it thus to the preceding sentences. A desiderative sentence would be a mere repetition of a wish similar to that expressed in the initial clause (vs. 1a). The action which the bridegroom is expected to carry out when he has his definitive meeting with the bride is the embrace of friendship as a symbolic gesture of the covenant enactment between the Davidic descendant and the leader of the people represented by the bride.

Vs. 4: The second refrain is the one taken up from the apostrophe in 2:7 with some modification. The omission of the allusion to "gazelles or hinds of the field," as a metaphor of the rural population, indicates that the discrimination which initially existed between repatriate and autochthonous Jews has been overcome. The particles *ʾim . . . wᵉʾim* replaced by *mah . . .*

ûmah used in the adjuration are similar in meaning (*GK* § 150dN; Joüon, *Gr* § 144h).

The apostrophe directed by the bride to the elite of the Jewish priesthood, i.e. the "daughters of Jerusalem," is a warning not to ally themselves to the leaders of the neighboring people by means of treaties. For the condition necessary for political relations to be established with other countries is the existence of the state resulting from the covenant, i.e. "love," between the king and the people of Judah. And only the members of this national covenant have the prerogative to assume commitments with other states in the degree to which they are in the interest (*ḥpṣ*) to all the nation (2:7).

The juxtaposition of the two refrains relates the bride with the bridegroom (vs. 3) and with the "daughters of Jerusalem" (vs. 4). While vs. 3 replies to the question: Where does the authority of the bride come from? vs. 4 replies to the question: Who is it who promotes the interests of the community, the bride or the daughters of Jerusalem?

Commentary: The Theme of the Capital (8:1-4)

The theme of this song is that of the aspirations of the inhabitants of Judah for the establishment of the capital of the country in Jerusalem, with the consequent elevation of the city to the status of the official residence of the heir to the throne. While he resides in Mizpah, a small town some thirteen kilometers to the north of Jerusalem, the future king has no national status; in fact he occupies a subaltern position as governor at the service of the Persians. It was hoped that with the transference of the future king and the executive branch of the government to Jerusalem, the residence of the head of government, the administrative center, and the seat of the citizens' assembly would be installed there. As a consequence of this, Jerusalem would become the capital of the country as seat of the Davidic monarchy and symbol of unity of all the social groups organized into a political community.

With the restoration of the capital, the town of Mizpah would be forgotten as the former and provisional residence of the governor of Judah, for it continued to remind the Jews of the national catastrophe through having been the seat of the Babylonian governor after the destruction of Jerusalem and the fall of the kingdom of Judah. However, it was even more important to give continuity to the institutions of Israel than to wipe out sad memories. Among the institutions to be continued there figured in the pre-exilic period the city of Jerusalem as capital of the kingdom and religious center of the Israelite nation. With the inauguration of the era of restoration of the history of Israel in 538 B.C. the reconstruction of the Jerusalem temple began. While the works in the sanctuary were going on, the prophet

Zechariah, glimpsing a glorious future of Jerusalem, prophesied that she would become once again the chosen city of God (Zech 1:17; 2:16) as the capital not only of Judah but also of the future kingdom of God (Zech 2:14-16). Before Jerusalem had been rebuilt, the same prophet proclaimed her to be the sign of divine election (Zech 3:2) for the community of Judah in the post-exilic period, as also for the Jews of the diaspora.

Throughout the Persian domination over the territory of Judah it had not been possible for the leader of the Jewish population to carry out in public any meetings of a political character in favor of the restoration of the Davidic monarchy without causing a confrontation with the foreign occupying forces (vs. 1). And neither could the Jews promote at that time the transfer of the seat of government to Jerusalem without awakening in the Persians the suspicion that they were attempting to restore the capital of the former kingdom of Judah and that they were working toward the linking of the community of Judah with the royal house of David (vs. 2).

The situation of dependence on Persian hegemony did not reduce, however, the social groups of Judah to a state of lethargy, but gave rise to strife between repatriate and autochthonous Jews in their attempt to secure a dominant position. For the elite of the Jewish priesthood, once back from Babylon, tried to secure its leadership and conquer its sources of income through political treaties with the leaders of the neighboring countries. Against the opportunistic and self-seeking measures, which worked in detriment to the cohesion of the community, the leader of the native population rose up demanding the suspension of these alliances (vs. 4). The leader of the people thus assumed a political function when coming in defense of the common good against the particular interests of a privileged social group, and they did this based not on a contest of rivaling forces but on the hierarchy of ends which had its foundation in the structure of the government whose head was to be the king of the house of David (vs. 3). The theme of this song complements the tenor of the previous song (2:4-7).

4. ✦ *The Return to the Apple Tree (8:5)*

5 Who is that coming up from the desert, *Chorus*
leaning upon her beloved?
Under the apple tree I awakened you. *Bride*
There your mother was in labor with you,
there she who bore you was in labor.

Accented Transliteration (8:5)

5 *mî zṓ't 'ōlā́h min-hammidbā́r*
mitrappéqet 'al-dôdā́h
táḥat hattappûᵃḥ 'ôrartíkā
šā́mmāh ḥibbᵉlátkā 'imméka
šā́mmāh ḥibbᵉlā́ yᵉlādátkā

Literary Analysis (8:5)

This brief song in dialogue style is composed of a distich, formulated as a rhetorical question, and a tristich in which the bride evokes an event from the past. The unity of this section has its base in the thematic content and in the literary form which is characterized by an initial question serving as transition between the refrain of the previous song and this one which evokes a past happening, in contrast with the section of descriptive praise contained in the following song.

Poetic and rhetorical devices used in the song are sound repetition: assonance *o–a* (vs. 5a-c), end rhyme *-kā* (vs. 5c-e); word repetition: anaphora *mi–mi* (vs. 5ab), *šāmmāh–šāmmāh* (vs. 5de); repetition of structural patterns: parallelism, e.g. adverb + verb + noun // adverb + verb + verb *šāmmāh ḥibbᵉlatkā 'immekā // šāmmāh ḥibbᵉlâ yᵉlādatkā;* rhetorical device: the "apple tree" used as an image of the Davidic monarchy.

Vocabulary Analysis (8:5)

Vs. 5: The initial phrase "Who is that coming up from the desert?" (*mî zō't 'ōlāh min hammidbār*) repeats the first hemistich of 3:6 spoken by the chorus. The difference between the two clauses is the use of feminine pronouns, interrogative and demonstrative, which occur in this verse referring to the woman, while in 3:6 these pronouns are in the neuter because they refer to something undefined. The ascent from the desert is the road which comes up from Jericho across the desert of Judah to the plateau where the city of Jerusalem is situated. The meaning of this geographical indication can be elucidated by the reference to the flight of Zedekiah, the last king of Judah, who managed to break through the besieging forces around Jerusalem on the eve of the capitulation of the city in 587 B.C. He was, however, captured by Babylonian troops in the valley of Jericho and deported to Babylon (2 Kgs 25:4-5; Jer 39:4-5). At the place from which the king of Judah had been taken to exile the descendant of the Davidic dynasty will begin his return to Jerusalem so as to occupy the royal throne which had remained empty during the exile of King Zedekiah and his family.

The person who is coming in the direction of the onlookers is identified as a woman "leaning upon her beloved" (*mitrappeqet ʿal dôdāh*). The participle *mitrappeqet* is a *hapax legomenon* usually taken to mean "she is leaning" on the basis of cognates in other Semitic languages. The presence of this woman alone with "her beloved" (*dôdāh*) is a peculiar literary device of introducing onto the scene the person who will take up the word in the following verse. With relation to the bridegroom, she is the bride who represents the leading figure of the autochthonous population of Judah. On the occasion of the repatriation of the heir to the throne it befell to the leaders of the Jewish population, who were longing for the restoration of the Davidic monarchy in Judah, to receive him on the road coming from the eastern frontier of the country and to accompany him to his official residence situated in Jerusalem. The support offered by the bridegroom to the bride symbolizes the function of the monarchical institution as the basis of the political structure of the restored nation.

With the intention of perfecting the stichometry of the Song it has been conjectured that a line of this verse has been suppressed, and that the distich should initially have been a tristich because of the symmetry with the following tristich (RUDOLPH, 180; ZAPLETAL, 145).

The bride turns to the bridegroom to tell him that every time she thought of kingship she remembered him. This idea is expressed in figurative language by the prepositional phrase "under the apple tree" (*taḥat hattappûaḥ*) and by the clause "I awakened you" (*ʿôrartîkā*). The apple tree is the image of the monarchy highlighting its function as protective shelter of the nation, already explained above in 2:3. The preposition "under" (*taḥat*) indicates the place in the shade of the apple tree occupied by the Israelite people during the monarchic period which ran for four centuries of its history up till the suppression of the monarchy and the deportation of the king in 587 B.C. However the idea of the monarchy remained alive in the collective memory of the Jews during the exilic period. After the promulgation of the imperial edict leading to the repatriation of the exiled Jews there arose a movement in favor of the restoration of the monarchy through the preaching of the prophets Haggai and Zechariah who, in 520 B.C., had stirred up the hope that in the near future a Davidic descendant, who had returned to the homeland, would occupy the throne (Hag 2:20-23; Zech 4:11-14; 6:12-14).

With the phrase "under the apple tree" the bride refers to kingship as the protecting power of the nation, and with the clause "I awakened you" she alludes to the movement in favor of the Davidites' accession to the throne.

The expression "your mother" (*ʾimmekā*) designates the mother of the bridegroom as a poetic personification of the royal house of David, already explained above in 3:11. Two almost identical clauses evoke the circumstances which preceded the birth of the Davidic crown prince destined to occupy the royal throne. One of these are the pangs of childbirth suffered by the mother. The verb *ḥbl* in *Piel* means "to be in labor" and also "to be pregnant" (Ps 7:15). Other meanings based on homonymous Hebrew words are not relevant here. The verbs *ḥibbᵉlatkā* (she was in labor with you) and *ḥibbᵉlâ* (she was in labor) suggest the expectancy of the crown prince's accession to the throne in analogy with the physiological phenomenon of childbirth.

The other circumstance related to birth is the place mentioned where the mother was going to bear her son. The Hebrew adverb *šāmmāh* (there), although written with the paragogic *he,* does not indicate the movement toward a place (JOÜON, *Gr* § 93i), but refers to the apple tree of the previous sentence.

The interpretation of the text has to take into consideration not only the meaning of the words but also the emphasis given to the idea by the repetition of terms used in both main clauses: the subject is "your mother" (*'immekā*) in parallel with "she who bore you" (*yᵉlādatkā*); the predicate is expressed by the same verb formulated in two different ways, e.g. "she was in labor with you" (*ḥibbᵉlatkā*) and "she was in labor" (*ḥibbᵉlâ*). The only word repeated without alteration is the adverb "there" (*šāmmāh*), i.e. "under the apple tree." That tree is part of the heraldic emblem of Davidic royalty. The heir apparent will have his name inscribed in the genealogical tree of the Davidic dynasty. His birth in a foreign land does not impede that he be recognized as the legitimate successor of the house of David and that he have the right of citizenship of Judah. The royal family exiled in Babylon kept alive the hope of seeing one of her sons returning to the homeland so as to occupy the throne of David.

The majority of commentators, however, suppose that this verse is merely a fragment from some lost poem inserted in this poetic unit; for this reason they explain it in the context of the preceding or subsequent song and have recourse to emendations of the MT so as to adapt the text to support their specific mode of interpretation.

Commentary: The Theme of Royalty (8:5)

Situated in the context of a journey, this song deals with the return of Davidic royalty to Judah. With the repatriation of the heir apparent to the homeland a new page is opened in the annals of the history of Israel. The interregnum, which began with the deportation of the king of Judah to Babylon in 587 B.C., has come to an end. From the same place where King Zedekiah had been captured by the Babylonians and taken prisoner to exile, the descendant of the house of David begins his journey home in the direction of the official seat of the king. His return means the repatriation of the royal house in the promised land where, ever since the establishment of the monarchy in Judah, the Davidic king had in his charge the government of the nation and was a visible sign of the divine election for the people bound to Yahweh.

The leading figure representative of the people which goes to receive him on the road, ascending from the desert of Judah, so as to accompany him on his journey to the capital, shows its loyalty to the house of David to which it had maintained its allegiance by the pact of submission, in exchange for the covenant between king and people.

The temporary exile of the king and royal family had resulted in the cessation of the monarchy. But the return of the Davidic descendant to the homeland and his nomination by the Persian emperor to the office of governor were hopeful signs of its imminent restoration in Judah, which would officially be instituted by the ceremony of enthronement described in another song (5:9-16).

The mother of the prince, as a personification of the house of David, is represented in an advanced state of pregnancy so as to illustrate the growing hope that the monarchy will shortly be restored in Judah. Thus the presence of the royal family in the homeland is the guarantee of the Davidic dynasty being preserved from extinction. It was not aimed, with the restoration of the monarchy, to recover the national grandeur of the golden age of Israelite history, but to revitalize an institution which, as a visible sign of the divine election of Israel, must contribute efficaciously toward the political organization of the inhabitants of Judah in the framework of the Davidic monarchy, under the kingship of God over Israel. The theme of this song complements the thematic content of another song (2:1-3).

Poem VIII *The Plenitude of Love* (8:6-14)

1 ✦ *The Power of Love (8:6-7)*

Bride

6 Set me as a seal upon your heart,
    as a seal upon your arm;
for love is strong as death,
    passion is fierce as hell.
Its flashes are flashes of fire,
    a raging flame.
7 Many waters cannot quench love,
    neither can floods drown it.
If a man offered for love
    all the wealth of his house,
    he would be utterly scorned.

Accented Transliteration (8:6-7)

6 *śîmḗnî kaḥôtā́m ʿal-libbékā*
    kaḥôtā́m ʿal-z^{e}rôʿékā
kî-ʿazzấ kammā́wet ʾah^{a}bấ
    qāšā́h kiš^{e}ʾốl qinʾấ
r^{e}šāféhā rišpế ʾḗš
    šalhébetyā́h
7 *máyim rabbî́m lōʾ yûk^{e}lû́*
    l^{e}kabbốt ʾet-hāʾah^{a}bấ
    ûn^{e}hārốt lōʾ yišṭ^{e}fû́hā

'im-yittḗn 'îš
'et-kol-hốn bêtố bā'aḥªbấ
bốz yābûzû lố

Literary Analysis (8:6-7)

Poem VIII on the plenitude of love (8:6-14) is divided into four songs which extol the power, legacy, treasure, and intimacy of love between bride and bridegroom who represent, respectively, the community of Judah and the descendant of the Davidic dynasty. Both are related through a political covenant which defines the relationship between the authority of the sovereign and the prerogatives of the subjects, following the law of the Davidic monarchy. The themes dealt with in poem I (1:2-17) are taken up, in the inverse order, and developed in each of the four songs of this poem.

This song is composed of two strophes: the first (vs. 6) is in three distichs, the second, in two tristichs. The bride expresses her desire to belong to the bridegroom as exclusive and inalienable property similar to a seal which is for the exclusive use of its owner. The link between the strophes is indicated by the word "love" which is repeated three times in the description of the love-relationship between these persons. In the definition of love the figure of amplification is used, explicitating its characteristics by means of comparisons drawn from mythology (e.g. death and hell), from the observation of nature (e.g. flashes of fire and a raging flame, floodwater and rivers), and from the experience of economic power (e.g. money buys all except love). It is to be noted that the word "love" is not to be taken in the sense of emotional affection between lovers, but as a technical term to express the relationship of political alliance between the Davidic king and the Jewish community as is explained above in 1:3.

Poetic and rhetorical devices that occur in the song are sound repetition: assonance *i–a, kî-'azzâ . . . qin'â* (vs. 6cd), homoeotelleuton *kaḥôtām 'al-libbekā // kaḥôtām 'al-zᵉrô'ekā* (vs. 6ab), internal rhyme *im–im* (vs. 7a), *ôt–ôt* (vs. 7bc); word repetition: "love" (thrice), "seal"; rhetorical devices: the etymological figure *bôz yābûzû*, the allusion to death and hell is taken as a figurative reference to Mot and Sheol, the hyperbole "love is strong as death, passion is fierce as hell," the simile "me as a seal," "love strong as death," "passion fierce as hell," and the metaphor "its flashes are flashes of fire, a raging flame."

Vocabulary Analysis (8:6-7)

Vs. 6: The relationship between king and people is expressed in figurative language which uses comparisons to relate two objects from which an underlying similarity can be deduced. The reference to the seal alludes to the custom by which important people would carry with them such an object tied to a cord hanging around their neck so that it fell over their heart, or on the other hand it was set into a ring used on their finger. The allusion to a seal upon the "arm" (*zᵉrôaʿ*) mentions an unusual detail not attested in other biblical or extra-biblical texts except by pictographical representations (KEEL, 246). For this reason some commentators substitute the word "seal" (*ḥôtām*) in the second hemistich for "bracelet" (*ṣāmîd*) upon the arm (RUDOLPH, 180; WÜRTHWEIN, 67). But the thought expressed here is the relation between person and person and not the relation between person and thing (DELITZSCH, 145). In other words, there is no attempt to relate the way in which the seal is used as a jewel around the neck or in the bracelet, but its function as a seal upon the heart and the arm to indicate the analogy between the seal and the bride in relationship to the king. Now, the inviolable and immortal part of the king is concentrated in his heart and on his right arm (VALERI, 764). For this reason, the request "set me!" (*śimēnî*) "upon your heart" (*ʿal libbekā*) and "upon your arm" (*ʿal zᵉrôʿekā*) expresses the desire of the bride for a lasting bond with the king, similar to the function of the seal which serves for its owner's use during his whole life.

The reason for this bond is the covenant between king and people expressed by the word "love" (*ʾahᵃbâ*), a technical term used in antiquity to indicate relationships between states, social groups, and individuals, characterized by the commitment of protection and collaboration so as to obtain mutual benefits. The relationship between the Davidic king and the Jewish community is reciprocal, because in the Old Testament the king is a sign that Israel was living within the sphere of a divine election: the monarch was God's vicegerent appointed to govern the chosen people. A characteristc aspect of the special kind of love meant here is its irresistible force which cannot be withstood and from which no one can withdraw. Two comparisons drawn from mythology place in parallel the powers of love and death. The emphasis on love results from the contrast between the destructive and constructive forces. "Death" (*māwet*) is represented in Canaanite mythology by the god Mot who, with an insatiable appetite, swallows mortals causing them to pass down the throat to his stomach (TROMP, 104). The belly of this deity is "hell" (*šᵉʾôl*) as a poetic personification of the dwelling place of the dead (Is 14:9). The hunger which gnaws at the belly of Mot is compared to the "passion" (*qinʾâ*) of love; the adjective *qāšāh* means "hard, fierce, inflexible, inexorable."

The infra-terrestrial scene is followed by an earthly one from which four natural phenomena are quoted all with destructive effect so as to serve as comparison with love. The Hebrew word *rᵉšāfèhā* (its flashes) evokes the name of Resheph, an important chthonian deity from the east-Semitic pantheon whose fiery arrows symbolize the scourge of epidemics and disasters which spread over the earth. It is not, however, the destructive aspect which inspired the comparison with love, but the fact that both are beyond human control as the flashes of the "bonfire" (*'ēš*) or a raging flame (*šalhebetyāh*). Two hypotheses have been presented to determine the meaning of *šalhebetyāh, a hapax legomenon.* The first explains its meaning by interpreting its ending *-yāh* as an abbreviated form of the name Yahweh, i.e. " a flame of Yahweh," with a religious sense (BUZY, 358; DELITZSCH, 147; KRINETZKI, 243; LYS, 290; PIATTI, 184; RAVASI, 135; TOURNAY-NICOLAŸ, 154; ZAPLETAL, 146). Another explanation, derived from this hypothesis, attributes to this word the meaning "flash of lightning" as an idiomatic expression (COLOMBO, 132; JOÜON, *Ct,* 316; RICCIOTTI, 278; ROBERT-TOURNAY, 302; RUDOLPH, 180; WÜRTHWEIN, 68). The second hypothesis explains *šalhebetyāh* as an equivalent form of the superlative used as a literary device which employs divine names to emphasize the meaning: "a raging flame" (BEA, 61; GERLEMAN, 217; WINANDY, 159).

However, none of the explanations of *šalhebetyāh* so far presented by the commentators is adequate because they do not take into consideration the metaplasm as a literary device used to highlight certain words. With relation to the syntactic analysis, *šalhebetyāh* is a nominal predicate of the subject "its flashes" (*rešāfehā*). In morphological analysis, this term is explained as a variant of *šalhebet* (Ez 21:3; Jb 15:30) which means "flame"; after there has been added to it the ending *-yāh* as an intensifying particle to emphasize its meaning, *šalhebetyāh* has the meaning "a raging flame." Other examples of lexical emphasis can be cited, e.g. *ma'apēl-ma'pēlyāh* (darkness), *'alîlâ–'alîlîyāh* (action), *pelîlâ–pelîlîyāh* (decision), *terûmâ–terûmîyāh* (contribution). In these cases the ending *-yāh* is not an abbreviated form of the name Yahweh but an intensifying particle. The comparison of love with flashes which rise up from the blaze and with a raging flame suggests the idea of the ardent desire shown by the Jews for the covenant with the Davidic king—a desire based not on a passing enthusiasm like a straw fire, but on the general expectancy which continues to assume ever wider proportions.

Vs. 7: The element opposed to fire is water, and two images deal with the destructive power of waters dropped by rainstorms or brought by torrents. The Hebrew expression *mayim rabbîm* in some texts has a cosmic connotation pointing to the primordial chaos or the netherworld. In figurative language it denotes the dangers which threaten the survival of the people who are faithful to Yahweh. The translation of *mayim rabbîm* by "many waters" suggests the idea of the spreading of water bringing destruction by flooding inhabited land. In this text there is an allusion to the fire which many waters "cannot quench" (*lō' yûkelû lekabbôt*), as an image of the deleterious factors which threaten to put out "love," i.e. the covenant between the Davidic king and the Jewish community.

The word *nᵉhārôt* (rivers) evokes the torrents of water from the primordial chaos which rushed against the just-created cosmos. In analogy with the victory of the creator over the destructive powers of chaos (Hab 3:8; Ps 93:3-4) it is affirmed that the covenant between king and people will rise victoriously from the battle against the hostile forces which threaten to submerge it in the whirlpool and to drag it (*šṭp*) into the rush of the flooding waters.

The transition from the sphere of nature to that of human life implies a change of scene: there appears the space where people exercise their dominion over consumer goods. In society man is capable of taking control over all goods of consumption by means of economic power, while in his contact with nature he has to face up to elements he cannot dominate. In the confrontation with the energies of matter and life man perceives a reality outside his grasp, i.e. "love." While wanting to possess it, he discovers that love is not a merchandise which can be bought nor an object for sale, because love is a gift which has an immanent bond with something which is transcendent, i.e. with relation to the chosen people and God. For the Jewish community, "love," i.e. the covenant with the Davidic king, is a sign of plenitude which consists in the full restoration of the chosen people in the mold of the political regime that had been in force during the monarchic period of the history of Israel.

The clause *bôz yābûzû lô* (he would be utterly scorned) has the verb in the active voice and the subject expressed by the indefinite "they," i.e. "they certainly would scorn him." The pronominal object of the verb *lô* (him) refers to *'îš* (a man) previously mentioned, while the ancient versions (LXX, Vg) refer it to the term *hôn* (wealth). The *Nova Vulgata* substitutes the pronoun *eam,* i.e. *substantiam,* for *eum,* i.e. *hominem,* supposing a scribal error. In fact the object of scorn is not the wealth offered in exchange for love, but the man who dares to lower it to a consumer good. The meaning of the conditional clause "if a man would offer" (*'im yittēn 'îš*) is an implicit warning against attempts to attribute to the covenant a merely economic value determined by the law of supply and demand.

Commentary: The Theme of the Covenant (8:6-7)

The theme of this song, which weaves emphatic praises to love, is the covenant between the Davidic king and the Jewish community. The use of the word "love" as a technical term to indicate relationships between states, social groups, and individuals is in line with the ancient custom of borrowing terms from common language for use in juridical texts. It is a linguistic phenomenon which occurred before the fixation of specific terminology for certain matters. The concept of love restricted to the political and social scene expresses the pact of submission, i.e. the relationship between people and king, from which the constitution of society results by the pact of association between the various social groups. The socio-political body thus constituted maintains individuals united not by the use of external force but by virtue of the covenant bond.

On the other hand, the interpretation of love as a sentiment of affection between lovers rests on the hypothesis that the object of this song is that of describing love in ideal terms. In the explanation of the descriptive data of love, presented in this text, the commentators base their arguments on the presupposition that here there is an implicit criticism of lack of love, of its failings, or of its debasement. Because they leave out the intrinsic meaning of the text, they thus describe the extrinsic context according to various theories: cult-mythical, naturalistic, spiritual, allegorical, or typological. As a result idealized interpretations have been imposed on this text, based upon the mind of each commentator without any foundation in the conceptual content or the thematic matter of this song.

The two people called "Solomon" and the "Shulamite" in the previous songs represent respectively the Davidic descendant and the leading figure representative of the Jewish population. The relationship between king and people is compared with the belonging of the seal to its owner. A relationship of lasting belonging is indicated by means of the image of guarding the seal on the heart and the arm, because the inviolable and immortal part of the king is concentrated in his heart and on his right arm.

The bond between king and people is defined by certain peculiarities developed in detail by means of comparisons drawn from mythology, e.g. death and hell, from the observation of nature, e.g. fire and a raging flame, floodwater and torrents, and from the experience of economic power, e.g. money buys all except for a gratuitous gift.

Above all it was necessary to convince the Jews that this covenant was indestructible. Despite the proofs to the contrary, such as the deportation of the royal family to Babylon, the extinction of the Jewish state, the destruction of the capital, and the exile of the inhabitants of Jerusalem, now the Jewish community had to be reminded that the chosen people had not been destroyed. Its survival was a fact proven by the existence of the autochthonous population in Judah, by the Jewish communities which had maintained their cohesion in the diaspora, by the return of the Davidic descendant to the homeland named by the Persian emperor to the office of governor of the territory of Judah, and by the aspirations of the Jews to see the Davidic monarchy shortly restored. Since the forces of destruction had not been capable of breaking this covenant, it had indeed earned the qualification "strong as death," not by its capacity to destroy its aggressors but by that of resisting aggression.

Another qualifying aspect of this covenant is the dynamic quality inherent in its nature. Similar to an intense passion, this covenant awoke in the survivors of the national catastrophe the hope of restoring the monarchy. Now, during the period of exile the Jewish communities kept annual days of national mourning in commemoration of the fall of Jerusalem (in the fourth month), of the destruction of the temple (in the fifth month), of the death of Gedaliah (in the seventh month), and of the extinction of the Jewish state (in the tenth month) [Zech 8:19]. However, the motive which inspired the recollection of these dates was not despair for those who had fallen in the disaster but the hope of restoration. Before going down to their graves, the survivors of the southern kingdom bequeathed to those that were left behind the traditions of Yahwism as a legacy of faith to be preserved from extinction and the devotion to its institutions which was to be cherished in the faith-community. The hope of the restoring of the old regime had not been buried but had been kept alive in the collective memory by the existence of the Davidic heir to the throne, a factor of cohesion among the Jewish communities. For this reason, the Davidic covenant with the Jewish people continued to exercise its influence over these communities even after the death of the last king of Judah, since the Jews had not considered themselves as defeated for as long as they possessed, in the heir to the royal throne, a sign of their divine election as chosen people.

The comparison of the covenant with a burning fire and the flame rising from the blaze illustrates the ardent desire of the Jews to see the institution of monarchy restored. The repressive measures which the Persian forces of occupation and the governors of the neighboring provinces had repeatedly taken to suffocate the Jewish nationalist movement had not been successful, nor was there any lack of offers of economic advantages to the Jewish community in exchange for its loyalty to the Davidic descendant. These proposals, however, had always been rejected as an insult to the chosen people, whose social and political organization was the expression of its identity and its autonomy, in the literal sense of being a law for itself: it is this which had to be preserved as an inalienable gift bestowed upon Israel. The theme of the covenant dealt with in this song complements the thematic content developed in other songs (1:12-17; 2:16-17; 7:11).

2. ✦ *The Legacy of Love (8:8-10)*

8 We have a little sister, *Brothers*
and she has no breasts.
What shall we do for our sister,
on the day when she is spoken for?
9 If she is a wall,
we will build upon her a silver cornice;

and if she is a gate,
we will fix upon her a cedar panel.
10 I am a wall, *Bride*
and my breasts are like towers;
thus I became in his eyes
the one who finds peace.

Accented Transliteration (8:8-10)

8 *'āḥôt lā́nû q*^{e}*ṭannấ*
w^{e}*šādáyim 'ên lā́h*
mah-nna'^{a}*śéh la'*^{a}*ḥōtḗnû*
bayyốm šeyy^{e}*dubbar-bā́h*
9 *'im-ḥômấ hî́'*
nibnéh 'ālèhā tî́rat kā́sef
w^{e}*'im-délet hî́'*
nāṣûr 'ālèhā lû́^{a}*ḥ 'ā́rez*
10 *'*^{a}*nî́ ḥômấ*
w^{e}*šādáy kammigdālốt*
'ā́z hāyî́tî b^{e}*'ênấw*
k^{e}*môṣ*^{e}*'ḗt šālốm*

Literary Analysis (8:8-10)

This song on the legacy of love is composed of three strophes, in which the conditions for the organization of a government, with proportional representation of the local population, are described in analogy with the arrangements to be made for the engagement of a maiden. The first strophe (vs. 8) presents the people, e.g. the "sister," treated as if she were a minor, and the "brothers," preoccupied with the dowry to be handed over to their sister. The second strophe (vs. 9) expresses, in two conditional sentences, the presupposition that the organization of an autonomous government precedes economic autonomy. "Wall" and "gate" represent the status of political autonomy; "silver cornice" and "cedar panel" are images of the economic yield destined for the development of the country. The third strophe (vs. 10) describes the emergence of a superior form of society as a political community (vs. 10a) in which there is assured to the citizens their social equality (vs. 10b) and the right to participate in the government in virtue of the covenant with the Davidic king (vs. 10cd). The word "peace" is a technical term used as synonym of the "covenant."

Poetic and rhetorical devices employed in the song are sound repetition: end rhyme *hîʾ–hîʾ* (vs. 9ac) and homophony *kāsef–ʾārez* (vs. 9bd); word repetition: "sister," "she," "upon her," "wall," "breasts"; rhetorical devices: hyperbole "if she is a wall," "I am a wall," "my breasts are like towers," simile "breasts like towers," and metaphor "she is a wall . . . gate."

Vocabulary Analysis (8:8-10)

Vs. 8: The community of Judah is facing the problem of social and political inequality caused by the exercise of control inside the community by some leaders of certain social groups over others. In figurative language, those holding public offices, recruited among the members of a privileged elite, are called "brothers." They discriminated against the local population, represented by the "sister," denying her the right of participating in the government and depriving her of social equality. If it were a question of discrimination among the various social groups of the Jewish population, words would be used which in the Song designate integrated collectivities, such as daughters, daughters of Jerusalem, and daughters of Zion. To indicate specific functions exercised by the people in the service of the community, terms such as king, sons of my mother, companions, shepherds, guards, keepers, and warriors are used. Since the term "brother" (*ʾāḥ*) only occurs as a title attributed to the "beloved" (8:1), the leaders who are on equal pegging with the "sister" (*ʾāḥôt*) are denominated as such by a circumlocution or by the equivalent expression "sons of my mother" (1:6). In the expression "for us it is = we have" (*lānû*) there is to be understood the group of brothers.

The qualifying adjective "little" (*q^{e}ṭannâ*), which modifies the term "sister" is in parallel with the clause "she has no breasts" (*šādayim ʾên lāh*), meaning that she has not reached adulthood. This however does not mean to say that she is not yet twelve years old, the legal age required to contract marriage. She is not a minor, but she is treated as immature.

The question of the brothers "What shall we do for our sister?" (*mah-nnaʿ^{a}śeh laʾ^{a}ḥōtēnû*) expresses their worry about the dowry which they must give to her. The use of the verb *ʿśh* (to do) with the *lamed* of the dative can denote despisal "What shall we do with her?" or worry "What shall we do for her?" It is the latter meaning that is demanded by the relation of the sentence with what is set out in the following verse. The motive of the question is explicitated by the temporal clause introduced by the compound preposition "on the day when" (*bayyôm še*). In the passive construction *y^{e}dubbar-bāh,* in *Pual,* the verb is used impersonally "it will be spoken of her," which means that "she is spoken for" by a suitor who asks for the woman's hand in marriage.

Vs. 9: The arrangements for the engagement to be made by the brothers depend on the future status of the sister: "if she is a wall" (*'im-ḥômâ hî'*). Now, the wall which surrounds a city or a fortified place symbolizes the political autonomy of a city-state or country whose capital is fortified. When the sister has acquired the status of political autonomy for the population which she represents, through her engagement, the brothers promise that "we will build upon her" (*nibneh 'ālèhā*) not crenellations above the wall for defensive purpose, as is generally translated, but a "silver cornice" (*tîrat kāsef*) which constitutes an architectural ornament of great value. The description of the sister by means of architectural details added to her figure is in keeping with the custom in vogue in antiquity whereby famous cities were personified by gracious and charming women sculptured in statues. These female figures were fully draped and wore a turreted crown, like the "silver cornice," with a stylized representation of the city-gate engraved upon it.

In parallel with the wall another image is added: "if she is a gate" (*'im-delet hî'*), since the access to a fortified city was defended by turrets built beside the entrance gate. The intention of the brothers is not thus to block the gate from within with boards but to adorn it from without: "we will fix upon her a cedar panel" (*nāṣûr 'ālèhā lûaḥ 'ārez*).

In order to understand the meaning of this verse, the content of the text and its form must be looked at. The two conditional sentences, expressing a hypothesis capable of being realized, let it be understood that the brothers are disposed to give to their sister a valuable patrimony as a dowry. The content of these sentences is expressed in figurative language. So as to clarify the meaning of the images we must notice the different descriptive details of the sister: her youthful state is related with her physical profile (vs. 8), while her adult age is described by images drawn from architecture, e.g. wall, gate, and towers. The "wall" and "gate" are characteristics of a fortified city and symbols of political autonomy (Ez 26:2-6); the "silver cornice" could be an allusion to the shields hanging from the walls for decorative effect (Ez 27:11); the "cedar panel" was used in sumptuous buildings (1 Kgs 6:9). The interpretation of the ornamental accessories on the wall and gate, as images of economic autonomy, is based on other historical data about affluent societies which accumulated great riches in periods of political and economic independence, but had become impoverished under the domination of a foreign government. Now, when the territory of Judah recovers its political autonomy, the economic goods proper to the community, administered by the members of a privileged elite at the service of the Samaritan governor, will be transferred to administrators from the local population. Even more, the income derived from these goods, up till then in great part confiscated by the Samaritans as tribute, will be destined for the development of the country whose richness is symbolized by the "silver cornice" and the "cedar panel."

Vs. 10: In this strophe the sister, contesting the evaluation which the brothers had made of her, declares peremptorily "I am a wall" (*'ᵃnî ḥômâ*), thanks to the installation of the political community in Judah. So as to refute the brothers' observation that she had not yet attained adult age she argues: "my breasts are like towers" (*šāday kammigdālôt*), basing herself on the fact that two social groups, repatriate and autochthonous Jews, live harmoniously in the same community.

The properties identified in the woman indicate her present state of being; for this reason the tense of the linking verbs, implied in the two Hebrew clauses, is the present and not the past as is erroneously translated by some commentators. The following adverb clause *'āz hayîtî* modifies the verbs of the previous compound sentence expressing a relation either of time, if *'āz* (then) is taken in the usual temporal sense, or of conclusion "for this reason, thus," or of consecution "in such a way that," since *'āz* can also express a logical sense (DELITZSCH, 154; POPE, 683).

The pronominal suffix of the noun *bᵉ'ênâw* (in his eyes) refers to the bridegroom, even though he is not explicitly mentioned in this song but in the following, where he is called "Solomon" (vss. 11-12). In a metaphorical sense, the "eyes" came to designate the mind or the opinion; thus the prepositional phrase "in his eyes" means "in his opinion."

The particle *kᵉ*, prefixed to the word *môṣᵉ'ēt,* is the *kaph veritatis;* here it is used pleonastically not to indicate a likeness but to introduce the predicate "the one who finds peace" (*GK* § 118x). For this reason the adverb "like," which expresses a comparison, is omitted in the translation, thus avoiding the ambiguity between a predicate and a simile.

In two Hebrew manuscripts the participle *môṣᵉ'ēt* appears in the contracted form *mōṣē't,* a variation on the previous form which contains a secondary syllable (*BL* § 77y).

The similarity in writing between the participle of *mṣ'* in the *Qal* "the one who finds" and the participle of *yṣ'* in *Hiphil* "the one who brings" has given rise to divergent translations of this text. The option for one of the two verbs depends on the point of view adopted in ascertaining the meaning of the word "peace" (*šālôm*). The various interpretations of the text are based on particular connotations attributed to the word "peace," such as "favor" (DELITZSCH, 154; KRINETZKI, 251 ; WÜRTHWEIN, 69), "happiness" (ASENSIO, 618; PIATTI, 193; RAVASI, 141), "surrender" (GERLEMAN, 221; KEEL, 253; ZAPLETAL, 151), "armistice" (BEA, 61), "matrimonial state" (BUZY, 361), "adult age" (WINANDY, 160), "security" (RICCIOTTI, 283; ROBERT-TOURNAY, 316), "liberation" (POUGET-GUITTON, 178), "fullness" (LYS, 299), a Hebrew allusion to the name of Solomon (COLOMBO, 135), a Hebrew allusion to the name of Jerusalem (JOÜON, *Ct,* 324; TOURNAY-NICOLAŸ, 158), "payment" based on the emendation of the Hebrew word (RUDOLPH, 182).

The word "peace" (*šālôm*) is used here as a technical term to designate the "covenant." That this be so can be shown from some texts of the Old Testament referring to political pacts which can be found in the literature of the people of the ancient Near East; they used this word as a synonym for covenant or alliance (KALLUVEETTIL, 34–42). Taken in this sense, the word "peace" indicates both the nature and the effect of the covenant including the requisites which are demanded for it to be established. In other Old Testament texts this word occurs as the direct object of the following transitive verbs, viz. *'śh šālôm* "to make peace" (Jos 9:15; Is 27:5), *'nh šālôm* "to accept peace" (Dt 20:11), and *qr' lešālôm* "to reaffirm peace" (Dt 20:10). All these verbs express the enactment of a covenant whose nature is explicitated in the respective texts.

Among the requisites for the covenant there can be mentioned the necessity that the superior party look favorably on the positive qualities with which the inferior is endowed so that this latter can be accepted as an ally. The expression which designates admission to a covenant is *māṣā' šālôm* "to find peace." The concrete conditions for obtaining this object are illustrated by two images: the first compares the installation of the political community with a "wall" which protects the space of autonomy for the establishment of basic social and political structures; the second mentions the "breasts like towers" to represent two human groups which are related among each other and which are harmoniously integrated into the same social body. On the basis of these facts the leading figure representative of the Jewish population is convinced that he has met the necessary conditions for entering into covenant with the future king of Judah.

Commentary: The Theme of the Government (8:8-10)

The theme developed in this song is the government exercised by a group of leaders who hold the political power in the Jewish community. This leadership function is expressed by the term "brother." The ties of family relationship designate not only the members of associate groups but also those holding public office (Neh 5:14). The equitable integration between them is the determining factor in the political integration of society, while a monopoly of power wielded by a privileged elite would cause the social body to fall apart.

The conditions necessary for a government with proportional representation of the local population to be established in Judah are described in analogy with the arrangements to be made for the engagement of a maiden. The first measure is to assure equality of status between those holding public offices and to recognize that the "sister" has the same legal capacity to take part in public administration, although she is considered "small," is treated as if she were underdeveloped, and is denied access to the sphere of those who by their position wield political power in the country (vs. 8a). The second measure deals with the possibility of the "sister" occupying a position on the same level as that of the "brothers." It is not, however, on the initiative of sister or brothers that this will be achieved but by means of the future king in whose competence it is to maintain cohesion between social groups through the pact of association between these groups and by their allegiance to the crown (vs. 8b).

The covenant relationship between the Jewish community and the Davidic king is compared to the marriage bond between the "sister" and her suitor. On the occasion of the celebration of betrothal the "brothers" would give a valuable dowry to their sister if the marriage were to bring political independence to the population which she represents (vs. 9). The transfer of the title deed to the sister depends on freedom with which to dispose of the goods of the community under the administration of the brothers; in other words, economic autonomy follows political autonomy. Now, during the period of exile and the first century of the era of restoration, the territory of Judah was under the mandate of Samaria, and the Jewish population did not have at its disposal the goods produced in the country; rather their income was confiscated by the Samaritans under the claim of taxation.

With the nomination of the Davidic descendant to the office of governor over Judah, the autochthonous Jewish population held high the hope that shortly it would be able to obtain the status of a province independent of Samaria. This would be the first step toward the restoration of the Davidic monarchy in the same style as the Phoenician monarchies which had been established by the Persians at around that time. The reason which permits the sister to declare herself to be a "wall"—an image of the political community—is the fact that the assembly of citizens with free participation and the co-responsibility in the governing of the community already exists (vs. 10a). This assembly is the full expression of the political body. In the woman who represents the Jewish community, the image of "breasts like towers" is an allusion to the harmonious integration of repatriate and autochthonous Jews in the same social body (vs. 10b). The analogy with a woman in the fullness of her vitality aims to awaken the spirit of solidarity between the two groups integrated into the post-exilic community, a spirit that will be shown in their fostering both the development of society and the improvement of the quality of life.

Thanks to advances in the political and social organization of the community, the population of Judah can pride itself on already presenting conditions favorable for a pact of political alliance with the heir to the throne of David so as to restore the monarchy (vs. 10cd). This song complements the theme developed in a previous song (1:7-11).

3. ✦ *The Treasure of Love (8:11-12)*

11 Solomon had a vineyard; *Bride*
as lord of holdings
he entrusted the vineyard to keepers;
a thousand silver shekels will be paid for its fruit.
12 My own vineyard is at my disposal;
the thousand is yours, O Solomon,
and two hundred for the keepers of its fruit.

Accented Transliteration (8:11-12)

11 *kérem hāyā́h lišlōmṓh*
bebá‘al hāmốn
nātán ’et-hakkérem lannōṭerî́m
’î́š yābî́’ befiryố ’élef kā́sef
12 *karmî́ šellî́ lefānā́y*
hā’élef lekā́ šelōmṓh
ûmā’táyim lenōṭerî́m ’et-piryố

Literary Analysis (8:11-12)

In this song the protagonists of two distinct communities are represented in figurative language as owners of vineyards. In the first strophe (vs. 11), local leaders are appointed to administrative posts in the community of the Jews in Babylon on the occasion of the repatriation of the Davidic descendant, called Solomon. The second strophe (vs. 12) refers to the Judean community, under local leadership, to be subordinated to the authority of the Davidic descendant. The nexus with the previous song is the matrimonial context in which the reference to assets is to be understood as the register of the patrimony which is required from those pledged to marry as a condition for the betrothal to be ratified.

Poetic and rhetorical devices used in the song are sound repetition: alliteration *n–m* (vs. 11c), end rhyme *-o* (vs. 12bc); word repetition: "vineyard" (thrice), "Solomon," "keepers," "thousand," "its fruit," anaphora *kerem–karmî* (vss. 11a, 12a). A rhetorical device is the use of "vineyard" as an image of the community.

Vocabulary Analysis (8:11-12)

Vs. 11: In the singular, the "vineyard" (*kerem*) represents both the community of Judah (1:6; 8:12) and the Jewish community of Babylon (8:11); in the plural, "vineyards" has the meaning of plantations of grapevines (1:6, 14; 2:15; 7:13) or, by metonymy, the settlements of autochthonous Jews in the rural districts of Judah. As a general collective noun, "vineyard" indicates the totality of the integrating parts; in a metaphorical sense it acquires a religious connotation, that of the chosen people (Is 5:1-7, etc.), or has a social connotation, that of the community (Ct 1:6; 8:11-12), or a political connotation, that of the nation (1:6; 8:12).

The tense of the verb used in the clause *hāyā . . . le* (he had) is the past in parallel with that of the verb *nātan* (he gave, entrusted).

Solomon is not here the historical Solomon but a descendant of the Davidic dynasty, a legitimate heir to the throne of David, and the factor of cohesion of the Jewish communities in the period of restoration after the exile. The exiled Judean king Jehoiachin and his sons Shealtiel and Shenazzar (= Sheshbazzar?) as also Zerubbabel, Shealtiel's son, carried out an important function in the governing of the Jewish community in Babylon (ODED, 481–483). Their immediate adjutants were the "elders among the exiles," the "elders of Judah," or "elders of Israel" (Jer 29:1; Ez 8:1; 14:1; 20:1). To these the term "keepers" (*nōṭerîm*) of the vineyard is referred, since they are the local leaders substituting the Davidic descendant in the administration of the Jewish community in the diaspora after the repatriation of the royal family.

The Hebrew expression *beba'al hāmôn* is commonly translated in a local sense, "in Baal-hamon," the name of an unknown place or identical to Tell Bel'ameh near Dothaim (Jdt 7:13), in the province of Samaria. However, the local meaning ought to be rejected because this expression qualifies the person of Solomon and not the vineyard.

Another hypothesis relates this expression with one of the honorific titles of the Persian kings "unique among many sovereigns," in Old Persian *aivam parūnām framātāram* (XPa 5-6), corresponding to the translation in Akkadian "first among many sovereigns" (*ištēn ina muṭe'emē mādūtu*) [*VAB* 3 107 § 1]. However, in the Hebrew expression *ba'al hāmôn* there is lacking the qualifier corresponding to *aivam* (unique), translated as *ištēn* (first). Besides, since it was notorious that the royal family was coming back from Babylon, it would be redundant to specify its exile by its relation of proximity with the king of Persia.

The Hebrew expression *beba'al hāmôn*, whose prefixed *be* is a *bet essentiae* meaning "like, as," is in apposition to Solomon designated *ba'al* (lord, owner, husband) and qualified by the term *hāmôn* which has various meanings; it can be: 1. agitation, 2. bustle, turmoil, 3. uproar, 4. procession, pomp,

5. wealth, riches, holdings. Seeing that *hāmôn* refers to the "vineyard," which represents a highly valued property, the function of this Hebrew word is to specify the value of the vineyard by the mention of an aggregate of real estate destined to viticulture. Thus, *hāmôn* here means "holdings" which designates, by metonymy, the various branches of the public administration under the care of Solomon, head of the Jewish community in Babylon.

The parallelism between *ba'al hāmôn* and *lᵉfānāy* (at my disposal), which occurs in the following verse, indicates the relation between Solomon and the Shulamite with regard to the administrative post which each occupies in the respective community. The mention of Solomon's possessions aims to refute the objection raised by some members of the Judean community against the restoration of the monarchic regime. It was argued that the means to be made available for the maintenance of a royal household far exceeded the economic output of the community so that the local population would have to carry the burden of keeping up all the panoply of the royal court.

The subject of the verb *yābi'* (will bring, pay) expressed by *'îš* is to be translated by the indefinite pronoun "someone" (JOÜON, *Gr* § 155g) and not by the distributive pronoun "each one," as if the "keepers" (*nōṭᵉrîm*) were the tenants of the vineyard. The income to be paid to Solomon does not derive from letting out the real estate belonging to the royal family in Babylon but is drawn from the proceeds (*piryô*, lit. "its fruit") of the local community.

Owing to the lack of a conjunction to connect the two clauses, it is only by inference from its context that we can determine which of the possible translations renders the idea expressed here. Now, a verbal-clause whose subject is indefinite and whose verb is in the active voice can be rendered in English by a passive construction; thus "someone will pay" comes to be equivalent to a passive "there will be paid." The verb *yābi'* (will pay) is translated by some commentators, rather than as an indicative, as a conditional, supposing that it is a question of a mere desire being expressed here rather than of a real fact (COLOMBO, 136; GERLEMAN, 222; POPE, 654; RUDOLPH, 184; WÜRTHWEIN, 70). Others translated it by "ought to pay" as an obligation imposed by the rental contract (BUZY, 362; DELITZSCH, 157; JOÜON, *Ct*, 328; KRINETZKI, 252; RICCIOTTI, 285; ROBERT-TOURNAY, 320; WINANDY, 92; ZAPLETAL, 148).

The total amount of the income is "a thousand pieces of silver" (*'elef kāsef*), supplying the word *šᵉqālîm* (shekels). This amount is equivalent to that in possession of the Shulamite (vs. 12). The parallelism between these sums aims to put the assets belonging to each of the future spouses on a par. According to the matrimonial statute, the parents or brothers of the bride would charge the bridegroom a "matrimonial tax" (*mōhar*), equivalent in worth to the amount of the "dowry" (*šillûḥîm*) as a condition for the betrothal to be ratified (TOSATO, 95–106).

Vs. 12: The expression "my own vineyard" (*karmî šellî*) designates the autochthonous Jewish community, i.e. "the people of the land [of Judah]" (*'am hā'āreṣ*), in opposition to the repatriate Jews, i.e. "the rest of the people" (*še'ērît hā'ām*). They are not antagonistic social groups; on the contrary, tied together by the same socio-religious traditions which both uphold, they constitute a single "restored people" (*'am nibrā'*) [Ps 102:19]. Their participation in the reconstruction of the Jerusalem temple under the direction of the governor Zerubbabel is a sign of belonging to the chosen people (Hag 2:2-4).

The leader of the autochthonous population not only voices the aspirations of the Judean community but is also responsible for its organization. The functions of administration and leadership in the community are indicated by the prepositional phrase "at my disposal" (*lefānay*), lit. "before me," in parallel with the leadership role of Solomon over the Jewish community in Babylon, as "lord of holdings." These communities were organized in cohesive social groups, under local leadership without interference from imperial authorities in their internal affairs. It is not aimed to evoke rivalry, since both communities are equally designated "vineyards," in whose service their leaders carry out administrative functions.

The Shulamite, handing over to Solomon "the thousand" (*hā'elef*) shekels of her patrimony, in allusion to the husband's right to enjoy the profits of the wife's dowry, establishes the analogy between political alliance and matrimonial bond, representing the link between the Davidic descendant and the community of Judah.

In the budget the sum of "two hundred" (*mā'tayim*) shekels is foreseen for the "keepers" (*nōṭerîm*); this is twenty percent of the total amount of the income proceeding from the commercialization of the products of the "vineyard" and means participation in its profits. With the recuperation of political autonomy, the province of Judah, now raised to a monarchy, will have at its disposal all the income from its economy so as to pay its officials and cover public expenditure. Thus administrative agents will be prevented from appropriating public funds to the detriment of the community. The economic resources of which the community of Judah disposes, as described in a previous song (4:9-11), are "its own fruit" (*piryô*).

Commentary: The Theme of the Nation (8:11-12)

This song deals with the Jewish nation to be restored in the land of their ancestors having as its ruler the heir to the throne of David. The decisive factor in the national restoration is the edict of Cyrus, promulgated in 538 B.C., which permitted the exiled Jews to return to their homeland. Permission for the reconstruction of the Jerusalem temple aimed at setting up a faith-community, according to the traditions of the Yahwistic cult under the ministry of the priesthood. But the central government did not take efficacious measures to overcome tensions between repatriate and autochthonous Jews and avoid interference by the governor of Samaria in the socioeconomic organization of the Judean community, which came under its administrative jurisdiction. So as to obtain political autonomy and economic independence, it was necessary that the territory of Judah be elevated to the rank of a province. This would only be viable with the organization of the Jewish population into a social and political community.

The first step toward overcoming the rupture of national unity, caused by the extinction of the Jewish state and the subsequent deportation of a considerable part of the country's inhabitants, was to integrate the various groups into one single community. A second step consisted in harmonizing diverse tendencies by suppressing the causes of discrimination. Before the edict of repatriation, the two groups were integrated into their own communitarian milieu designated by the concrete image of the "vineyard." The repatriate Jews called themselves "the rest of the people" (Hag 1:12, 14; 2:2; Zech 8:6, 12; Neh 7:72), in allusion to the leading position which their ancestors had occupied in the southern kingdom. This emerges in the reconstruction of the Jerusalem temple where the initiative of the repatriate Jews is contrasted with the inertia of the autochthonous Jews called "the people of the land [of Judah]" (Hag 2:4; Zech 7:5).

Another important factor for living together in harmony was mutual appreciation for the social structure of the two groups. The natural leader of the exiles was the heir apparent and a Davidic descendant. The leadership over the Judean community was exercised by a group representative of the local population. The two communities were organized in analogous form, viz. all the members were integrated into their respective community space, i.e. "vineyard," and the role of the leader and of the administrators was defined with a view to the common good.

The repatriation of the Davidic descendant was not intended as a political move to keep repatriate and autochthonous Jews in check. Rather it was so to integrate them into a social body, which would require the setting up of a particular system of government by which the Judean community would be organized, governed, and held together. The leader of the autochthonous Jews proposed the transference of all executive functions to the heir to the throne of David as the sole ruler of the community which would be organized into a nation. As in the monarchic period of Israel, the relationship of dependence between subjects and ruler would have to be reestablished. This is expressed in terms of a marriage bond between Solomon and the Shulamite, the representative of the population of Judah. The perception of the nexus with the previous song (8:8-10), having been established by said analogy, allows us to understand the double reference to the "thousand pieces of silver." The betrothal would be ratified after the payment of the "matrimonial tax," equivalent to the sum of the "dowry"; and it is in the matrimonial context that the Shulamite hands over to

Solomon a thousand shekels of her patrimony, since the husband has the right to enjoy the profits of the wife's dowry.

In the project of the public administration of the future nation a fund of a thousand shekels is set up. This sum is to come from the income of the community of Judah. An additional sum of a thousand shekels is to be paid by the community of Babylon so as to cover the expenditure of the royal household. The community of Judah also offers a fund of two hundred shekels to cover the salaries of administrative officials. The mention of Solomon's possessions aims to refute the objection of some members of the Judean community, viz. the royal household would live at the expense of the local population whose scarce economic resources would not permit them to keep up the whole panoply of the royal court.

In the organization of the nation, economic independence must be secured. This would be possible once the interference of the Samaritan authorities in administrative affairs had been got rid of and public resources had been released from the obligations imposed by the mandatory fiscal system. Here the theme of the nation which had been developed in another song (1:5-6) finds its complement.

4. ✦ *The Intimacy of Love (8:13-14)*

13 O you who dwell in the gardens, *Bridegroom*
  while companions are listening,
  let me hear your voice.
14 Make haste, my beloved, *Bride*
  like a gazelle or a young stag,
  up to the spice-bearing mountains.

Accented Transliteration (8:13-14)

13 *hayyôšébet bagganî́m*
  ḥ^{a}bērî́m maqšîbî́m
  l^{e}qôlḗk hašmî‘î́nî
14 *b^{e}ráḥ dôdî́*
  ûd^{e}mēh-l^{e}kā́ liṣbî́
’ô l^{e}‘ṓfer hā’ayyālî́m
  ‘al hārḗ b^{e}śāmî́m

Literary Analysis (8:13-14)

This song deals with the consent of the Judean community to the covenant between king and people as a prerequisite for the establishment of the monarchy in Judah. In the first strophe (vs. 13), the bridegroom, in the presence of the ministers of state, proposes the covenant to the bride who, in the second strophe (vs. 14), demonstrates her acceptance by inviting the bridegroom to meet with her as rapidly as possible in the mountainous region of Judah.

Poetic and rhetorical devices that occur in the song are sound repetition: assonance *a–i*, end rhyme *-îm* and *-î*; repetition of a sentence: refrain (vs. 14bc); figures of speech: simile "my beloved makes haste like a gazelle or a young stag"; the figurative use of the "gardens" denoting the settlements of the local population.

Vocabulary Analysis (8:13-14)

Vs. 13: The feminine participle, preceded by the definite article functioning as the vocative, *hayyôšebet* (O you who dwell), designates the Shulamite in terms of an inhabitant of the country. The circumstantial complement "in the gardens" (*bagganîm*), specifying the place where she dwells, represents the settlements of the autochthonous Jews, while the singular term "garden" is an image of the Jewish nation (4:12-15).

The subordinate clause "while the companions are listening" (*ḥaberîm maqšîbîm*) is an absolute adverbial adjunct, called in Latin ablative absolute, and indicates a circumstance referring to the role of the witnesses at the enactment of the covenant. This adjunct is absolute since it has no specific relation with any term of the clause. The Masoretic punctuation connects *maqšîbîm* (listening) with the following *leqôlēk* (your voice), while the Vulgate separates the words, *amici auscultant: fac me audire vocem tuam.* These "companions" are not to be identified as the Shulamite's "childhood playmates" as has been suggested (DELITZSCH, 159; POPE, 695). The term "companions" is drawn from administrative terminology in use among the Persians who designated the king's immediate auxiliaries as his "companions" (1:7).

It is the finite verb *hašmîʿînî* (let me hear) and not the participle *maqšîbîm* (listening) which governs the object *leqôlēk* (your voice), because phrases like *šmʿ le* (8:13) and *šmʿ ʾet* (2:14) are typical expressions of the terminology used in covenant texts (see the interpretation of the text in 2:14). The clause "let me hear your voice" is the key to understanding the strophe, as indeed the whole song, since it is a question of the consent to the covenant to be given by the bride in the presence of the bridegroom. These are the two protagonists of the Song who represent respectively the community of Judah and the Davidic king. The political alliance is ratified according to the pattern set out in a formal act, in analogy with the formalities prescribed for the ratification of pacts between heads of government, leaders of social groups, king and people, in use in the ancient Near East (KALLUVEETTIL, 135–138). There can be found in extra-biblical texts referring to treaties that the sovereign would exhort his vassal to "listen to the words," i.e. the stipulations of the treaty. The consent of the inferior to the superior ratified the treaty, without it being necessary for the superior party formally to confirm what had been established.

It is to be noted that the initiative of ratifying the covenant between king and people is taken by the protagonist of this scene. This covenant of a political relationship constitutes the most intimate cooperation between Solomon, who represents the Davidic dynasty, and the Shulamite, a representative figure of the population of Judah. Given the political nature of this covenant, which aims to restore the monarchic regime in the land of their ancestors, the ratification of the pact of the covenant constitutes the formal act by which the Davidic monarchy is instituted in Judah.

Vs. 14: In reply to the bridegroom's exhortation, the bride begs him to meet with her. At first sight it seems that by making this request she is imposing a condition without which the covenant will not be made, which would be an unheard of attitude for a subject in relation to her superior. But this is not the case. Given the political situation of the territory of Judah under foreign domination, the Persian authorities would not permit that a Judean delegation appear before a Jewish governor, at his residence in Mizpah, where the ceremony of the ratification of the covenant would be held. For this reason the leader of the native population suggests to the governor that he escape from the vigilance of the "watchmen of the walls" (5:7). The imperative *b^eraḥ* (flee, escape), since it does not have a specific relation with any term of the sentence, could be understood as in incitation to flee far from the bride; if, however, it is translated "make haste," it expresses the idea of going to meet the bride.

The community of Judah shows its deference for the Jewish governor, a member of the house of David, calling him "my beloved" (*dôdî*). This is a title attributed to him by which he is identified as ally (1:13), because of his bond with this community through ties of "friendship" (*dōdîm*) created by the covenant (1:2, 4; 4:10; 7:13).

The request made to the bridegroom to hurry his coming is expressed by the imperative *d^emēh-l^ekā* (be like), translated as "like." The comparison "with a gazelle or a young stag" (*liṣbî ʾô l^eʿōfer hāʾayyālîm*) is based on the proverbial speed of these animals: may the bridegroom show his speed undertaking the journey to the region inhabited by the autochthonous Jews (2:9, 17)! The road which goes up to the "spice-bearing mountains" (*ʿal hārê* *beśāmîm*) is the one which leads to the settlements located in the territory of Judah. In the parallel text (2:17) it is the question of the same road leading up to "terraced mountains" (*'al-hārê beter*), described with topographical features. That these mountains are here specified with a particular variety of scented plants is to indicate the settlements of the native population of Judah by reference to their local flora, in parallel with the local fauna mentioned in the previous clause.

Commentary: The Theme of the Monarchy (8:13-14)

The theme of this song is the monarchy to be restored in Judah in the post-exilic period. An undertaking of such dimensions would be subject to the risk of failing at the outset, if the Jewish leadership did not proceed with great caution so as to prevent a possible confrontation with the foreign forces of occupation. For the Persian authorities, should they perceive the first steps toward the reorganization of the political life of the Jewish people, would inevitably react with severe sanctions against the leaders of the movement for their daring attempt to shake off the yoke of foreign domination.

Under such circumstances, for the monarchy to be established a consensus on policy and program will be needed, with an appeal to all the leaders of the social groups whose support is sought. The first measure to be taken is to demand discretion from all those initiated in the plan of intended proceedings, a demand that can be inferred from the formulation of this plan in the disguise of an idyll. The second is to send an invitation to the heir to the throne to go to meet the leader of the Jewish population in the mountainous region without the interference of the palace guard. The third is to summon officials to act as witnesses for the enactment of the covenant between the Davidic descendant and the community of Judah, thus complying with the legal conditions for the legitimacy of the pact. With the submission of the people to the king and the unification of the various social groups, cohesion would be created among the inhabitants of Judah through their covenant relationship with the Davidic king. Since the house of David was the principle of stability of the kingdom of Judah in the pre-exilic period, it was hoped that thus the institution of the monarchy might once again become the decisive factor in the restoration of the Jewish nation in the post-exilic period. The theme of this final song complements the theme of the first song (1:2-4).

Bibliography of Works Cited

AHARONI, Y., *The Land of the Bible.* A Historical Geography. Transl. from the Hebrew by A. F. Rainey. 2nd rev. ed., Westminster Press, Philadelphia 1979.

ALONSO SCHÖKEL, L., *Estudios de Poética Hebrea,* J. Flors, Barcelona 1963.

——. "Poésie hebraïque," *DBS* VIII, cols. 47-90, Létouzey et Ané, Paris 1972.

ALT, A., *Kleine Schriften zur Geschichte des Volkes Israel.* Vols. 2, 3. Beck, München ^{3}1964, ^{2}1968.

ASENSIO, F., *Cantar de los Cantares* (Los Salmos y los Libros Salomónicos, ed. J. Leal, La Sagrada Escritura VI, B.A.C. 293), Biblioteca de Autores Cristianos, Madrid 1969, pp. 583–619.

BEA, A., *Canticum Canticorum,* Pontificio Instituto Biblico, Roma 1953.

BENGTSON, H. (ed.), *Griechen und Perser:* Die Mittelmeerwelt im Altertum I (Fischer Weltgeschichte V), Fischer Bücherei, Frankfurt–Hamburg 1965.

BRUNO, A. D., *Das Hohe Lied—Das Buch Hiob:* Eine rhythmische und text-kritische Untersuchung nebst einer Einführung in das Hohe Lied, Almqvist & Wiksell, Stockholm 1956, pp. 11-54.

BUZY, D., *Le Cantique des Cantiques* (La Sainte Bible VI/3), Létouzey et Ané, Paris 1946.

COLOMBO, D., *Cantico dei Cantici* (Nuovissima Versione della Bibbia dai Testi Originali 21), Ed. Paoline, Roma 1970.

DALMAN, G. H., *Arbeit und Sitte in Palästina.* 7 vols., Bertelsman, Gütersloh 1928-42; reprinted, Olms, Hildesheim 1964.

DELITZSCH, F., *Commentary on the Song of Songs and Ecclesiastes* (Commentary on the Old Testament by C. F. Keil and F. Delitzsch, Vol. VI). Transl. from the German by M. G. Easton, T. & T. Clark, Edinburgh 1877; reprinted, Eerdmans, Grand Rapids, Michigan 1969, pp. 1-161.

DE VAUX, R., *Ancient Israel.* Its Life and Institutions. Transl. from the French by J. McHugh. 2nd ed., Darton, Longman & Todd, London 1965.

DHORME, E., *L'emploi métaphorique des noms de parties du corps en hébreu et en akkadien,* Paul Geuthner, Paris 1963.

DUBARLE, A.-M., "Le Cantique des Cantiques dans l'exégèse récente," in *Aux grands carrefours de la révélation et de l'exégèse de l'Ancien Testament,* ed. Ch. Hauret (Recherches Bibliques VIII), Desclée De Brouwer, Bruges 1967, pp. 139–152.

DUSSAUD, R., *Les religions des Hittites et des Hourites, des Phéniciens et des Syriens* (Mana I/2: Les anciennes religions orientales II), Presses Universitaires, Paris 1949.

EXUM, J. C., "A Literary and Structural Analysis of the Song of Songs," *ZAW* 85 (1973), 47–79.

FEUILLET, A., *Le Cantique des Cantiques.* Étude de théologie biblique et réflexions sur une méthode d'exégèse (Lectio Divina 10), Du Cerf, Paris 1953.

FISHER, M. B., *The Middle East.* A Physical, Social, and Regional Geography. 4th ed., Methuen, London; Dutton, New York 1961.

GALLING, K., *Biblisches Reallexikon* (Handbuch zum Alten Testament I/1), 2nd ed., Mohr, Tübingen 1977.

GAUDEMET, J., *Institutions de l'Antiquité,* 2nd ed., Sirey, Paris 1982.

GERLEMAN, G., *Ruth. Das Hohelied* (Biblischer Kommentar. Altes Testament XVIII), 2nd ed., Neukirchener Verlag, Neukirchen-Vluyn 1981.

GESENIUS, W.—KAUTZSCH, E., *Gesenius' Hebrew Grammar.* Transl. from the German by A. E. Cowley. 2nd ed., Clarendon, Oxford 1910.

GORDON, C. H., *Ugaritic Textbook.* Grammar, Texts in Transliteration, Cuneiform Selections, Glossary, Indices (Analecta Orientalia 38), Pontifical Biblical Institute, Rome 1965.

JOÜON, P., *Grammaire de l'hébreu biblique.* 2nd ed., Biblical Institute, Rome 1947; reprinted, 1965.

——, *Le Cantique des Cantiques,* Beauchesne, Paris 1908.

KALLUVEETTIL, P., *Declaration and Covenant.* A Comprehensive Review of Covenant Formulae from the Old Testament and the Ancient Near East (Analecta Biblica 88) Biblical Institute Press, Rome 1982.

KEEL, O., *Das Hohelied* (Zürcher Bibelkommentare: AT 18), Theologischer Verlag, Zürich 1986.

KENT, R. G., *Old Persian.* Grammar, Texts, Lexicon (American Oriental Series 33), 2nd rev. ed., American Oriental Society, New Haven, Connecticut 1961.

KENYON, K. M., *Archaeology in the Holy Land,* Praeger, New York 1960.

KRAŠOVEC, J., *Der Merismus im Biblisch-Hebräischen und Nordwestsemitischen* (Biblica et Orientalia 33), Biblical Institute Press, Rome 1977.

KRINETZKI, G., *Hoheslied* (Die Neue Echter Bibel: Kommentar zum AT mit der Einheitsübersetzung), Echter Verlag, Stuttgart 1980.

KRINETZKI, L. (= G), *Das Hohe Lied.* Kommentar zu Gestalt und Kerygma eines alttestamentlichen Liebesliedes, Patmos-Verlag, Düsseldorf 1964.

LANDY, F., "Beauty and the Enigma: An Inquiry into Some Interrelated Episodes of the Song of Songs," *JSOT* 17 (1980), 55–106.

LICHTHEIM, M., *Ancient Egyptian Literature,* Vols. 2, 3. University of California Press, Berkeley and Los Angeles 1978, 1980.

LORETZ, O., *Das althebräische Liebeslied.* Untersuchungen zur Stichometrie und Redaktionsgeschichte des Hohenliedes und des 45. Psalms, *AOAT* 14/1 (1971), 1–56.

LYS, D., *Le plus beau chant de la création.* Commentaire du Cantique des Cantiques (Lectio Divina 51), Du Cerf, Paris 1968.

MCCARTHY, D. J., *Treaty and Covenant.* A Study in Form in the Ancient Oriental Documents and in the Old Testament (Analecta Biblica 21A). New edition completely rewritten. Biblical Institute Press, Rome 1978.

MOLDENKE, H. N.—MOLDENKE, A. L., *Plants of the Bible,* Ronald Press, New York 1952.

MORAN, W. L., "The Ancient Near Eastern Background of the Love of God in Deuteronomy," *CBQ* 25 (1963), 77–87.

NEGEV, A. (ed.), *Archaeological Encyclopedia of the Holy Land,* Weidenfeld and Nicolson, London and Jerusalem 1972.

ODED, B., "Judah and the Exile," in *Israelite and Judaean History,* eds. J. H. Hayes—J. M. Miller, S.C.M. Press, London 1977, pp. 435–488.

OLMSTEAD, A. T., *History of the Persian Empire* (Phoenix Books), University of Chicago, Chicago and London 1959.

PIATTI, T., *Il Cantico dei Cantici,* Ed. Paoline, Roma 1958.

PIJOÁN, J., *Summa Artis. Historia General del Arte.* Vol. II *Arte del Asia Occidental,* 4th ed., Espasa-Calpe, Madrid 1957.

POPE, M. H., *Song of Songs* (The Anchor Bible 7C), Doubleday & Co., Garden City, NY 1977.

PORTEN, B. *Archives from Elephantine.* The Life of an Ancient Jewish Military Colony. University of California Press, Berkeley and Los Angeles 1968.

POUGET, G.—GUITTON, J. *Le Cantique des Cantiques* (Études Bibliques), 2nd ed., Gabalda, Paris 1948.

RAVASI, G., *Cântico dos Cânticos.* Transl. from the Italian by J. R. Vidigal. Ed. Paulinas, São Paulo 1988.

RICCIOTTI, G., *Il Cantico dei Cantici,* S.E.I., Turin 1928.

ROBERT, A.—TOURNAY, R., in collaboration with FEUILLET, A., *Le Cantique des Cantiques* (Études bibliques), Gabalda, Paris 1963.

RUDOLPH, W., *Das Buch Ruth. Das Hohe Lied. Die Klagelieder* (Kommentar zum Alten Testament XVIII/1–3), Mohn, Gütersloh 1962.

SEGAL, M. H., "The Song of Songs," *VT* 12 (1962), 470–490.

STADELMANN, L., "Fidelidade em época de crise: A importância dos remanescentes em Judá para a preservação da fé javista," *PT* 19 (1987), 181–202.

TOSATO, A., *Il Matrimonio Israelitico.* Una teoria generale (Analecta Biblica 100), Biblical Institute Press, Rome 1982.

TOURNAY, R. J., *Quand Dieu parle aux hommes le langage de l'amour.* Études sur le Cantique des Cantiques (Cahiers de la Revue Biblique 21), Gabalda, Paris 1982.

——, "The Song of Songs and its Concluding Section," *Immanuel* 10 (1980), 5–14.

TOURNAY, R.—NICOLAŸ, M., *Le Cantique des Cantiques.* Commentaire abrégé. Du Cerf, Paris 1967.

TROMP, N. J., *Primitive Conceptions of Death and the Nether World in the Old Testament* (Biblica et Orientalia 21), Biblical Institute Press, Rome 1969.

VALERI, V., "Regalità," in *Enciclopedia Einaudi* XI, G. Einaudi, Turin 1980, pp. 742–771.

WIDENGREN, G., "The Persians," in *Peoples of Old Testament Times,* ed. D. J. Wiseman, Clarendon, Oxford 1973, pp. 312–357.

WINANDY, J., *Le Cantique des Cantiques.* Poème d'amour mué en écrit de sagesse (Bible et Vie Chrétienne), Casterman et Ed. de Maredsous, Tournay 1960.

WÜRTHWEIN, E., *Das Hohelied* (Die fünf Megilloth: Handbuch zum Alten Testament I/18), 2nd ed., Mohr (Paul Siebeck), Tübingen 1969, pp. 25–71.

ZAPLETAL, V., *Das Hohelied.* Kritisch und metrisch untersucht, Universitäts-Buchhandlung, Freiburg 1907.

ZIEGLER, K.—SONTHEIMER, W. (eds.), *Der Kleine Pauly.* Lexikon der Antike. 5 Vols., Deutscher Taschenbuch Verlag, München 1979.

ZORELL, F., *Lexicon Hebraicum Veteris Testamenti,* Pontificium Institutum Biblicum, Romae 1940–1954, 1984.

Index of Passages

SONG OF SONGS
1:1 13, 101
1:2-17 7, 10, 15, 16, 208
1:2-4 7, 10, 15, 16, 26, 228
1:2 16, 17, 18, 29, 122, 133, 193, 197, 227
1:3 18, 19, 20, 23, 64, 162, 183, 208
1:4 17, 18, 20, 23, 24, 25, 63, 78, 79, 122, 133, 193, 227
1:5-6 7, 10, 29, 30, 34, 225
1:5 19, 20, 30, 57, 141, 164
1:6 32, 33, 34, 79, 93, 163, 175, 197, 215, 221
1:7-11 7, 10, 37, 38, 45, 219
1:7 23, 38, 39, 90, 112, 194, 226
1:8 25, 41, 151, 157, 194
1:9 45
1:10 44
1:11 38, 45
1:12-17 7, 10, 47, 48, 49, 53, 85, 213
1:12 18, 127, 194
1:13 50, 98, 128, 227
1:14 33, 50, 192, 221
1:15 51, 75, 111, 122, 157
1:16 52
1:17 52
2:1-17 7, 10, 55, 189
2:1-3 8, 10, 55, 56, 60, 205
2:1-2 84, 152
2:1 56, 84, 114, 152
2:2 19, 20, 57, 84, 114, 152, 164
2:3 57, 58, 203
2:4-7 8, 10, 61, 62, 68, 85, 158, 201
2:4 18, 23, 62
2:5 23, 64, 104, 141
2:6 64, 199
2:7 19, 20, 23, 57, 64, 67, 94, 141, 158, 164, 199, 200
2:8-15 8, 10, 70, 71, 72, 73, 80, 192, 195
2:8 73
2:9 73, 227
2:10 74, 77, 192
2:11 75
2:12 75, 192
2:13 75, 192, 193, 194
2:14 77, 78, 138, 163, 226
2:15 33, 78, 79, 193, 221
2:16-17 8, 10, 54, 77, 78, 82, 83, 85, 189, 191, 213
2:16 83, 84, 114, 153, 190

SONG OF SONGS (*cont.*)
2:17 84, 114, 227, 228
3:1-11 8, 10, 87, 88
3:1-5 8, 10, 87, 88, 89, 95, 140, 142, 158
3:1 23, 39, 89, 90, 140
3:2 23, 39, 90, 140
3:3 23, 39, 91, 140
3:4 23, 39, 93, 105, 163, 197, 198
3:5 19, 20, 23, 57, 67, 94, 141, 158, 164
3:6-10 25
3:6-8 8, 10, 25, 88, 96, 97, 100, 114, 154
3:6 97, 127, 128, 202
3:7 99, 105
3:8 100, 105, 179
3:9-11 8, 10, 25, 88, 101, 102, 106, 149
3:9 103, 149
3:10 19, 20, 23, 25, 57, 104, 164, 204
3:11 105
4:1–5:1 8, 10, 109, 110, 156
4:1-7 8, 10, 109, 110, 111, 115, 158, 159
4:1 40, 111, 112, 122, 125, 141, 156, 157
4:2 112, 156, 158
4:3 40, 112, 141, 156, 158
4:4 113, 176
4:5 84, 113, 114, 152, 176
4:6 114
4:7 115, 138, 157, 163
4:8 8, 10, 116, 117, 118, 121, 123, 125, 128, 169
4:9-11 8, 10, 54, 120, 121, 123, 181, 223
4:9 32, 121, 125, 138, 157
4:10 17, 18, 32, 122, 133, 193, 227
4:11 18, 122, 123, 128
4:12-15 8, 10, 123, 124, 125, 128, 187, 226
4:12 32, 121, 125, 151, 187, 226
4:13 126, 165, 192, 194
4:14 122, 127, 131
4:15 128, 164
4:16–5:1 8, 10, 129, 130, 133, 187
4:16 122, 126, 130, 151, 164, 194
5:1 18, 25, 32, 121, 126, 130, 131, 151, 164, 185
5:2–6:3 8, 11, 88, 135, 137
5:2-8 8, 11, 90, 96, 135, 136, 137, 141, 158
5:2 32, 77, 115, 121, 137, 138, 146, 163
5:3 139
5:4 139, 147
5:5 139
5:6 140
5:7 91, 92, 140, 227
5:8 19, 20, 23, 57, 94, 141, 164
5:9-16 8, 11, 101, 107, 108, 143, 144, 148, 205
5:9 25, 41, 97, 145, 151, 157
5:10 146, 149
5:11 138, 146
5:12 146, 149, 194
5:13 139, 147, 149, 199
5:14 147, 149
5:15 148
5:16 19, 20, 57, 148, 164
6:1-3 8, 11, 101, 107, 149, 150, 151, 153
6:1 25, 41, 97, 151, 157
6:2 84, 114, 151, 152, 164
6:3 84, 114, 152, 153, 190
6:4–7:10 8, 11, 110, 155, 156

6:4-7	8, 11, 116, 155, 156, 158
6:4	156, 157, 164
6:5	157
6:6	112, 158
6:7	40, 112, 141, 158
6:8-12	8, 11, 120, 159, 160, 161, 167
6:8	19, 161, 162
6:9	19, 20, 57, 77, 93, 115, 162, 163, 164, 197
6:10	25, 97, 157, 163, 164
6:11	151, 164, 193
6:12	42, 165, 172, 173, 179
7:1-6	9, 11, 124, 169, 170, 171, 180
7:1	25, 171
7:2	21, 93, 164, 173
7:3	174
7:4	176
7:5	119, 147, 176, 194
7:6	100, 178
7:7-10	9, 11, 129, 134, 181, 182, 183, 186
7:7	23, 122, 183
7:8	183
7:9	18, 184
7:10	18, 184, 199
7:11–8:5	8, 9, 11, 56, 189
7:11	9, 11, 54, 86, 153, 189, 190, 213
7:12-14	9, 11, 82, 191, 192, 193, 194
7:12	192
7:13	17, 33, 79, 133, 192, 193, 198, 221, 227
7:14	18, 126, 192, 193, 194
8:1-4	9, 11, 70, 158, 193, 195, 196, 200
8:1	32, 93, 163, 196, 197, 215
8:2	18, 93, 163, 185, 197
8:3	199
8:4	19, 20, 23, 57, 67, 141, 158, 164, 199
8:5	9, 11, 25, 56, 58, 61, 94, 97, 98, 106, 201, 202, 204
8:6-14	7, 9, 11, 16, 207, 208
8:6-7	9, 11, 54, 207, 208, 211
8:6	23, 208
8:7	23, 141, 210
8:8-10	9, 11, 47, 213, 214, 218, 224
8:8	32, 215
8:9	141, 216
8:10	25, 172, 217
8:11-12	9, 11, 34, 37, 220, 221, 223
8:11	33, 172, 221
8:12	33, 34, 172, 221, 223
8:13-14	9, 11, 29, 225, 226, 228
8:13	78, 164, 226
8:14	84, 122, 227

GENESIS

3:16	190
4:7	190
15:10	84
24:43	19, 162
30:14-16	194
32:3	172
32:7-8	172
41:43	165

EXODUS

2:8	19, 162
3:8, 17	122
15:15	66
15:20	19, 162
32:18	173
33:3	122

NUMBERS

21:18	166

DEUTERONOMY
6:3 122
7:6-8 163
11:9 122
20:10 218
20:11 218
26:15 122

JOSHUA
9:15 218
15:34, 53 58
16:8 58
17:7-8 58

JUDGES
9:7-15 59
9:16, 19 115
21:21 19, 162

1 SAMUEL
2:8 166
21:21 173
29:5 173

2 SAMUEL
1:10 147
5:7-9 22, 105
6:19 64
15:30 98, 114
25:4 100
25:5 101

1 KINGS
5:9-14 14
6:9 219
6:30 148
11:3 19, 162
19:18 197
22:39 177

2 KINGS
5 165
18:31 76
25:4 202
25:5 202

1 CHRONICLES
16:3 64

2 CHRONICLES
28:21 166
32:9 190
35:24 165

EZRA
1:1 80
1:2-4 81
1:3 93
2:66 47
3:7 119
5:14 92
6:3-12 81
6:7 92
6:16-18 81, 159
7:13 81
9–10 22
10:7-9 93

NEHEMIAH
1:1-3 27
2:7 81
2:8 126
2:17 93
3:1-32 68
3:7 68, 94
3:9-18 91, 94
5:1-5 187
5:14 218
6:18 22
7:72 224
10:31 22
12 93
12:27-43 82, 140
13:23-29 22, 33, 67

ESTHER
1:1 161
1:5 164

1:6 147
7:7 164
7:8 164

JOB
12:21 166
15:30 210
34:18 166
38:31 159

PSALMS
2 147
7:15 204
37:11, 22, 29, 34 81
45:9 177
68:14 44
68:31 66
75:9 174
83:12 166
90:10 157
93:3-4 211
101 147
102:19 223
113:8 166
118:9 166
137:4 77
138:3 157
146:3 166

PROVERBS
2:21-22 81
3:8 174
6:3 157
6:18 166
7:13 197
7:17 139
7:18 17, 133, 193
8:30 174
10:30 81
19:6 166
23:30 174
23:31 184
24:26 17
25:12 174
30:19 19, 162

ECCLESIASTES
2:5 126
7:2 63

ISAIAH
2:2 114
3:5 157
5:1-7 33, 221
5:3 21
7:14 19, 162
7:22-25 122
14:9 66, 209
16:7 64
16:8 126
27:5 218
40:3-4 85
42:16 85
49:11 85

JEREMIAH
8:13 76
16:5, 8 63
29 27
29:1 221
30:3 81
34:18 84
39:4-5 202
49:27 177
51:39-64 27
52:15 174

LAMENTATIONS
1:2 133
4:7 146
4:20 28

EZEKIEL
8:1 221
14:1 221
16:4 174
16:8 17, 133, 193

EZEKIEL (*cont.*)
17:3-4 59
17:22-24 59
19:10-14 59
20:1 221
21:3 210
23:17 17, 133, 193
26:2-6 216
27:11 113, 216
31:3-9 59
36:28 81
37:15-28 27

DANIEL
4:7-9 59
4:11-19 59

HOSEA
2:15 174
3:1 64
13:2 197

JOEL
1:12 58

AMOS
3:15 177
4:1 66

MICAH
1:16 183
2:9 183
4:1 114

HABAKKUK
3:8 211

HAGGAI
1:1 92
1:6 79, 187
1:10 187
1:12 224
1:14 92, 224
2:1 92
2:2-4 223
2:2 224
2:4 224
2:16-17 187
2:20 92
2:20-23 4, 28, 203

ZECHARIAH
1–8 91
1:16-17 4
1:17 4, 93, 201
2:6-9 93
2:14-17 4, 93, 201
2:16 4, 201
3:2 4, 201
4:6-10 28
4:11-14 203
5:3-4 79
6:12-14 4, 203
7:1-7 18
7:5 224
8:2-7, 15 93
8:6, 12 224
8:7-8 4
8:19 18, 213

MALACHI
2:10-16 67
2:11 22

JUDITH
7:13 221

1 MACCABEES
4:57 113

2 MACCABEES
15:39 174